ISBN 0-8373-3232-X

C-3232   CAREER EXAMINATION SERIES

This is your PASSBOOK® for...

Data Base Coordinator

Test Preparation Study Guide

Questions & Answers

NLC

NATIONAL LEARNING CORPORATION

Copyright © 2015 by

National Learning Corporation

212 Michael Drive, Syosset, New York 11791

All rights reserved, including the right of reproduction in whole or in part, in any form or by any means, electronic or mechanical, including photocopying, recording, or by any information storage and retrieval system, without permission in writing from the Publisher.

(516) 921-8888
(800) 645-6337
FAX: (516) 921-8743
www.passbooks.com
sales @ passbooks.com
info @ passbooks.com

PRINTED IN THE UNITED STATES OF AMERICA

PASSBOOK®
NOTICE

This book is SOLELY intended for, is sold ONLY to, and its use is RESTRICTED to *individual*, bona fide applicants or candidates who qualify by virtue of having seriously filed applications for appropriate license, certificate, professional and/or promotional advancement, higher school matriculation, scholarship, or other legitimate requirements of educational and/or governmental authorities.

This book is NOT intended for use, class instruction, tutoring, training, duplication, copying, reprinting, excerption, or adaptation, etc., by:

(1) Other publishers

(2) Proprietors and/or Instructors of "Coaching" and/or Preparatory Courses

(3) Personnel and/or Training Divisions of commercial, industrial, and governmental organizations

(4) Schools, colleges, or universities and/or their departments and staffs, including teachers and other personnel

(5) Testing Agencies or Bureaus

(6) Study groups which seek by the purchase of a single volume to copy and/or duplicate and/or adapt this material for use by the group as a whole without having purchased individual volumes for each of the members of the group

(7) Et al.

Such persons would be in violation of appropriate Federal and State statutes.

PROVISION OF LICENSING AGREEMENTS. — Recognized educational commercial, industrial, and governmental institutions and organizations, and others legitimately engaged in educational pursuits, including training, testing, and measurement activities, may address a request for a licensing agreement to the copyright owners, who will determine whether, and under what conditions, including fees and charges, the materials in this book may be used by them. In other words, a licensing facility exists for the legitimate use of the material in this book on other than an individual basis. However, it is asseverated and affirmed here that the material in this book *CANNOT* be used without the receipt of the express permission of such a licensing agreement from the Publishers.

NATIONAL LEARNING CORPORATION
212 Michael Drive
Syosset, New York 11791

Inquiries re licensing agreements should be addressed to:
The President
National Learning Corporation
212 Michael Drive
Syosset, New York 11791

PASSBOOK® SERIES

THE *PASSBOOK® SERIES* has been created to prepare applicants and candidates for the ultimate academic battlefield — the examination room.

At some time in our lives, each and every one of us may be required to take an examination — for validation, matriculation, admission, qualification, registration, certification, or licensure.

Based on the assumption that every applicant or candidate has met the basic formal educational standards, has taken the required number of courses, and read the necessary texts, the *PASSBOOK® SERIES* furnishes the one special preparation which may assure passing with confidence, instead of failing with insecurity. Examination questions — together with answers — are furnished as the basic vehicle for study so that the mysteries of the examination and its compounding difficulties may be eliminated or diminished by a sure method.

This book is meant to help you pass your examination provided that you qualify and are serious in your objective.

The entire field is reviewed through the huge store of content information which is succinctly presented through a provocative and challenging approach — the question-and-answer method.

A climate of success is established by furnishing the correct answers at the end of each test.

You soon learn to recognize types of questions, forms of questions, and patterns of questioning. You may even begin to anticipate expected outcomes.

You perceive that many questions are repeated or adapted so that you can gain acute insights, which may enable you to score many sure points.

You learn how to confront new questions, or types of questions, and to attack them confidently and work out the correct answers.

You note objectives and emphases, and recognize pitfalls and dangers, so that you may make positive educational adjustments.

Moreover, you are kept fully informed in relation to new concepts, methods, practices, and directions in the field.

You discover that you are actually taking the examination all the time: you are preparing for the examination by "taking" an examination, not by reading extraneous and/or supererogatory textbooks.

In short, this PASSBOOK®, used directedly, should be an important factor in helping you to pass your test.

DATA BASE COORDINATOR

DUTIES
The work involves development and implementation of policies and procedures to improve the delivery and availability of data processing services through coordinated systems analysis and data base activities. Responsibility is included for developing short- and long-term plans for the design and implementation of data bases to effect more efficient use of computer resources. The incumbent assists the Director of Management Information Systems and the Assistant Manager of Data Processing in establishing priorities and scheduling systems development with an emphasis on data base optimization.

Develops new software applications and programs; writes computer programs in Fortran and in job control languages. Establishes backup files and recovery procedures for data bases; establishes forms and procedures for data entry and retrieval. Plans, assigns and supervises the work of data entry personnel, determines priorities of the work and coordinates user needs with system ability. Does related work as required.

SCOPE OF THE EXAMINATION
The written test will cover knowledge, skills and/or abilities in such areas as:

1. Terminology and concepts applicable to data communications software and hardware;
2. Principles and practices of data base administration;
3. Data structures and their application to data base management systems;
4. Systems analysis;
5. Symbolic logic;
6. Project management; and
7. Administrative supervision.

HOW TO TAKE A TEST

I. YOU MUST PASS AN EXAMINATION

A. *WHAT EVERY CANDIDATE SHOULD KNOW*

Examination applicants often ask us for help in preparing for the written test. What can I study in advance? What kinds of questions will be asked? How will the test be given? How will the papers be graded?

As an applicant for a civil service examination, you may be wondering about some of these things. Our purpose here is to suggest effective methods of advance study and to describe civil service examinations.

Your chances for success on this examination can be increased if you know how to prepare. Those "pre-examination jitters" can be reduced if you know what to expect. You can even experience an adventure in good citizenship if you know why civil service exams are given.

B. *WHY ARE CIVIL SERVICE EXAMINATIONS GIVEN?*

Civil service examinations are important to you in two ways. As a citizen, you want public jobs filled by employees who know how to do their work. As a job seeker, you want a fair chance to compete for that job on an equal footing with other candidates. The best-known means of accomplishing this two-fold goal is the competitive examination.

Exams are widely publicized throughout the nation. They may be administered for jobs in federal, state, city, municipal, town or village governments or agencies.

Any citizen may apply, with some limitations, such as the age or residence of applicants. Your experience and education may be reviewed to see whether you meet the requirements for the particular examination. When these requirements exist, they are reasonable and applied consistently to all applicants. Thus, a competitive examination may cause you some uneasiness now, but it is your privilege and safeguard.

C. *HOW ARE CIVIL SERVICE EXAMS DEVELOPED?*

Examinations are carefully written by trained technicians who are specialists in the field known as "psychological measurement," in consultation with recognized authorities in the field of work that the test will cover. These experts recommend the subject matter areas or skills to be tested; only those knowledges or skills important to your success on the job are included. The most reliable books and source materials available are used as references. Together, the experts and technicians judge the difficulty level of the questions.

Test technicians know how to phrase questions so that the problem is clearly stated. Their ethics do not permit "trick" or "catch" questions. Questions may have been tried out on sample groups, or subjected to statistical analysis, to determine their usefulness.

Written tests are often used in combination with performance tests, ratings of training and experience, and oral interviews. All of these measures combine to form the best-known means of finding the right person for the right job.

II. HOW TO PASS THE WRITTEN TEST

A. NATURE OF THE EXAMINATION

To prepare intelligently for civil service examinations, you should know how they differ from school examinations you have taken. In school you were assigned certain definite pages to read or subjects to cover. The examination questions were quite detailed and usually emphasized memory. Civil service exams, on the other hand, try to discover your present ability to perform the duties of a position, plus your potentiality to learn these duties. In other words, a civil service exam attempts to predict how successful you will be. Questions cover such a broad area that they cannot be as minute and detailed as school exam questions.

In the public service similar kinds of work, or positions, are grouped together in one "class." This process is known as *position-classification*. All the positions in a class are paid according to the salary range for that class. One class title covers all of these positions, and they are all tested by the same examination.

B. FOUR BASIC STEPS

1) Study the announcement

How, then, can you know what subjects to study? Our best answer is: "Learn as much as possible about the class of positions for which you've applied." The exam will test the knowledge, skills and abilities needed to do the work.

Your most valuable source of information about the position you want is the official exam announcement. This announcement lists the training and experience qualifications. Check these standards and apply only if you come reasonably close to meeting them.

The brief description of the position in the examination announcement offers some clues to the subjects which will be tested. Think about the job itself. Review the duties in your mind. Can you perform them, or are there some in which you are rusty? Fill in the blank spots in your preparation.

Many jurisdictions preview the written test in the exam announcement by including a section called "Knowledge and Abilities Required," "Scope of the Examination," or some similar heading. Here you will find out specifically what fields will be tested.

2) Review your own background

Once you learn in general what the position is all about, and what you need to know to do the work, ask yourself which subjects you already know fairly well and which need improvement. You may wonder whether to concentrate on improving your strong areas or on building some background in your fields of weakness. When the announcement has specified "some knowledge" or "considerable knowledge," or has used adjectives like "beginning principles of…" or "advanced … methods," you can get a clue as to the number and difficulty of questions to be asked in any given field. More questions, and hence broader coverage, would be included for those subjects which are more important in the work. Now weigh your strengths and weaknesses against the job requirements and prepare accordingly.

3) Determine the level of the position

Another way to tell how intensively you should prepare is to understand the level of the job for which you are applying. Is it the entering level? In other words, is this the position in which beginners in a field of work are hired? Or is it an intermediate or advanced level? Sometimes this is indicated by such words as "Junior" or "Senior" in the class title. Other jurisdictions use Roman numerals to designate the level – Clerk I, Clerk II, for example. The word "Supervisor" sometimes appears in the title. If the level is not indicated by the title, check the description of duties. Will you be working under very close supervision, or will you have responsibility for independent decisions in this work?

4) Choose appropriate study materials

Now that you know the subjects to be examined and the relative amount of each subject to be covered, you can choose suitable study materials. For beginning level jobs, or even advanced ones, if you have a pronounced weakness in some aspect of your training, read a modern, standard textbook in that field. Be sure it is up to date and has general coverage. Such books are normally available at your library, and the librarian will be glad to help you locate one. For entry-level positions, questions of appropriate difficulty are chosen – neither highly advanced questions, nor those too simple. Such questions require careful thought but not advanced training.

If the position for which you are applying is technical or advanced, you will read more advanced, specialized material. If you are already familiar with the basic principles of your field, elementary textbooks would waste your time. Concentrate on advanced textbooks and technical periodicals. Think through the concepts and review difficult problems in your field.

These are all general sources. You can get more ideas on your own initiative, following these leads. For example, training manuals and publications of the government agency which employs workers in your field can be useful, particularly for technical and professional positions. A letter or visit to the government department involved may result in more specific study suggestions, and certainly will provide you with a more definite idea of the exact nature of the position you are seeking.

III. KINDS OF TESTS

Tests are used for purposes other than measuring knowledge and ability to perform specified duties. For some positions, it is equally important to test ability to make adjustments to new situations or to profit from training. In others, basic mental abilities not dependent on information are essential. Questions which test these things may not appear as pertinent to the duties of the position as those which test for knowledge and information. Yet they are often highly important parts of a fair examination. For very general questions, it is almost impossible to help you direct your study efforts. What we can do is to point out some of the more common of these general abilities needed in public service positions and describe some typical questions.

1) General information

Brod, general information has been found useful for predicting job success in some kinds of work. This is tested in a variety of ways, from vocabulary lists to questions about current events. Basic background in some field of work, such as sociology or economics, may be sampled in a group of questions. Often these are principles which have become familiar to most persons through exposure rather than through formal training. It is difficult to advise you how to study for these questions; being alert to the world around you is our best suggestion.

2) Verbal ability

An example of an ability needed in many positions is verbal or language ability. Verbal ability is, in brief, the ability to use and understand words. Vocabulary and grammar tests are typical measures of this ability. Reading comprehension or paragraph interpretation questions are common in many kinds of civil service tests. You are given a paragraph of written material and asked to find its central meaning.

3) Numerical ability
Number skills can be tested by the familiar arithmetic problem, by checking paired lists of numbers to see which are alike and which are different, or by interpreting charts and graphs. In the latter test, a graph may be printed in the test booklet which you are asked to use as the basis for answering questions.

4) Observation
A popular test for law-enforcement positions is the observation test. A picture is shown to you for several minutes, then taken away. Questions about the picture test your ability to observe both details and larger elements.

5) Following directions
In many positions in the public service, the employee must be able to carry out written instructions dependably and accurately. You may be given a chart with several columns, each column listing a variety of information. The questions require you to carry out directions involving the information given in the chart.

6) Skills and aptitudes
Performance tests effectively measure some manual skills and aptitudes. When the skill is one in which you are trained, such as typing or shorthand, you can practice. These tests are often very much like those given in business school or high school courses. For many of the other skills and aptitudes, however, no short-time preparation can be made. Skills and abilities natural to you or that you have developed throughout your lifetime are being tested.

Many of the general questions just described provide all the data needed to answer the questions and ask you to use your reasoning ability to find the answers. Your best preparation for these tests, as well as for tests of facts and ideas, is to be at your physical and mental best. You, no doubt, have your own methods of getting into an exam-taking mood and keeping "in shape." The next section lists some ideas on this subject.

IV. KINDS OF QUESTIONS

Only rarely is the "essay" question, which you answer in narrative form, used in civil service tests. Civil service tests are usually of the short-answer type. Full instructions for answering these questions will be given to you at the examination. But in case this is your first experience with short-answer questions and separate answer sheets, here is what you need to know:

1) Multiple-choice Questions
Most popular of the short-answer questions is the "multiple choice" or "best answer" question. It can be used, for example, to test for factual knowledge, ability to solve problems or judgment in meeting situations found at work.
A multiple-choice question is normally one of three types—
- It can begin with an incomplete statement followed by several possible endings. You are to find the one ending which *best* completes the statement, although some of the others may not be entirely wrong.
- It can also be a complete statement in the form of a question which is answered by choosing one of the statements listed.

- It can be in the form of a problem – again you select the best answer.

Here is an example of a multiple-choice question with a discussion which should give you some clues as to the method for choosing the right answer:

When an employee has a complaint about his assignment, the action which will *best* help him overcome his difficulty is to
   A. discuss his difficulty with his coworkers
   B. take the problem to the head of the organization
   C. take the problem to the person who gave him the assignment
   D. say nothing to anyone about his complaint

In answering this question, you should study each of the choices to find which is best. Consider choice "A" – Certainly an employee may discuss his complaint with fellow employees, but no change or improvement can result, and the complaint remains unresolved. Choice "B" is a poor choice since the head of the organization probably does not know what assignment you have been given, and taking your problem to him is known as "going over the head" of the supervisor. The supervisor, or person who made the assignment, is the person who can clarify it or correct any injustice. Choice "C" is, therefore, correct. To say nothing, as in choice "D," is unwise. Supervisors have and interest in knowing the problems employees are facing, and the employee is seeking a solution to his problem.

2) True/False Questions

The "true/false" or "right/wrong" form of question is sometimes used. Here a complete statement is given. Your job is to decide whether the statement is right or wrong.

SAMPLE: A roaming cell-phone call to a nearby city costs less than a non-roaming call to a distant city.

This statement is wrong, or false, since roaming calls are more expensive.

This is not a complete list of all possible question forms, although most of the others are variations of these common types. You will always get complete directions for answering questions. Be sure you understand *how* to mark your answers – ask questions until you do.

V. RECORDING YOUR ANSWERS

Computer terminals are used more and more today for many different kinds of exams.
For an examination with very few applicants, you may be told to record your answers in the test booklet itself. Separate answer sheets are much more common. If this separate answer sheet is to be scored by machine – and this is often the case – it is highly important that you mark your answers correctly in order to get credit.
An electronic scoring machine is often used in civil service offices because of the speed with which papers can be scored. Machine-scored answer sheets must be marked with a pencil, which will be given to you. This pencil has a high graphite content which responds to the electronic scoring machine. As a matter of fact, stray dots may register as answers, so do not let your pencil rest on the answer sheet while you are pondering the correct answer. Also, if your pencil lead breaks or is otherwise defective, ask for another.

Since the answer sheet will be dropped in a slot in the scoring machine, be careful not to bend the corners or get the paper crumpled.

The answer sheet normally has five vertical columns of numbers, with 30 numbers to a column. These numbers correspond to the question numbers in your test booklet. After each number, going across the page are four or five pairs of dotted lines. These short dotted lines have small letters or numbers above them. The first two pairs may also have a "T" or "F" above the letters. This indicates that the first two pairs only are to be used if the questions are of the true-false type. If the questions are multiple choice, disregard the "T" and "F" and pay attention only to the small letters or numbers.

Answer your questions in the manner of the sample that follows:

32. The largest city in the United States is
    A. Washington, D.C.
    B. New York City
    C. Chicago
    D. Detroit
    E. San Francisco

1) Choose the answer you think is best. (New York City is the largest, so "B" is correct.)
2) Find the row of dotted lines numbered the same as the question you are answering. (Find row number 32)
3) Find the pair of dotted lines corresponding to the answer. (Find the pair of lines under the mark "B.")
4) Make a solid black mark between the dotted lines.

VI. BEFORE THE TEST

Common sense will help you find procedures to follow to get ready for an examination. Too many of us, however, overlook these sensible measures. Indeed, nervousness and fatigue have been found to be the most serious reasons why applicants fail to do their best on civil service tests. Here is a list of reminders:

- Begin your preparation early – Don't wait until the last minute to go scurrying around for books and materials or to find out what the position is all about.
- Prepare continuously – An hour a night for a week is better than an all-night cram session. This has been definitely established. What is more, a night a week for a month will return better dividends than crowding your study into a shorter period of time.
- Locate the place of the exam – You have been sent a notice telling you when and where to report for the examination. If the location is in a different town or otherwise unfamiliar to you, it would be well to inquire the best route and learn something about the building.
- Relax the night before the test – Allow your mind to rest. Do not study at all that night. Plan some mild recreation or diversion; then go to bed early and get a good night's sleep.
- Get up early enough to make a leisurely trip to the place for the test – This way unforeseen events, traffic snarls, unfamiliar buildings, etc. will not upset you.
- Dress comfortably – A written test is not a fashion show. You will be known by number and not by name, so wear something comfortable.

- Leave excess paraphernalia at home – Shopping bags and odd bundles will get in your way. You need bring only the items mentioned in the official notice you received; usually everything you need is provided. Do not bring reference books to the exam. They will only confuse those last minutes and be taken away from you when in the test room.
- Arrive somewhat ahead of time – If because of transportation schedules you must get there very early, bring a newspaper or magazine to take your mind off yourself while waiting.
- Locate the examination room – When you have found the proper room, you will be directed to the seat or part of the room where you will sit. Sometimes you are given a sheet of instructions to read while you are waiting. Do not fill out any forms until you are told to do so; just read them and be prepared.
- Relax and prepare to listen to the instructions
- If you have any physical problem that may keep you from doing your best, be sure to tell the test administrator. If you are sick or in poor health, you really cannot do your best on the exam. You can come back and take the test some other time.

VII. AT THE TEST

The day of the test is here and you have the test booklet in your hand. The temptation to get going is very strong. Caution! There is more to success than knowing the right answers. You must know how to identify your papers and understand variations in the type of short-answer question used in this particular examination. Follow these suggestions for maximum results from your efforts:

1) Cooperate with the monitor

The test administrator has a duty to create a situation in which you can be as much at ease as possible. He will give instructions, tell you when to begin, check to see that you are marking your answer sheet correctly, and so on. He is not there to guard you, although he will see that your competitors do not take unfair advantage. He wants to help you do your best.

2) Listen to all instructions

Don't jump the gun! Wait until you understand all directions. In most civil service tests you get more time than you need to answer the questions. So don't be in a hurry. Read each word of instructions until you clearly understand the meaning. Study the examples, listen to all announcements and follow directions. Ask questions if you do not understand what to do.

3) Identify your papers

Civil service exams are usually identified by number only. You will be assigned a number; you must not put your name on your test papers. Be sure to copy your number correctly. Since more than one exam may be given, copy your exact examination title.

4) Plan your time

Unless you are told that a test is a "speed" or "rate of work" test, speed itself is usually not important. Time enough to answer all the questions will be provided, but this does not mean that you have all day. An overall time limit has been set. Divide the total time (in minutes) by the number of questions to determine the approximate time you have for each question.

5) Do not linger over difficult questions

If you come across a difficult question, mark it with a paper clip (useful to have along) and come back to it when you have been through the booklet. One caution if you do this – be sure to skip a number on your answer sheet as well. Check often to be sure that you have not lost your place and that you are marking in the row numbered the same as the question you are answering.

6) Read the questions

Be sure you know what the question asks! Many capable people are unsuccessful because they failed to *read* the questions correctly.

7) Answer all questions

Unless you have been instructed that a penalty will be deducted for incorrect answers, it is better to guess than to omit a question.

8) Speed tests

It is often better NOT to guess on speed tests. It has been found that on timed tests people are tempted to spend the last few seconds before time is called in marking answers at random – without even reading them – in the hope of picking up a few extra points. To discourage this practice, the instructions may warn you that your score will be "corrected" for guessing. That is, a penalty will be applied. The incorrect answers will be deducted from the correct ones, or some other penalty formula will be used.

9) Review your answers

If you finish before time is called, go back to the questions you guessed or omitted to give them further thought. Review other answers if you have time.

10) Return your test materials

If you are ready to leave before others have finished or time is called, take ALL your materials to the monitor and leave quietly. Never take any test material with you. The monitor can discover whose papers are not complete, and taking a test booklet may be grounds for disqualification.

VIII. EXAMINATION TECHNIQUES

1) Read the general instructions carefully. These are usually printed on the first page of the exam booklet. As a rule, these instructions refer to the timing of the examination; the fact that you should not start work until the signal and must stop work at a signal, etc. If there are any *special* instructions, such as a choice of questions to be answered, make sure that you note this instruction carefully.

2) When you are ready to start work on the examination, that is as soon as the signal has been given, read the instructions to each question booklet, underline any key words or phrases, such as *least, best, outline, describe* and the like. In this way you will tend to answer as requested rather than discover on reviewing your paper that you *listed without describing*, that you selected the *worst* choice rather than the *best* choice, etc.

3) If the examination is of the objective or multiple-choice type – that is, each question will also give a series of possible answers: A, B, C or D, and you are called upon to select the best answer and write the letter next to that answer on your answer paper – it is advisable to start answering each question in turn. There may be anywhere from 50 to 100 such questions in the three or four hours allotted and you can see how much time would be taken if you read through all the questions before beginning to answer any. Furthermore, if you come across a question or group of questions which you know would be difficult to answer, it would undoubtedly affect your handling of all the other questions.

4) If the examination is of the essay type and contains but a few questions, it is a moot point as to whether you should read all the questions before starting to answer any one. Of course, if you are given a choice – say five out of seven and the like – then it is essential to read all the questions so you can eliminate the two that are most difficult. If, however, you are asked to answer all the questions, there may be danger in trying to answer the easiest one first because you may find that you will spend too much time on it. The best technique is to answer the first question, then proceed to the second, etc.

5) Time your answers. Before the exam begins, write down the time it started, then add the time allowed for the examination and write down the time it must be completed, then divide the time available somewhat as follows:
    - If 3-1/2 hours are allowed, that would be 210 minutes. If you have 80 objective-type questions, that would be an average of 2-1/2 minutes per question. Allow yourself no more than 2 minutes per question, or a total of 160 minutes, which will permit about 50 minutes to review.
    - If for the time allotment of 210 minutes there are 7 essay questions to answer, that would average about 30 minutes a question. Give yourself only 25 minutes per question so that you have about 35 minutes to review.

6) The most important instruction is to *read each question* and make sure you know what is wanted. The second most important instruction is to *time yourself properly* so that you answer every question. The third most important instruction is to *answer every question*. Guess if you have to but include something for each question. Remember that you will receive no credit for a blank and will probably receive some credit if you write something in answer to an essay question. If you guess a letter – say "B" for a multiple-choice question – you may have guessed right. If you leave a blank as an answer to a multiple-choice question, the examiners may respect your feelings but it will not add a point to your score. Some exams may penalize you for wrong answers, so in such cases *only*, you may not want to guess unless you have some basis for your answer.

7) Suggestions
    a. Objective-type questions
        1. Examine the question booklet for proper sequence of pages and questions
        2. Read all instructions carefully
        3. Skip any question which seems too difficult; return to it after all other questions have been answered
        4. Apportion your time properly; do not spend too much time on any single question or group of questions

5. Note and underline key words – *all, most, fewest, least, best, worst, same, opposite,* etc.
6. Pay particular attention to negatives
7. Note unusual option, e.g., unduly long, short, complex, different or similar in content to the body of the question
8. Observe the use of "hedging" words – *probably, may, most likely,* etc.
9. Make sure that your answer is put next to the same number as the question
10. Do not second-guess unless you have good reason to believe the second answer is definitely more correct
11. Cross out original answer if you decide another answer is more accurate; do not erase until you are ready to hand your paper in
12. Answer all questions; guess unless instructed otherwise
13. Leave time for review

b. Essay questions
1. Read each question carefully
2. Determine exactly what is wanted. Underline key words or phrases.
3. Decide on outline or paragraph answer
4. Include many different points and elements unless asked to develop any one or two points or elements
5. Show impartiality by giving pros and cons unless directed to select one side only
6. Make and write down any assumptions you find necessary to answer the questions
7. Watch your English, grammar, punctuation and choice of words
8. Time your answers; don't crowd material

8) Answering the essay question

Most essay questions can be answered by framing the specific response around several key words or ideas. Here are a few such key words or ideas:

M's: manpower, materials, methods, money, management
P's: purpose, program, policy, plan, procedure, practice, problems, pitfalls, personnel, public relations

   a. Six basic steps in handling problems:
      1. Preliminary plan and background development
      2. Collect information, data and facts
      3. Analyze and interpret information, data and facts
      4. Analyze and develop solutions as well as make recommendations
      5. Prepare report and sell recommendations
      6. Install recommendations and follow up effectiveness

   b. Pitfalls to avoid
      1. *Taking things for granted* – A statement of the situation does not necessarily imply that each of the elements is necessarily true; for example, a complaint may be invalid and biased so that all that can be taken for granted is that a complaint has been registered

2. *Considering only one side of a situation* – Wherever possible, indicate several alternatives and then point out the reasons you selected the best one
3. *Failing to indicate follow up* – Whenever your answer indicates action on your part, make certain that you will take proper follow-up action to see how successful your recommendations, procedures or actions turn out to be
4. *Taking too long in answering any single question* – Remember to time your answers properly

IX. AFTER THE TEST

Scoring procedures differ in detail among civil service jurisdictions although the general principles are the same. Whether the papers are hand-scored or graded by machine we have described, they are nearly always graded by number. That is, the person who marks the paper knows only the number – never the name – of the applicant. Not until all the papers have been graded will they be matched with names. If other tests, such as training and experience or oral interview ratings have been given, scores will be combined. Different parts of the examination usually have different weights. For example, the written test might count 60 percent of the final grade, and a rating of training and experience 40 percent. In many jurisdictions, veterans will have a certain number of points added to their grades.

After the final grade has been determined, the names are placed in grade order and an eligible list is established. There are various methods for resolving ties between those who get the same final grade – probably the most common is to place first the name of the person whose application was received first. Job offers are made from the eligible list in the order the names appear on it. You will be notified of your grade and your rank as soon as all these computations have been made. This will be done as rapidly as possible.

People who are found to meet the requirements in the announcement are called "eligibles." Their names are put on a list of eligible candidates. An eligible's chances of getting a job depend on how high he stands on this list and how fast agencies are filling jobs from the list.

When a job is to be filled from a list of eligibles, the agency asks for the names of people on the list of eligibles for that job. When the civil service commission receives this request, it sends to the agency the names of the three people highest on this list. Or, if the job to be filled has specialized requirements, the office sends the agency the names of the top three persons who meet these requirements from the general list.

The appointing officer makes a choice from among the three people whose names were sent to him. If the selected person accepts the appointment, the names of the others are put back on the list to be considered for future openings.

That is the rule in hiring from all kinds of eligible lists, whether they are for typist, carpenter, chemist, or something else. For every vacancy, the appointing officer has his choice of any one of the top three eligibles on the list. This explains why the person whose name is on top of the list sometimes does not get an appointment when some of the persons lower on the list do. If the appointing officer chooses the second or third eligible, the No. 1 eligible does not get a job at once, but stays on the list until he is appointed or the list is terminated.

X. HOW TO PASS THE INTERVIEW TEST

The examination for which you applied requires an oral interview test. You have already taken the written test and you are now being called for the interview test – the final part of the formal examination.

You may think that it is not possible to prepare for an interview test and that there are no procedures to follow during an interview. Our purpose is to point out some things you can do in advance that will help you and some good rules to follow and pitfalls to avoid while you are being interviewed.

What is an interview supposed to test?

The written examination is designed to test the technical knowledge and competence of the candidate; the oral is designed to evaluate intangible qualities, not readily measured otherwise, and to establish a list showing the relative fitness of each candidate – as measured against his competitors – for the position sought. Scoring is not on the basis of "right" and "wrong," but on a sliding scale of values ranging from "not passable" to "outstanding." As a matter of fact, it is possible to achieve a relatively low score without a single "incorrect" answer because of evident weakness in the qualities being measured.

Occasionally, an examination may consist entirely of an oral test – either an individual or a group oral. In such cases, information is sought concerning the technical knowledges and abilities of the candidate, since there has been no written examination for this purpose. More commonly, however, an oral test is used to supplement a written examination.

Who conducts interviews?

The composition of oral boards varies among different jurisdictions. In nearly all, a representative of the personnel department serves as chairman. One of the members of the board may be a representative of the department in which the candidate would work. In some cases, "outside experts" are used, and, frequently, a businessman or some other representative of the general public is asked to serve. Labor and management or other special groups may be represented. The aim is to secure the services of experts in the appropriate field.

However the board is composed, it is a good idea (and not at all improper or unethical) to ascertain in advance of the interview who the members are and what groups they represent. When you are introduced to them, you will have some idea of their backgrounds and interests, and at least you will not stutter and stammer over their names.

What should be done before the interview?

While knowledge about the board members is useful and takes some of the surprise element out of the interview, there is other preparation which is more substantive. It *is* possible to prepare for an oral interview – in several ways:

1) Keep a copy of your application and review it carefully before the interview

This may be the only document before the oral board, and the starting point of the interview. Know what education and experience you have listed there, and the sequence and dates of all of it. Sometimes the board will ask you to review the highlights of your experience for them; you should not have to hem and haw doing it.

2) Study the class specification and the examination announcement

Usually, the oral board has one or both of these to guide them. The qualities, characteristics or knowledges required by the position sought are stated in these documents. They offer valuable clues as to the nature of the oral interview. For example, if the job involves supervisory responsibilities, the announcement will usually indicate that knowledge of modern supervisory methods and the qualifications of the candidate as a supervisor will be tested. If so, you can expect such questions, frequently in the form of a hypothetical situation which you are expected to solve. NEVER go into an oral without knowledge of the duties and responsibilities of the job you seek.

3) Think through each qualification required
Try to visualize the kind of questions you would ask if you were a board member. How well could you answer them? Try especially to appraise your own knowledge and background in each area, *measured against the job sought*, and identify any areas in which you are weak. Be critical and realistic – do not flatter yourself.

4) Do some general reading in areas in which you feel you may be weak
For example, if the job involves supervision and your past experience has NOT, some general reading in supervisory methods and practices, particularly in the field of human relations, might be useful. Do NOT study agency procedures or detailed manuals. The oral board will be testing your understanding and capacity, not your memory.

5) Get a good night's sleep and watch your general health and mental attitude
You will want a clear head at the interview. Take care of a cold or any other minor ailment, and of course, no hangovers.

What should be done on the day of the interview?
Now comes the day of the interview itself. Give yourself plenty of time to get there. Plan to arrive somewhat ahead of the scheduled time, particularly if your appointment is in the fore part of the day. If a previous candidate fails to appear, the board might be ready for you a bit early. By early afternoon an oral board is almost invariably behind schedule if there are many candidates, and you may have to wait. Take along a book or magazine to read, or your application to review, but leave any extraneous material in the waiting room when you go in for your interview. In any event, relax and compose yourself.

The matter of dress is important. The board is forming impressions about you – from your experience, your manners, your attitude, and your appearance. Give your personal appearance careful attention. Dress your best, but not your flashiest. Choose conservative, appropriate clothing, and be sure it is immaculate. This is a business interview, and your appearance should indicate that you regard it as such. Besides, being well groomed and properly dressed will help boost your confidence.

Sooner or later, someone will call your name and escort you into the interview room. *This is it.* From here on you are on your own. It is too late for any more preparation. But remember, you asked for this opportunity to prove your fitness, and you are here because your request was granted.

What happens when you go in?
The usual sequence of events will be as follows: The clerk (who is often the board stenographer) will introduce you to the chairman of the oral board, who will introduce you to the other members of the board. Acknowledge the introductions before you sit down. Do not be surprised if you find a microphone facing you or a stenotypist sitting by. Oral interviews are usually recorded in the event of an appeal or other review.

Usually the chairman of the board will open the interview by reviewing the highlights of your education and work experience from your application – primarily for the benefit of the other members of the board, as well as to get the material into the record. Do not interrupt or comment unless there is an error or significant misinterpretation; if that is the case, do not hesitate. But do not quibble about insignificant matters. Also, he will usually ask you some question about your education, experience or your present job – partly to get you to start talking and to establish the interviewing "rapport." He may start the actual questioning, or turn it over to one of the other members. Frequently, each member undertakes the questioning on a particular area, one in which he is perhaps most competent, so you can expect each member to participate in the examination. Because time is limited, you may also expect some rather abrupt switches in the direction the questioning takes, so do not be upset by it. Normally, a board member will not pursue a single line of questioning unless he discovers a particular strength or weakness.

After each member has participated, the chairman will usually ask whether any member has any further questions, then will ask you if you have anything you wish to add. Unless you are expecting this question, it may floor you. Worse, it may start you off on an extended, extemporaneous speech. The board is not usually seeking more information. The question is principally to offer you a last opportunity to present further qualifications or to indicate that you have nothing to add. So, if you feel that a significant qualification or characteristic has been overlooked, it is proper to point it out in a sentence or so. Do not compliment the board on the thoroughness of their examination – they have been sketchy, and you know it. If you wish, merely say, "No thank you, I have nothing further to add." This is a point where you can "talk yourself out" of a good impression or fail to present an important bit of information. Remember, *you close the interview yourself.*

The chairman will then say, "That is all, Mr. _____, thank you." Do not be startled; the interview is over, and quicker than you think. Thank him, gather your belongings and take your leave. Save your sigh of relief for the other side of the door.

How to put your best foot forward
Throughout this entire process, you may feel that the board individually and collectively is trying to pierce your defenses, seek out your hidden weaknesses and embarrass and confuse you. Actually, this is not true. They are obliged to make an appraisal of your qualifications for the job you are seeking, and they want to see you in your best light. Remember, they must interview all candidates and a non-cooperative candidate may become a failure in spite of their best efforts to bring out his qualifications. Here are 15 suggestions that will help you:

1) Be natural – Keep your attitude confident, not cocky
If you are not confident that you can do the job, do not expect the board to be. Do not apologize for your weaknesses, try to bring out your strong points. The board is interested in a positive, not negative, presentation. Cockiness will antagonize any board member and make him wonder if you are covering up a weakness by a false show of strength.

2) Get comfortable, but don't lounge or sprawl
Sit erectly but not stiffly. A careless posture may lead the board to conclude that you are careless in other things, or at least that you are not impressed by the importance of the occasion. Either conclusion is natural, even if incorrect. Do not fuss with your clothing, a pencil or an ashtray. Your hands may occasionally be useful to emphasize a point; do not let them become a point of distraction.

3) Do not wisecrack or make small talk
This is a serious situation, and your attitude should show that you consider it as such. Further, the time of the board is limited – they do not want to waste it, and neither should you.

4) Do not exaggerate your experience or abilities
In the first place, from information in the application or other interviews and sources, the board may know more about you than you think. Secondly, you probably will not get away with it. An experienced board is rather adept at spotting such a situation, so do not take the chance.

5) If you know a board member, do not make a point of it, yet do not hide it
Certainly you are not fooling him, and probably not the other members of the board. Do not try to take advantage of your acquaintanceship – it will probably do you little good.

6) Do not dominate the interview
Let the board do that. They will give you the clues – do not assume that you have to do all the talking. Realize that the board has a number of questions to ask you, and do not try to take up all the interview time by showing off your extensive knowledge of the answer to the first one.

7) Be attentive
You only have 20 minutes or so, and you should keep your attention at its sharpest throughout. When a member is addressing a problem or question to you, give him your undivided attention. Address your reply principally to him, but do not exclude the other board members.

8) Do not interrupt
A board member may be stating a problem for you to analyze. He will ask you a question when the time comes. Let him state the problem, and wait for the question.

9) Make sure you understand the question
Do not try to answer until you are sure what the question is. If it is not clear, restate it in your own words or ask the board member to clarify it for you. However, do not haggle about minor elements.

10) Reply promptly but not hastily
A common entry on oral board rating sheets is "candidate responded readily," or "candidate hesitated in replies." Respond as promptly and quickly as you can, but do not jump to a hasty, ill-considered answer.

11) Do not be peremptory in your answers
A brief answer is proper – but do not fire your answer back. That is a losing game from your point of view. The board member can probably ask questions much faster than you can answer them.

12) Do not try to create the answer you think the board member wants
He is interested in what kind of mind you have and how it works – not in playing games. Furthermore, he can usually spot this practice and will actually grade you down on it.

13) Do not switch sides in your reply merely to agree with a board member
Frequently, a member will take a contrary position merely to draw you out and to see if you are willing and able to defend your point of view. Do not start a debate, yet do not surrender a good position. If a position is worth taking, it is worth defending.

14) Do not be afraid to admit an error in judgment if you are shown to be wrong

The board knows that you are forced to reply without any opportunity for careful consideration. Your answer may be demonstrably wrong. If so, admit it and get on with the interview.

15) Do not dwell at length on your present job

The opening question may relate to your present assignment. Answer the question but do not go into an extended discussion. You are being examined for a *new* job, not your present one. As a matter of fact, try to phrase ALL your answers in terms of the job for which you are being examined.

Basis of Rating

Probably you will forget most of these "do's" and "don'ts" when you walk into the oral interview room. Even remembering them all will not ensure you a passing grade. Perhaps you did not have the qualifications in the first place. But remembering them will help you to put your best foot forward, without treading on the toes of the board members.

Rumor and popular opinion to the contrary notwithstanding, an oral board wants you to make the best appearance possible. They know you are under pressure – but they also want to see how you respond to it as a guide to what your reaction would be under the pressures of the job you seek. They will be influenced by the degree of poise you display, the personal traits you show and the manner in which you respond.

ABOUT THIS BOOK

This book contains tests divided into Examination Sections. Go through each test, answering every question in the margin. We have also attached a sample answer sheet at the back of the book that can be removed and used. At the end of each test look at the answer key and check your answers. On the ones you got wrong, look at the right answer choice and learn. Do not fill in the answers first. Do not memorize the questions and answers, but understand the answer and principles involved. On your test, the questions will likely be different from the samples. Questions are changed and new ones added. If you understand these past questions you should have success with any changes that arise. Tests may consist of several types of questions. We have additional books on each subject should more study be advisable or necessary for you. Finally, the more you study, the better prepared you will be. This book is intended to be the last thing you study before you walk into the examination room. Prior study of relevant texts is also recommended. NLC publishes some of these in our Fundamental Series. Knowledge and good sense are important factors in passing your exam. Good luck also helps. So now study this Passbook, absorb the material contained within and take that knowledge into the examination. Then do your best to pass that exam.

EXAMINATION SECTION

EXAMINATION SECTION
TEST 1

DIRECTIONS: Each question or incomplete statement is followed by several suggested answers or completions. Select the one that BEST answers the question or completes the statement. *PRINT THE LETTER OF THE CORRECT ANSWER IN THE SPACE AT THE RIGHT.*

1. Which of the following is NOT a characteristic of a relational database   1.____

    A. It is a two-dimensional table.
    B. Each row is distinct.
    C. The key fields are created by a programmer.
    D. Each column has a distinct name.
    E. The order of columns is immaterial.

2. Each row of a relational database is called a   2.____

    A. table   B. row   C. column
    D. tuple   E. none of the above

3. Each column of a relational database is called a   3.____

    A. table   B. row   C. column
    D. tuple   E. attribute

4. The _____ is NOT a component of a database application system.   4.____

    A. hardware   B. programs
    C. data   D. procedures
    E. decision support system

5. The structure of the entire database is called a   5.____

    A. DBMS   B. schema
    C. application mechanism   D. DBA
    E. hierarchy

6. Which of the following is the national query language?   6.____

    A. IDMS   B. dBase III Plus
    C. SQL   D. DB2
    E. none of the above

7. Metadata is a term MOST closely associated with the _____ of a data base management system.   7.____

    A. forms generator
    B. data dictionary
    C. database programming language
    D. query languages
    E. data models

8. The _____ is responsible for the development, operation, maintenance, and administration of the database.   8.____

    A. DDL   B. DBM   C. DBA   D. DL/1   E. DBTG

9. In a local area network, the common database is located in the microcomputer

   A. subdirectory
   B. LAN
   C. file server
   D. Distributed Transaction Manager (DTM)
   E. Device Media Control Locator (DMCL)

10. The _____ data model is also called the *tree* model.

    A. hierarchical   B. relational   C. network
    D. inverted   E. none of the above

11. A group of one or more attributes (columns in a relation) that uniquely identifies a record in a file is called a

    A. descriptor   B. indicator   C. key
    D. field   E. pointer

12. The *lock manager* is responsible for

    A. securing the DBMS from unauthorized users
    B. securing the DBMS from disasters such as fire or flood
    C. preventing undesirable results from occurring during concurrent processing
    D. rollback and recovery procedures
    E. all of the above

13. The MOST common computer programming language used with database management systems is

    A. PL/1   B. Fortran   C. Basic
    D. QBE   E. COBOL

14. Which of the following is NOT a microcomputer database management system?

    A. Rbase   B. dBase   C. Oracle
    D. DB2   E. None of the above

15. Which of the following symbols is NOT used with data flow diagrams?

    A. (circle)   B. (square)   C. (curved arrow)
    D. (diamond) E. (open-ended rectangle)

16. The *father* of the relational database model is   16.____

    A. Codd   B. Martin   C. Djikstra
    D. Kroenke   E. Boyce

17. The process of grouping together fields in a database to form a well-structured relation is   17.____
    called

    A. dependency   B. data modeling
    C. normalization   D. logical database design
    E. relational design

18. A relationship between fields in a database is called   18.____

    A. relational dependency
    B. functional dependency
    C. first normal form
    D. logical database design
    E. domain/key normal form

19. The notation used for describing a one-to-many relationship between data is   19.____

    A. 1:M   B. 1:!   C. M:1
    D. 1:N   E. none of the above

20. The data in a database is the property of the   20.____

    A. users
    B. database administrator
    C. manufacturer of the database software
    D. government
    E. none of the above

21. The data dictionary lists the   21.____

    A. standard names for data items in the database
    B. files in a database system
    C. relationships between data in a database
    D. all of the above
    E. none of the above

22. The process of recreating a database system from start is called   22.____

    A. recovery   B. rollback   C. rebuilding
    D. back-up   E. reduplication

23. The process of correcting an error or group of errors is called   23.____

    A. recovery   B. rollback   C. data validation
    D. back-up   E. re-initiation

24. *Deadlock* occurs when

   A. multiple users *log on* with identical passwords
   B. users cannot decide on who owns the data in the database system
   C. one group of users will not let other users have access to data
   D. two users are waiting for data that each other has locked
   E. database software does not operate properly on certain hardware

25. The PRIMARY responsibility of the database administrator (DBA) is to

   A. maintain the data dictionary
   B. meet with end users to determine their needs from the database management system
   C. safeguard the database and optimize the benefits users derive from it
   D. develop database applications
   E. specify the software to be used for the database management system

---

KEY (CORRECT ANSWERS)

1.	C	11.	C
2.	D	12.	C
3.	E	13.	E
4.	E	14.	E
5.	B	15.	D
6.	C	16.	A
7.	B	17.	C
8.	C	18.	B
9.	C	19.	D
10.	A	20.	A

21.	D
22.	A
23.	B
24.	D
25.	C

TEST 2

DIRECTIONS: Each question or incomplete statement is followed by several suggested answers or completions. Select the one that BEST answers the question or completes the statement. *PRINT THE LETTER OF THE CORRECT ANSWER IN THE SPACE AT THE RIGHT.*

1. The database administrator (DBA) must TYPICALLY address _____ problems. 1._____

    A. technical
    B. psychological
    C. organizational political
    D. managerial
    E. all of the above

2. The PRIMARY goal of normalization in a database is to 2._____

    A. reduce data redundancy
    B. maintain database security
    C. reduce data integrity
    D. reduce storage requirements
    E. reduce data entry volume

3. Which of the following is NOT typical of a microcomputer database management system? They 3._____

    A. use simpler administration than of mainframe database systems
    B. are primarily single-user systems
    C. are developed by end users
    D. handle up to five different applications
    E. use the hierarchial or network data model

4. The _____ data model requires the MOST maintenance by a professional database staff. 4._____

    A. relational   B. network   C. hierarchial
    D. tree   E. none of the above

5. Concatenation is 5._____

    A. the joining of two fields (attributes) to uniquely identify a record in a field
    B. the splitting of one field into two separate parts
    C. a method of changing the definition of a field
    D. a type of relationship between two files
    E. a type of random access

6. A general language used to communicate with the database management system is 6._____
    A. DDL   B. CODASYL   C. DBTG   D. DAD   E. QBE

7. A mathematical formula for calculating a disk address for a key field is called

   A. linear projection
   B. location numeration
   C. hierarchial sequential access method
   D. indexing
   E. hashing

8. The transferring of data from a personal computer to a mainframe computer is called

   A. downloading B. uploading C. modeming
   D. handshaking E. none of the above

9. The initial one-time cost of starting up a database management system is called

   A. software maintenance
   B. software development
   C. computer system overhead
   D. DBMS installation
   E. training

10. Which of the following is NOT a benefit that is derived from having a well-designed database management system?

    A. Improved security of data
    B. Better information provided to users
    C. Reduced administration resources
    D. More accurate information
    E. Reduced maintenance and program development costs

11. In many companies, user departments are charged for using the database management system.
    Resource utilization billing charges the area user based upon

    A. a fixed amount per period
    B. a fixed amount, dependent on the type of application being used
    C. time, transactions processed, computer resources
    D. a fixed amount per user
    E. the number of transactions processed

12. _____ is NOT a function of the database administrator(DBA).

    A. Training
    B. Data dictionary management
    C. Database loading
    D. Entering data and querying database for users
    E. Database security

13. The process of evaluating the proper hardware environment for the database management system is called

    A. tuning   B. performance monitoring
    C. sizing   D. feature evaluation
    E. feature implementation

14. A data model is the

    A. method for organizing a database
    B. physical structure of the database
    C. language used to query the database
    D. database management system software
    E. conceptual view of the database

15. The data model which is GENERALLY considered to be the *slowest* in performance is the _____ model.

    A. network   B. hierarchial   C. inverted
    D. relational   E. all of the above

16. Which data model provides the link in which data is related together within the data itself?

    A. Network   B. Hierarchial   C. Plex
    D. Tree   E. Relational

Questions 17-20.

DIRECTIONS: Use the following relational database to answer Questions 17 through 20.

23	SIMMONS	1B	.324
31	WILSON	OF	.309
19	FARMER	P	.144

17. How many *tuples* are depicted?

    A. One   B. Two   C. Three
    D. Four   E. None of the above

18. How many *tables* are depicted?

    A. One   B. Two   C. Three
    D. Four   E. None of the above

19. How many *data elements* are depicted?

    A. One   B. Two   C. Three
    D. Four   E. None of the above

20. How many *attributes* are depicted?

    A. One   B. Two   C. Three
    D. Four   E. None of the above

21. A database administrator (DBA) is analogous to a

    A. salesperson   B. accountant   C. vice president
    D. auditor   E. controller

22. _____ is the preferred method of recovering a database system from a system failure.

    A. Reprocessing
    B. Rollback
    C. Rollforward
    D. Rollback/rollforward
    E. Restoring from backup tapes or disks

23. A set of possible values for a data field that defines a range of valid data entries for that field is called a

    A. derived range
    B. validation check
    C. domain
    D. enumerated range
    E. condition name

24. The _____ database operation produces a new relationship by combining two existing relations.

    A. extract
    B. join
    C. combine
    D. selection
    E. all of the above

25. Which of the following is a selection criteria for a data model?

    A. Vendor support
    B. Security
    C. Performance
    D. User interface
    E. All of the above

KEY (CORRECT ANSWERS)

1. E
2. A
3. E
4. B
5. A

6. A
7. E
8. B
9. D
10. C

11. C
12. D
13. C
14. A
15. D

16. E
17. C
18. A
19. E
20. D

21. E
22. D
23. C
24. B
25. E

EXAMINATION SECTION
TEST 1

DIRECTIONS: Each question or incomplete statement is followed by several suggested answers or completions. Select the one that BEST answers the question or completes the statement. *PRINT THE LETTER OF THE CORRECT ANSWER IN THE SPACE AT THE RIGHT.*

1. A database management system is

    A. hardware that monitors user log-ons and log-offs
    B. software that merges data into one pool
    C. firmware that allows high level languages to be used
    D. ROM used to store data
    E. RAM used to store data

    1.____

2. A database manager

    A. is a software package
    B. is a collection of related files
    C. permits data to be easily retrieved and manipulated
    D. permits data to be easily stored
    E. all of the above

    2.____

3. A specific advantage of a database management system is

    A. consolidation of files
    B. program dependence
    C. making programming harder
    D. restricting data flexibility
    E. all of the above

    3.____

4. Which of the following is NOT an advantage of a database management system?

    A. Easing program maintenance
    B. Restricting data flexibility
    C. Providing data security
    D. Restricting data accessibility
    E. All of the above are advantages

    4.____

5. One of the advantages of a database management system is

    A. standardization of program names
    B. standardization of paragraph names
    C. standardization of screen formats
    D. standardization of data names
    E. all are advantages of a database management system

    5.____

6. A database management system promotes

    A. data distribution   B. program distribution
    C. data security   D. special situation values
    E. access distribution

    6.____

7. Which of the following is NOT a type of database?

   A. Network
   B. Flat file
   C. Relational
   D. Hierarchical
   E. All are types of databases

8. In a hierarchical database management system,

   A. one data set is subservient to another
   B. a data set can be subservient to two or more other data sets
   C. data sets can be viewed as two-dimensional tables
   D. child data sets govern two or more parent data sets
   E. child data sets govern a single parent data set

9. In a network database management system,

   A. one data set is subservient to another
   B. a data set can be subservient to two or more other data sets
   C. data sets can be viewed as two-dimensional tables
   D. child data sets govern two or more parent data sets
   E. child data sets govern a single parent data set

10. In a relational database management system,

    A. one data set is subservient to another
    B. a data set can be subservient to two or more other data sets
    C. data sets can be viewed as two-dimensional tables
    D. child data sets govern two or more parent data sets
    E. child data sets govern a single parent data set

11. In a hierarchical database management system, a parent data set can govern how many other data sets?

    A. 1   B. 2   C. 3
    D. 4   E. All of the above

12. In a hierarchical database management system, a child data set is subservient to how many parent data sets?

    A. 1   B. 2   C. 3
    D. 4   E. All of the above

13. In a network database management system, a child data set is subservient to how many parent data sets?

    A. 1   B. 2   C. 3
    D. 4   E. All of the above

14. In a network database management system, a parent data set can govern how many other data sets?

    A. 1   B. 2   C. 3
    D. 4   E. All of the above

15. Which of the following database management systems is classified as relational?

    A. SQL   B. IMAGE   C. DDL   D. DML   E. IMS

    15.____

16. Which of the following database management systems is classified as network?

    A. SQL   B. IMAGE   C. DDL   D. DML   E. IMS

    16.____

17. Which of the following database management systems is classified as hierarchical?

    A. SQL   B. IMAGE   C. DDL   D. DML   E. IMS

    17.____

18. In a relational database management system, a record is called a(n)

    A. relation   B. attribute   C. tuple
    D. join   E. none of the above

    18.____

19. In a relational database management system, a file is called a(n)

    A. relation   B. attribute   C. tuple
    D. join   E. none of the above

    19.____

20. In a relational database management system, a field is called a(n)

    A. relation   B. domain   C. tuple
    D. join   E. none of the above

    20.____

KEY (CORRECT ANSWERS)

1. B
2. E
3. A
4. B
5. D

6. C
7. B
8. A
9. B
10. C

11. E
12. A
13. E
14. E
15. A

16. B
17. E
18. C
19. A
20. B

TEST 2

DIRECTIONS: Each question or incomplete statement is followed by several suggested answers or completions. Select the one that BEST answers the question or completes the statement. *PRINT THE LETTER OF THE CORRECT ANSWER IN THE SPACE AT THE RIGHT.*

1. Which of the following is NOT a basic operation for a relational database management system?

    A. Delete a table
    B. Create a table
    C. Join a table
    D. Union a table
    E. Delete a tuple

2. A database management system that contains its own language for manipulating the database management system is called

    A. self-contained
    B. host language
    C. network
    D. QUERY
    E. relational

3. A database management system that uses a high level language like COBOL to manipulate the database management system is called

    A. self-contained
    B. host language
    C. network
    D. QUERY
    E. relational

4. Which of the following is a language designed for novice users to locate and retrieve data?

    A. IMS   B. DDL   C. QUERY   D. COBOL   E. Pascal

5. Which of the following is NOT a common database management system utility routine?

    A. Initialization
    B. Copying
    C. Capacity changes
    D. Transaction logging
    E. None of the above

6. Generally given credit for development of relational database management systems is

    A. Grace Hopper
    B. Ada Lovelace
    C. Blaise Pascal
    D. Edgar Codd
    E. Warnier Orr

7. Relational database management systems were developed in the

    A. 1950's   B. 1960's   C. 1970's   D. 1980's   E. 1940's

8. Relational database management system can be found on _____ computers.

    A. personal   B. main frame   C. mini
    D. hobby   E. all types of

9. Which of the following relational operations means to combine relations?

    A. Copy   B. Print   C. Create
    D. Join   E. Add an attribute

10. We define a database management system with a

    A. DML B. COBOL program C. schema or DDL
    D. IMS E. QUERY

11. We can read, store, or modify data in a database management system with a(n)

    A. DML B. COBOL program C. schema or DDL
    D. IMS E. QUERY

12. A novice user can interrogate a database management system with

    A. DML B. COBOL program C. schema or DDL
    D. IMS E. QUERY

13. A commonly used database management system is

    A. DML B. COBOL program C. schema or DDL
    D. IMS E. QUERY

14. Which of the following is NOT an example of a database management system control system?

    A. Transaction logging B. Checking access rights
    C. Back down D. Back up
    E. All are control systems

15. Which of the following database management system control system records all changes made to the database management system?

    A. Transaction logging B. Checking access rights
    C. Back down D. Back up
    E. All are control systems

16. Which of the following database management system control systems tests for read or write capability?

    A. Transaction logging B. Checking access rights
    C. Back down D. Back up
    E. All are control systems

17. Which of the following database management system control systems copies the database management system to another disk or tape?

    A. Transaction logging B. Checking access rights
    C. Back down D. Back up
    E. All are control systems

18. IMAGE is a

    A. network database management system
    B. operation on Hewlett Packard computers
    C. system that has an Inquiry language called QUERY
    D. host language system
    E. All of the above

19. IBM's IMS

    A. is a network database management system
    B. operates on Hewlett Packard computers
    C. has an Inquiry language called QUERY
    D. is a host language system
    E. is none of the above

20. Burroughs DMS-II

    A. is a network database management system
    B. operates on Hewlett Packard computers
    C. has an Inquiry language called QUERY
    D. is a host language system
    E. is all of the above

KEY (CORRECT ANSWERS)

1.	D	11.	B
2.	A	12.	E
3.	B	13.	D
4.	C	14.	C
5.	E	15.	A
6.	D	16.	B
7.	C	17.	D
8.	E	18.	E
9.	D	19.	E
10.	C	20.	A

EXAMINATION SECTION
TEST 1

DIRECTIONS: Each question or incomplete statement is followed by several suggested answers or completions. Select the one that BEST answers the question or completes the statement. *PRINT THE LETTER OF THE CORRECT ANSWER IN THE SPACE AT THE RIGHT.*

1. A database uses _____ to identify information.
    - A. record numbers
    - B. register addresses
    - C. field names
    - D. directories

2. _____ could be added to a database in order to increase the number of search and access points available to a user.
    - A. Subject discriptors
    - B. Partitions
    - C. Term authority lists
    - D. Call programs

3. The central idea behind the management of a database is
    - A. procedural and nonprocedural interfaces
    - B. minimal redundancy and minimal storage space
    - C. physical data independence
    - D. the separation of data description and data manipulation

4. Which of the following is NOT a type of query language operator used in database searches?
    - A. Object-oriented
    - B. Logical
    - C. Relational
    - D. Mathematical

5. When accessing a record in an indexed file, which of the following steps would be performed FIRST?
    - A. Accessing the index
    - B. Disk access to the record or bucket
    - C. Data transfer from disk to main program memory
    - D. Relative address conversion to absolute address

6. A database management system (DBMS) that employs a hierarchy, but may relate each lower-level data element to more than one parent element, is classified specifically as a(n) _____ DBMS.
    - A. object-oriented
    - B. network
    - C. relational
    - D. aggregational

7. A value-added field might be added to a database in order to
    - A. standardize field formats
    - B. estimate the disk capacity for a full database
    - C. provide indexing consistency
    - D. improve retrieval

8. Each of the following disks is a type of direct-access disk-storage system EXCEPT

   A. magnetic disk
   B. floppy
   C. moving-capstan
   D. fixed-head

9. In determining an appropriate file organization, three principal factors must be considered.
   Which of the following is NOT one of these factors?

   A. Volatility
   B. Conversion
   C. Activity
   D. Size

10. A _____ file is used to update or modify data in a master file.

    A. descriptor
    B. transaction
    C. secondary
    D. conversion

11. Which of the following steps in designing and using a database would be performed FIRST?

    A. Selecting a name for the file
    B. Deciding the form into which information should be stored
    C. Data definition
    D. Defining the type of data to be stored in each field

12. Each of the following is an advantage associated with the use of a DBMS over a flat-file system EXCEPT

    A. fewer storage requirements
    B. better data integrity
    C. lower software costs
    D. lower operating costs

13. Memory storage space that is not directly addressable by processor instructions, but by specialized I/O instructions, is called

    A. allocated memory
    B. secondary storage
    C. internal storage
    D. main memory

14. Which of the following is NOT a disadvantage associated with sequential file processing?

    A. Master files must be sorted into key field sequence.
    B. Files are only current immediately after an update.
    C. Files are difficult to design.
    D. Transaction files must be stored in the same key.

15. When data is updated in some, but not all, of the files in which it appears, _____ has occurred.

    A. data confusion
    B. data dependence
    C. cross-keying
    D. data redundancy

16. The MOST common medium for direct-access storage is

    A. optical disk
    B. magnetic tape
    C. hard card
    D. magnetic disk

17. The purpose of *hashing* is to

    A. discover an unpartitioned sector onto which data may be written
    B. determine a schedule by which batch-processed data may be submitted to the computer
    C. create a buffer delay between data entry and output during interactive processing
    D. convert the key field value for a record to the address of the record on a file

18. What is the term for the description of a specific set of data corresponding to a model of an enterprise, which is obtained by using a particular data description language?

    A. Schema
    B. Descriptor
    C. Object instance
    D. Conceptualization

19. In a sequential file, records are arranged in sequence according to one or more

    A. query languages
    B. column numbers
    C. key fields
    D. hash marks

20. Which of the following is NOT a mathematical query language operator used in database searches?

    A. +
    B. >=
    C. ^
    D. /

21. In _____ file organization, the cost per each transaction processed remains about the same as the percent of records accessed on a file increases.

    A. sequential
    B. hashed
    C. indexed sequential
    D. random

22. For more complex data types, such as those used in multimedia applications, what type of DBMS would be MOST useful?

    A. Hierarchical
    B. Relational
    C. Object-oriented
    D. Network

23. When determining how many generations of a file to retain in a database, the PRIMARY factor is usually

    A. hardware capabilities
    B. storage space
    C. whether files are keyed or indexed
    D. probability of need to access old data for recovery purposes

24. When data is transferred from a user program to secondary storage, it first passes through

    A. program private memory
    B. file system buffers
    C. I/O buffers
    D. program code

25. In order to maintain files in a database, each of the following operations is typically required EXCEPT

    A. balancing index trees
    B. altering the file system's directory
    C. changing field widths
    D. adding fields to records

KEY (CORRECT ANSWERS)

1.	C	11.	B
2.	A	12.	C
3.	D	13.	B
4.	A	14.	C
5.	A	15.	A
6.	B	16.	D
7.	D	17.	D
8.	C	18.	A
9.	B	19.	C
10.	B	20.	B

21. D
22. C
23. D
24. D
25. B

———

TEST 2

DIRECTIONS: Each question or incomplete statement is followed by several suggested answers or completions. Select the one that BEST answers the question or completes the statement. *PRINT THE LETTER OF THE CORRECT ANSWER IN THE SPACE AT THE RIGHT.*

1. An installation has two tape drives and one disk drive. An application program requires access to three sequential files: an old master file, a transaction file, and an updated master file.
   Typically, the _____ file should be stored on the disk.

   A. old master
   B. transaction
   C. updated master
   D. both versions of the master

2. The purpose of *record blocking* is to

   A. allow multiple records to be brought into main memory in a single access to secondary storage
   B. create the illusion of a *virtual device* for the program until the spooler copies a record to the real device
   C. allocate more free buffer space to a file prior to run-unit determination
   D. offload responsibilities for building data paths from the CPU

3. Entries in a database's secondary key tables (index files), which tell the computer where a data is stored on the disk, are

   A. logical records   B. data addresses
   C. physical records   D. secondary keys

4. Of the types of file organization below, which involves the LOWEST volatility?

   A. Direct   B. Sequential
   C. Master-keyed   D. Indexed

5. Typically each of the following elements is defined during the *data definition* process EXCEPT

   A. field types   B. field names
   C. number of columns   D. width of fields

6. A database's master index contains

   A. the key values for an indexed sequential file
   B. the machine code for every field in a given set of records
   C. the logical record for every randomly-accessed file
   D. each field's physical location on a disk pack

7. Which of the following types of information would MOST likely be stored in a logic field?

   A. Calendar month/day/year
   B. A patient or customer's mailing address
   C. Numbers that may later be involved in some mathematical calculations
   D. The designation of an employee's status is hourly or salaried

8. When determining how frequently a sequential master file should be updated, each of the following factors should be considered EXCEPT

   A. activity ratio
   B. rate of data change
   C. storage space
   D. urgency for current data

9. Which of the following programs is a file manager, rather than a DBMS?

   A. Q&A   B. FoxPro   C. Approach   D. Paradox

10. Which of the following is NOT an advantage associated with the use of indexed file processing?

    A. No need for hashing algorithm
    B. Random access is faster than direct processing
    C. Can function with applications required for both sequential and direct processing
    D. Access to specific records faster than sequential processing

11. Of the query language operators listed below, which is mathematical?

    A. AND   B. SUB   C. <   D. SQRT(N)

12. A collection of records may sometimes be structured as a file on secondary storage, rather than as a data structure in main memory.
    Which of the following is NOT a possible reason for this?

    A. Permanence of storage
    B. Security concerns
    C. Size of collection
    D. Selective access requirements

13. What is the term for the disk rotation time needed for the physical record to pass under read/write heads?

    A. Transaction time
    B. Latency time
    C. Head displacement time
    D. Transfer time

14. The subset of a database schema required by a particular application program is referred to as a(n)

    A. root
    B. user's view
    C. logical structure
    D. node

15. Which of the following steps in designing and using a database would be performed LAST?

    A. Defining the type of data that will be stored in each field
    B. Assigning field names
    C. Data definition
    D. Defining the width of alphanumeric and numeric fields

16. What type of database structure organizes data in the form of two-dimensional tables?

    A. Relational
    B. Network
    C. Logical
    D. Hierarchical

17. What is the term for the specific modules that are capable of reading and writing buffer contents on devices? 17.____

    A. Spoolers
    B. Device handlers
    C. I/O managers
    D. Memory allocators

18. Each of the following is a disadvantage associated with the use of a DBMS EXCEPT 18.____

    A. extensive conversion costs
    B. possible wide distribution of data losses and damage
    C. reduced data security
    D. start-up costs

19. _____ decisions about a database begin after a feasibility study and continue to be refined throughout the design and creation process. 19.____

    A. Procedural
    B. Structural
    C. Conversion
    D. Content

20. Each of the following is an advantage associated with direct file processing EXCEPT 20.____

    A. ability to update several files at the same time
    B. no need for separate transaction files
    C. files do not have to be sorted into key field sequence
    D. fewer storage space required than for sequential processing

21. The core of any file management system accesses secondary storage through 21.____

    A. the I/O manager
    B. file system buffers
    C. relative addressing
    D. key access

22. Each of the following is a responsibility typically belonging to a file system EXCEPT 22.____

    A. maintaining directories
    B. interfacing the CPU with a secondary storage device
    C. establishing paths for data flow between main memory and secondary storage
    D. buffering data for delivery to the CPU or secondary devices

23. In a hierarchical database, there are several phone numbers belonging to a single address.
    This is an example of 23.____

    A. vector data aggregate
    B. data dependence
    C. data confusion
    D. data redundancy

24. A DBMS might access the data dictionary for each of the following purposes EXCEPT 24.____

    A. change the description of a data field
    B. to determine if a data element already exists before adding
    C. request and deliver information from the database to the user
    D. determine what application programs can access what data elements

25. _____ would MOST likely be stored in a memo field.

    A. A revisable listing of symptoms specific to a particular ailment
    B. The designation of a patient's gender (male/female)
    C. A patient's billing number
    D. The date of a patient's last visit

KEY (CORRECT ANSWERS)

1.	B	11.	D
2.	A	12.	B
3.	A	13.	B
4.	B	14.	B
5.	C	15.	D
6.	A	16.	A
7.	D	17.	B
8.	C	18.	C
9.	A	19.	B
10.	B	20.	D

21. A
22. B
23. A
24. C
25. A

EXAMINATION SECTION
TEST 1

DIRECTIONS: Each question or incomplete statement is followed by several suggested answers or completions. Select the one that BEST answers the question or completes the statement. *PRINT THE LETTER OF THE CORRECT ANSWER IN THE SPACE AT THE RIGHT.*

1. What is the term for a device that enables a single communications channel to carry data transmissions from many different sources simultaneously? 1._____

   A. Compiler
   C. Concentrator
   B. Multitasker
   D. Multiplexer

2. Which of the following represents the earliest stage in the computer language translation process? 2._____

   A. Linkage editor
   C. Compiler
   B. Load module
   D. Object code

3. Within data flow diagrams, the transformations that occur within the lowest level are described by 3._____

   A. development methodologies
   B. structure charts
   C. selection constructs
   D. process specifications

4. The time or number of operations after which a process in a system repeats itself is expressed in a measure known as 4._____

   A. periodicity
   C. loop
   B. synchronicity
   D. iteration

5. What is the term for the single steps or actions in the logic of a program that do NOT depend on the existence of any condition? 5._____

   A. Logical construct
   C. Sequence construct
   B. Run control
   D. Rule base

6. Which of the following terms is most different in meaning from the others? 6._____

   A. Data file approach
   B. Relational data model
   C. Flat file organization
   D. Traditional file environment

7. Which of the following is a tool for locating data on the Internet that performs key word searches of an actual database of documents, software, and data files available for downloading? 7._____

   A. WAIS   B. Archie   C. Acrobat   D. Gopher

8. Typical transaction processing (TPS) systems include all of the following types EXCEPT _____ systems. 8._____

   A. finance/accounting
   C. engineering/design
   B. sales/marketing
   D. human resources

9. The main weakness of the enterprise analysis approach to systems development is that it

   A. involves little input at the managerial level
   B. is relatively unstructured
   C. produces an enormous amount of data that is expensive to collect and analyze
   D. only generally identifies an organization's informational requirements

10. What is the term for special system software that translates a higher-level language into machine language for execution by the computer?

    A. Compiler   B. Translator   C. Renderer   D. Assembler

11. Compared to private branch exchanges, LANs
    I. are more expensive to install
    II. have a smaller geographical range
    III. are more inflexible
    IV. require specially trained staff

    The CORRECT answer is

    A. I only   B. I, III
    C. I, II, IV   D. III, IV

12. Each of the following is considered to be a basic component of a database management system EXCEPT a

    A. transform algorithm
    B. data manipulation language
    C. data definition language
    D. data dictionary

13. Which of the following is a technical approach to the study of information systems?

    A. Management science   B. Sociology
    C. Political science   D. Psychology

14. In desktop publishing applications, a user may sometimes elect to alter the standard spacing between two characters. This is a technique known as

    A. weighting   B. kerning   C. pointing   D. leading

15. In systems design, the generic framework used to think about a problem is known as the

    A. schema   B. reference model
    C. prototype   D. operational model

16. What is the term for a small computer that manages communications for the host computer in a network?

    A. Concentrator   B. Multiplexer
    C. Controller   D. Front-end processor

17. Which of the following is a competitive strategy for developing new market niches, where a business can compete in a target area better than its competitors?   17.____

    A. Vertical integration	B. Focused differentiation
    C. Multitasking	D. Forward engineering

18. An electronic meeting system (EMS) is considered to be a type of collaborative   18.____

    A. executive support system (ESS)
    B. management information system (MIS)
    C. office automation system (OAS)
    D. group decision support system (GDSS)

19. In systems theory, the minimum description required to distinguish a system from its environment is known as a(n)   19.____

    A. blip	B. margin	C. mediation	D. boundary

20. The principal advantage of the hierarchical and network database models is   20.____

    A. adaptability
    B. architecture simplicity
    C. minimal programming requirements
    D. processing efficiency

21. Which of the following is a character–oriented tool for locating data on the Internet which allows a user to locate textual information through a series of hierarchical menus?   21.____

    A. FTP	B. Gopher	C. Lug	D. Archie

22. The principal logical database models include each of the following types EXCEPT   22.____

    A. network	B. object–oriented
    C. relational	D. hierarchical

23. Computer programming includes a logic pattern where a stated condition determines which of two or more actions can be taken, depending on the condition. This pattern is known as the   23.____

    A. object linkage	B. selection construct
    C. key field	D. iteration construct

24. Which of the following is the tool used by database designers to document a conceptual data model?   24.____

    A. Entity–relationship diagram
    B. Partition statement
    C. Gantt chart
    D. Data–flow diagram

25. The phenomenon of _____ refers to the idea that people will avoid new uncertain alternatives and stick with traditional and familiar rules and procedures.   25.____

    A. the Hawthorne effect
    B. bounded rationality
    C. system–oriented reasoning
    D. case–based reasoning

KEY (CORRECT ANSWERS)

1.	D	11.	C
2.	C	12.	A
3.	D	13.	A
4.	A	14.	B
5.	C	15.	B
6.	B	16.	D
7.	B	17.	B
8.	C	18.	D
9.	C	19.	D
10.	A	20.	D

21.	B
22.	B
23.	B
24.	A
25.	B

TEST 2

DIRECTIONS: Each question or incomplete statement is followed by several suggested answers or completions. Select the one that BEST answers the question or completes the statement. *PRINT THE LETTER OF THE CORRECT ANSWER IN THE SPACE AT THE RIGHT.*

1. In systems theory, the history of a system's structural transformations is referred to as its   1.____

   A. ontology
   B. entailment
   C. ontogeny
   D. epistemology

2. Programming language that consists of the 1s and 0s of binary code is referred to as   2.____

   A. machine language
   B. assemblage
   C. object language
   D. pseudocode

3. Generally, the EBCDIC standard can be used to code up to _____ characters in one byte of information.   3.____

   A. 128   B. 256   C. 512   D. 1024

4. In MIS terminology, which of the following offers the best definition of *network*?   4.____

   A. The devices and software that link components and transfer data from one location to another
   B. The media and software governing the storage and organization of data for use
   C. Two or more computers linked to share data or resources such as a printer
   D. Formal rules for accomplishing tasks

5. Which of the following is a type of MIS application used for analysis?   5.____

   A. Database
   B. Operations research
   C. Desktop publishing
   D. Presentation

6. In computer processing, an overload sometimes results when trying to test more rules to reach a solution that the computer is capable of handling. This type of overload is referred to as   6.____

   A. combinatorial explosion
   B. data crashing
   C. transaction jam
   D. conversion error

7. In the normal processing of a workgroup information system, which of the following is an operations procedure, as opposed to a user procedure?   7.____

   A. Maintaining backup
   B. Placing constraints on processing
   C. Initiating access to network
   D. Starting hardware and programs

8. A company's European units want to share information about production schedules and inventory levels to ship excess products from one country to another. The telecommunications technology most appropriate for this is   8.____

   A. teleconferencing
   B. voice mail
   C. e-mail
   D. videoconferencing

9. As opposed to systems development, approximately how much of an organization's efforts can be expected to be spent on systems maintenance during the total system life cycle?

   A. 25   B. 45   C. 65   D. 85

10. The most critical, and often most difficult, task of the systems analyst is usually to

    A. define the specific problem that must be solved with an information system
    B. identify the causes of the problem
    C. specify the nature of the solution that will address the problem
    D. define the specific information requirements that must be met by the system solution

11. Which of the following is not a commonly recognized difference between workgroup and enterprise management information systems?

    A. An enterprise MIS is a subfunction of a company.
    B. Workgroup MIS users know and work with each other.
    C. An enterprise MIS uses several different applications.
    D. A workgroup MIS is a peripheral system.

12. The first step in testing the accuracy of a spreadsheet application is usually to

    A. verify the input
    B. stresstest the spreadsheet
    C. check the output
    D. involve others in the process

13. Programs in information systems make use of complete, unambiguous procedures for solving specified problems in a finite number of steps. These procedures are known as

    A. schema   B. protocols
    C. algorithms   D. criteria

14. Weaknesses in a system's _____ controls may permit unauthorized changes in processing.

    A. software   B. computer operations
    C. data file security D. implementation

15. In the model of case–based reasoning, after a user describes a problem, the system

    A. modifies its solution to better fit the problem
    B. asks the user questions to narrow its search
    C. retrieves a solution
    D. searches a database for a similar problem

16. The particular form that information technology takes in a specific organization to achieve selected goals or functions is referred to as the organization's

    A. information configuration
    B. knowledge base
    C. operability
    D. information architecture

17. Which of the following applications is most likely to require real-time response from a telecommunications network? 17.____

   A. Intercomputer data exchange
   B. Administrative message switching
   C. Process control
   D. On-line text retrieval

18. The main DISADVANTAGE associated with the use of application software packages to solve organizational problems is that 18.____

   A. the initial costs of purchase are often prohibitive
   B. they often involve the added costs of customization and additional programming
   C. maintenance and support will usually have to come from within the purchasing organization
   D. the new program usually requires intensive training

19. Which of the following is a disadvantage associated with distributed data processing? 19.____

   A. Drains on system power
   B. Reliance on high-end telecommunications technology
   C. Increased vulnerability of storage location
   D. Reduced responsiveness to local users

20. In the current environment of systems development, end-user computing contributes most effectively to the _____ aspects of the process. 20.____

   A. problem identification and systems study
   B. installation and maintenance
   C. systems study and installation
   D. programming and detail design

21. Which of the following steps in the machine cycle of a computer occurs during the execution cycle (e-cycle)? 21.____

   A. Instruction fetched
   B. Data sent from main memory to storage register
   C. Instruction decoded
   D. Instruction placed into instruction register

22. Of the following, which offers the least accurate definition of *information* as it applies to the study of MIS? 22.____

   A. Data placed within a context
   B. The amount of uncertainty that is reduced when a message is received
   C. A thing or things that are known to have occurred, to exist, or to be true
   D. Knowledge derived from data

23. Programming languages in which each source code statement generates multiple statements at the machine-language level are described as 23.____

   A. incremental   B. high-level
   C. first-generation   D. hierarchical

24. Which of the following types of visual representations is used as an overview, to depict an entire system as a single process with its major inputs and outputs?

   A. Context diagram
   B. Decision tree
   C. Data flow diagram
   D. Nomograph

25. Once an organization has developed a business telecommunications plan, it must determine the initial scope of the project, taking several factors into account. The first and most important of these factors is

   A. security
   B. connectivity
   C. distance
   D. multiple access

KEY (CORRECT ANSWERS)

1. C
2. A
3. B
4. C
5. B

6. A
7. D
8. C
9. C
10. D

11. A
12. C
13. C
14. A
15. D

16. D
17. D
18. B
19. B
20. D

21. B
22. C
23. B
24. A
25. C

TEST 3

DIRECTIONS: Each question or incomplete statement is followed by several suggested answers or completions. Select the one that BEST answers the question or completes the statement. *PRINT THE LETTER OF THE CORRECT ANSWER IN THE SPACE AT THE RIGHT.*

1. Which of the following is a commonly used term for the programming environment of an expert system?

    A. Model   B. Ada   C. Schema   D. AI shell

2. In the language of dataflow diagrams, the external entity that absorbs a dataflow is known as a

    A. store   B. sink   C. cache   D. source

3. Which of the following is most clearly a fault tolerant technology?

    A. Random access memory
    B. On–line transaction processing
    C. Secondary storage
    D. Mobile data networks

4. Each of the following is a type of input control used with applications EXCEPT

    A. data conversion   B. run control totals
    C. edit checks   D. batch control totals

5. In a typical organization, approximately what percentage of total system maintenance time is spent making user enhancements, improving documentation, and recoding system components?

    A. 20   B. 40   C. 60   D. 80

6. Which of the following is NOT considered to be an operations control used with information systems?

    A. Error detection circuitry
    B. Control of equipment maintenance
    C. Regulated access to data centers
    D. Control of archival storage

7. Which of the following styles of systems development is most often used for information systems at the workgroup level?

    A. Traditional life cycle
    B. Life cycle for licensed programs
    C. Prototyping
    D. Outsourcing

8. Which of the following systems exists at the management level of an organization?

    A. Decision support system (DSS)
    B. Executive support system (ESS)
    C. Office automation system (OAS)
    D. Expert system

9. What is the term for a special language translator that translates each source code statement into machine code and executes it one at a time?

   A. Adapter
   B. Assembler
   C. Compiler
   D. Interpreter

10. Which of the following is NOT perceived to be a difference between a decision support system and a management information system?

    A. In an MIS, systems analysis is aimed at identifying information requirements.
    B. The philosophy of a DSS is to provide integrated tools, data, and models to users.
    C. The design process of an MIS is never really considered to be finished.
    D. The design of a DSS is an interative process.

11. Which of the following is a programming language that resembles machine language but substitutes mnemonics for numeric codes?

    A. Pseudocode
    B. BASIC
    C. C
    D. Assembly language

12. Each of the following is a rule of thumb for handling type in desktop publishing applications EXCEPT

    A. use small capitals for acronyms
    B. use sans serif typefaces when presenting a lot of text
    C. generally limit the different number of typefaces in a document to two
    D. use distinctly different typefaces together in the same document

13. Typically, a microcomputer is classified as a desktop or portable machine that has up to

    A. 1 gigabyte of secondary storage space
    B. 5 gigabytes of secondary storage space
    C. 64 megabytes of RAM
    D. 1 gigabyte of RAM

14. Which of the following is NOT considered to be a basic component of a decision support system?

    A. Electronic meeting system
    B. Database
    C. DSS software system
    D. Model base

15. Information systems that monitor the elementary activities and transactions of the organization are said to be functioning at the _____ level.

    A. tactical
    B. operational
    C. strategic
    D. managerial

16. Which of the following applications would be most likely to use the sequential method of file organization in a database?

    A. Personnel evaluations
    B. Inventory
    C. Asset turnover calculations
    D. Payroll

17. Each of the following is a reason for the increased vulnerability of computerized systems to external threats EXCEPT

    A. invisible appearance of procedures
    B. inability to replicate manually
    C. wider overall impact than manual systems
    D. multiple points of access

18. Membership functions are nonspecific terms that are used to solve problems in applications of

    A. decision support   B. expert systems
    C. neural networks   D. fuzzy logic

19. Rules or standards used to rank alternatives in order of desirability are known as

    A. norms   B. algorithms
    C. parameters   D. criteria

20. In most organizations, the database administration group performs each of the following functions EXCEPT

    A. developing security procedures
    B. performing data quality audits
    C. maintaining database management software
    D. defining and organizing database structure and content

21. What is the term for on-line data that appears in the form of fixed-format reports for management executives?

    A. Browsers   B. Briefing books
    C. Modules   D. Web pages

22. Which of the following is a likely application of the optimization models of a decision-support system?

    A. Forecasting sales
    B. Determining the proper product mix within a given market
    C. Predicting the actions of competitors
    D. Goal seeking

23. In database management, a group of related fields is known as a(n)

    A. domain   B. register   C. record   D. file

24. Storage of _____ is NOT a function of a computer's primary storage.   24._____
    A. operating system programs
    B. data being used by the program
    C. all or part of the program being executed
    D. long-term data in a nonvolatile space

25. Which of the following is equal to 1 billion bytes of information?   25._____
    A. Nanobyte   B. Gigabyte   C. Terabyte   D. Megabyte

KEY (CORRECT ANSWERS)

1. D   11. D
2. B   12. B
3. B   13. C
4. B   14. A
5. C   15. B

6. A   16. D
7. B   17. C
8. A   18. D
9. D   19. D
10. C   20. B

21. B
22. B
23. C
24. D
25. B

EXAMINATION SECTION
TEST 1

DIRECTIONS: Each question or incomplete statement is followed by several suggested answers or completions. Select the one that BEST answers the question or completes the statement. *PRINT THE LETTER OF THE CORRECT ANSWER IN THE SPACE AT THE RIGHT.*

1. What is the term for the methodical simplification of a logical data model?   1.____

    A. Elucidation B. Normalization
    C. Partitioning D. Bit streaming

2. Systems development projects _____ are most likely to benefit from the use of internal integration tools.   2.____

    A. with high levels of technical complexity
    B. in which end-user participation is voluntary
    C. which experience counterimplementation
    D. that are small in scale and involve only specific departments

3. In a typical telecommunications system, a message that has just passed through the front-end multiplexer will then pass through   3.____

    A. a front-end processor B. a modem or modems
    C. a controller D. the host computer

4. Which of the following is a characteristic of data warehouse data? They   4.____

    A. are organized from a functional view
    B. are volatile to support operations within a company
    C. include enterprise-wide data, collected from legacy systems
    D. involve individual fields that may be inconsistent across the enterprise

5. Which of the following terms is used to enumerate the bits that can be moved at one time between a CPU, primary storage, and other devices of a computer?   5.____

    A. Bandwidth B. RAM cache
    C. Data bus width D. Register

6. In enterprise analysis, data elements are organized into groups that support related sets of organizational processes. These groups are known as   6.____

    A. data sub-units B. critical success factors
    C. end-user interfaces D. logical application groups

7. Which of the following terms is used to describe a system's order of complexity?   7.____

    A. Resilience B. Eudemony
    C. Ordinality D. Dialectics

8. Of the following file organization methods, the only one that can be used on magnetic tape is   8.____

    A. random B. indexed sequential
    C. alphabetic D. sequential

9. What is the term for a set of rules and procedures that govern transmissions between the components of a telecommunications network?

   A. Criteria
   B. Norms
   C. Algorithms
   D. Protocols

10. In what type of processing can more than one instruction be processed at once, by breaking down a problem into smaller parts and processing them simultaneously?

    A. Parallel
    B. Indexed
    C. Sequential
    D. Batch

11. Which of the following terms is used to describe a system in which the internal parameters can be changed when necessary through feedback?

    A. Homeostatic
    B. Elastic
    C. Capacitive
    D. Heuristic

12. Each of the following is a rule of thumb for handling graphics in desktop publishing applications EXCEPT

    A. using pie charts for showing parts of a whole
    B. showing data relationships with line plots
    C. using serif typefaces in graph labels
    D. using bar charts to shown quantities of a single item

13. The central liability-related ethical issue raised by new information technologies is generally considered to be

    A. whether software or other intellectual property may be copied for personal use
    B. the point at which it is justifiable to release software or services for consumption by others
    C. the conditions under which it is justifiable to invade the privacy of others
    D. whether individuals and organizations that create, produce, and sell systems are morally responsible for the consequences of their use

14. Which of the following personnel would be considered part of the development team in an MIS department?

    A. Control clerk
    B. Maintenance programmer
    C. Education specialist
    D. Data administrator

15. Which of the following is an object-oriented programming language that can deliver only the software functionality needed for a particular task, and which can run on any computer or operating system?

    A. Perl
    B. C
    C. Linux
    D. Java

16. Which of the following is NOT typically an example of the inquiry/response type of telecommunications application?

    A. Point-of-sale system
    B. Airline reservation system
    C. Hospital information system
    D. Credit checking

17. Which of the following is an example of work-flow management?

    A. Financial officers at a firm use a computer program to calculate the rate of return for specific investments.
    B. A manager views a company's quarterly revenues from her own workstation without the need for printed matter.
    C. Loan officers at a bank enter application information into a central system so that the application can be evaluated by many people at once.
    D. Cashiers at a retail outlet scan the bar codes on items of merchandise to more quickly move customers through the checkout.

18. According to Simon's description, there are four stages in any decision-making process. Decision support systems are designed primarily to help monitor the _____ stage.

    A. implementation B. design
    C. choice   D. intelligence

19. A form of organization resembling a fishnet or network, in which authority is determined by knowledge and function, is a

    A. hierarchy   B. matrix
    C. heterarchy D. homeostat

20. What is the term used to describe the approach to software development that combines data and procedures into a single item?

    A. Operational   B. Object-oriented
    C. Output controlled D. Transactional

21. Which of the following is a computer language that is an application generator?

    A. SQL   B. Nomad   C. AMAPS   D. FOCUS

22. Approximately what percentage of an organization's software development budget will be expended on testing?

    A. 10-20   B. 15-35   C. 30-50   D. 55-75

23. The process embodied in an input-output device, which enables it to convert or code without memory a type of signal, motion, or sequence of characters into another, is known as

    A. telematics   B. polarity
    C. reification D. transduction

24. Which of the following steps in the business systems planning (BSP) process is typically performed FIRST?

    A. Defining business processes
    B. Analyzing current systems support
    C. Defining information architecture
    D. Developing recommendations

25. What is the term for a networking technology that parcels information into 8-byte cells, allowing data to be transmitted between computers of different vendors at any speed? 25.____

    A. Indexed sequential access method (ISAM)
    B. Asynchronous transfer mode (ATM)
    C. Private branch exchange (PBX)
    D. Domestic export

KEY (CORRECT ANSWERS)

1.	B	11.	D
2.	A	12.	C
3.	B	13.	D
4.	C	14.	B
5.	C	15.	D
6.	D	16.	C
7.	C	17.	C
8.	D	18.	A
9.	D	19.	C
10.	A	20.	B

21. D
22. C
23. D
24. A
25. B

TEST 2

DIRECTIONS: Each question or incomplete statement is followed by several suggested answers or completions. Select the one that BEST answers the question or completes the statement. *PRINT THE LETTER OF THE CORRECT ANSWER IN THE SPACE AT THE RIGHT.*

1. *Intelligent agent* software is an appropriate tool for each of the following applications EXCEPT

    A. finding cheap airfares
    B. conducting data conferences
    C. scheduling appointments
    D. deleting junk e-mail

2. Which of the following is the general term for high-speed digital communications networks that are national or worldwide in scope and accessible by the general public?

    A. Wide-area networks (WANs)
    B. Internet
    C. World Wide Web
    D. Information superhighway

3. Which of the following types of organizations is LEAST likely to make use of a hierarchical database?

    A. Insurance companies
    B. Consultancies/service organizations
    C. Banks
    D. National retailers

4. A transmission rate of _____ per second falls within the normal range for a local-area network.

    A. 70 bits   B. 100 kilobits
    C. 100 megabits   D. 3 gigabits

5. In the history of artificial intelligence, the effort to build a physical analog to the human brain has been referred to as the _____ approach.

    A. schematic   B. sequential
    C. neuronet   D. bottom-up

6. In an individual MIS, the most commonly-used technique for conducting operations research is _____ programming.

    A. productivity   B. statistical
    C. management   D. linear

7. Of the types of organizational change that are enabled by information technology, which tends to be the most common?

    A. Paradigm shift
    B. Automation
    C. Business reengineering
    D. Rationalization of procedures

8. Which of the following is offered the clearest protection under the Electronic Communications Privacy Act of 1986?

    A. Personal e-mail received from outside by the organization's system
    B. Interoffice fax transmissions
    C. Business-related phone calls received from outside by the organization's system
    D. Interoffice e-mail

9. Which of the following systems exists at the operational level of an organization?

    A. Transaction processing system (TPS)
    B. Executive support system (ESS)
    C. Office automation system (OAS)
    D. Management information system (MIS)

10. The representation of data as they appear to an application programmer or end user is described as a(n) _____ view.

    A. schematic
    B. analogous
    C. logical
    D. physical

11. Which of the computer hardware *generations* involved vacuum tube technology?

    A. First   B. Second   C. Third   D. Fourth

12. Which of the following is an example of the administrative message switching application of telecommunications technology?

    A. Inventory control
    B. Electronic mail
    C. Library systems
    D. International transfer of bank funds

13. Which of the following styles of systems development is most often used for information systems at the enterprise level?

    A. Prototyping
    B. Outsourcing
    C. End-user development
    D. Traditional life cycle

14. Which of the following is an element of the physical design of an information system?

    A. Manual procedures
    B. Input descriptions
    C. Processing functions
    D. Controls

15. Which of the following functions to connect dissimilar networks by providing the translation from one protocol to another?

    A. Gateway   B. Assembler   C. Gopher   D. Buffer

16. The primary memory of most microcomputers is measured in

    A. megabytes   B. gigabytes   C. kilobytes   D. bytes

17. _____ tools is a project management technique that structures and sequences tasks, and budgets the time, money, and technical resources required to complete these tasks.

    A. Internal integration
    B. Formal control
    C. External integration
    D. Formal planning

18. What is the term for the capacity of a communications channel as measured by the difference between the highest and lowest frequencies that can be transmitted by that channel?

    A. Transmissivity
    B. Broadband
    C. Baud rate
    D. Bandwidth

18.____

19. Which of the following are LEAST likely to be an input into a management information system (MIS)?

    A. Design specifications
    B. Simple models
    C. Summary transaction data
    D. High-volume data

19.____

20. Which of the following is a shared network service technology that packages data into bundles for transmission but does not use error correction routines?

    A. Private branch exchange
    B. Packet switching
    C. Internal integration
    D. Frame relay

20.____

21. A purpose of a file server in a network is to

    A. collect messages for batch transmission
    B. route communications
    C. store programs
    D. connect dissimilar networks

21.____

22. _____ testing provides the final certification that a new system is ready to be used in a production setting.

    A. Parallel
    B. Unit
    C. Acceptance
    D. System

22.____

23. The number of _____ is NOT an example of software metrics.

    A. payroll checks printed per hour
    B. known users who are dissatisfied with an application's performance
    C. transactions that can be processed in one business day
    D. known bugs per hundred lines of code

23.____

24. What is the term for a set or rules that govern the manipulation of characters in a system?

    A. Synergy
    B. Entropy
    C. Aggregation
    D. Calculus

24.____

25. During the process of enterprise analysis, the results of a large managerial survey are broken down into each of the following EXCEPT

    A. processes
    B. goals
    C. data matrices
    D. functions

25.____

KEY (CORRECT ANSWERS)

1.	B	11.	A
2.	D	12.	B
3.	B	13.	D
4.	C	14.	A
5.	D	15.	A
6.	D	16.	C
7.	B	17.	D
8.	A	18.	D
9.	A	19.	A
10.	C	20.	D

21. C
22. C
23. B
24. D
25. B

———

EXAMINATION SECTION
TEST 1

DIRECTIONS: Each question or incomplete statement is followed by several suggested answers or completions. Select the one that BEST answers the question or completes the statement. *PRINT THE LETTER OF THE CORRECT ANSWER IN THE SPACE AT THE RIGHT.*

1. Representations of human knowledge used in expert systems generally include each of the following EXCEPT

    A. frames
    B. semantic nets
    C. fuzzy logic
    D. rules

    1.____

2. Routines performed to verify input data and correct errors prior to processing are known as

    A. edit checks
    B. pilots
    C. control aids
    D. data audits

    2.____

3. Which of the following statements about database management systems is generally FALSE?
They

    A. are able to separate logical and physical views of data
    B. eliminate data confusion by providing central control of data creation and definitions
    C. reduce data redundancy
    D. involve slight increases in program development and maintenance costs

    3.____

4. In systems theory, there is a *what-if* method of treating uncertainty that explores the effect on the alternatives of environmental change. This method is generally referred to as _____ analysis.

    A. sensitivity
    B. contingency
    C. a fortiori
    D. systems

    4.____

5. One of the core capabilities of a decision support system (DSS) is the logical and mathematical manipulation of data_____ a capability referred to as

    A. control aids
    B. representations
    C. memory aids
    D. operations

    5.____

6. What is the term for the ability to move software from one generation of hardware to another more powerful generation?

    A. Adaptability
    B. Interoperability
    C. Multitasking
    D. Migration

    6.____

7. In an enterprise information system, which of the following is considered to be an input control?

    A. Documentation of operating procedures
    B. Reviews of processing logs
    C. Verification of control totals
    D. Program testing

    7.____

8. Low-speed transmission of data that occurs one character at a time is described as 8.____

   A. asynchronous   B. unchained
   C. phased   D. unstructured

9. Which of the following is a disadvantage associated with the use of relational databases? 9.____

   A. Limited ability to combine information from different sources
   B. Simplicity in maintenance
   C. Relatively slower speed of operation
   D. Limited flexibility regarding ad hoc queries

10. When all the elements in a system are in the same category, _____ is said to be at a minimum. 10.____

    A. uncertainty   B. synergy
    C. inefficiency   D. entropy

11. Which of the following is most likely to rely on parallel processing? 11.____

    A. Minicomputer   B. Workstation
    C. Microcomputer D. Supercomputer

12. In imaging systems, what is the term for the device that allows a user to identify and retrieve a specific document? 12.____

    A. Forward chain   B. Index server
    C. Knowledge base D. Search engine

13. Which of the following systems exists at the strategic level of an organization? 13.____

    A. Decision support system (DSS)
    B. Executive support system (ESS)
    C. Knowledge work system (KWS)
    D. Management information system (MIS)

14. What is the term for the secondary storage device on which a complete operating system is stored? 14.____

    A. Central Processing Unit   B. Microprocessor
    C. Optical code recognizer   D. System residence drive

15. Which of the following is NOT a type of knowledge work system (KWS)? 15.____

    A. Investment workstations
    B. Virtual reality systems
    C. Computer-aided design (CAD)
    D. Decision support system (DSS)

16. A transmission over a telecommunications network in which data can flow two ways, but in only one direction at a time, is described as 16.____

    A. simplex   B. half duplex
    C. full duplex D. multiplex

17. The functions of knowledge workers in an organization generally include each of the following EXCEPT

    A. updating knowledge
    B. managing documentation of knowledge
    C. serving as internal consultants
    D. acting as change agents

17.____

18. The predominant programming language for business was

    A. Perl   B. COBOL   C. FORTRAN   D. SGML

18.____

19. In general, the technology associated with reduced instruction set (RISC) computers is most appropriate for

    A. decision support systems (DSS)
    B. network communications
    C. scientific and workstation computing
    D. desktop publishing

19.____

20. Which of the following signifies the international reference model for linking different types of computers and networks?

    A. WAN   B. ISDN   C. TCP/IP   D. OSI

20.____

21. The main difference between neural networks and expert systems is that neural networks

    A. seek a generalized capability to learn
    B. program solutions
    C. are aimed at solving one specific problem at a time
    D. seek to emulate or model a person's way of solving a set of problems

21.____

22. Which of the following is not a management benefit associated with end-user development of information systems?

    A. Reduced application backlog
    B. Increased user satisfaction
    C. Simplified testing and documentation procedures
    D. Improved requirements determination

22.____

23. Which of the following is NOT an example of an output control associated with information systems?

    A. Balancing output totals with input and processing totals
    B. formal procedures and documentation specifying recipients of reports and checks
    C. Error handling
    D. Review of computer processing logs

23.____

24. Of the following statements about the evolutionary planning method of strategic information systems design, which is FALSE?
    It is

    A. a top-down method
    B. high adaptive
    C. best for use in a dynamic environment
    D. susceptible to domination by a few users

25. In a relational database, a row or record is referred to as a(n)

    A. applet
    B. key field
    C. tuple
    D. bitmap

KEY (CORRECT ANSWERS)

1. C	11. D
2. A	12. B
3. D	13. B
4. B	14. D
5. D	15. D
6. D	16. B
7. C	17. B
8. A	18. B
9. C	19. C
10. A	20. D

21. A
22. C
23. C
24. A
25. C

TEST 2

DIRECTIONS: Each question or incomplete statement is followed by several suggested answers or completions. Select the one that BEST answers the question or completes the statement. *PRINT THE LETTER OF THE CORRECT ANSWER IN THE SPACE AT THE RIGHT.*

1. The technical staff of an organization are most likely to be users of a(n)　　1.____

    A. transaction processing system (TPS)
    B. management information system (MIS)
    C. decision support system (DSS)
    D. knowledge work system (KWS)

2. The predefined packet of data in some LANs, which includes data indicating the sender, receiver, and whether the packet is in use, is known as a　　2.____

    A. bus　　B. check　　C. token　　D. parity

3. Which of the following is NOT a typical characteristic of hypertext and hypermedia applications?　　3.____

    A. Users given commands to delete frames
    B. Independence from GUI environment
    C. Frames displayed in windows
    D. In shared systems, concurrent access to hypermedia data

4. Which of the following is a commercial digital information service that exists to provide business information?　　4.____

    A. Prodigy　　B. Dialog　　C. Quotron　　D. Lexis

5. Which of the following is NOT a characteristic of an enterprise MIS?　　5.____

    A. Standardization
    B. Requires systems managers
    C. Homogeneous data
    D. Supports multiple applications

6. In workgroup information systems, the simplest type of group conferencing is referred to as a(n)　　6.____

    A. videoconference　　　　B. group meeting
    C. asynchronous meeting　　D. electronic bulletin board

7. Which of the following is an advantage associated with the LAN model of multi-user systems?　　7.____

    A. Reliability of many computers
    B. Unlimited performance
    C. Centralized control
    D. Relative independence from technology

8. The main advantage of digital private branch exchanges over other local networking options is that they　　8.____

A. make use of existing phone lines
B. have a greater geographical range
C. perform important traffic control functions
D. can generally transmit larger volumes of data

9. In a typical organization, tactical and operational planning of an MIS would be the responsibility of the

A. steering committee and MIS managers
B. project teams
C. operations personnel and end users
D. chief information officer

10. _____ code is the term for program instructions written in a high-level language before translation into machine language.

A. Spaghetti   B. Source   C. Macro   D. Pseudo

11. In its current form, the technology of electronic data interchange (EDI) is appropriate for transmitting all of the following EXCEPT

A. purchase orders   B. bills of lading
C. solicitations   D. invoices

12. Which of the following types of applications is generally most dependent on the graphical user interface (GUI) environment?

A. Electronic communication
B. Desktop publishing
C. Word processing
D. Spreadsheet

13. Which of the following is a logical design element of an information system?

A. Hardware specifications   B. Output media
C. Data models   D. Software

14. A processing system rejects an order transaction for 10,000 units, on the basis that no order larger than 70 units had been placed previously. This is an example of a

A. check digit   B. format check
C. reasonableness check   D. dependency check

15. The concentric circle on the surface area of a disk, on which data are stored as magnetized spots, is known as a

A. cylinder   B. track   C. register   D. sector

16. Which of the following storage media generally has the slowest access speed?

A. Optical disk   B. RAM
C. Magnetic disk   D. Cache

17. The most time-consuming element of system conversion plans is

A. hardware upgrading   B. personnel training
C. documentation   D. data conversion

18. In most organizations, the chief information officer is given a rank equivalent to 18.____

    A. project manager B. data administrator
    C. team leader D. vice president

19. Which of the following statements about the prototyping approach to systems development is FALSE? 19.____
    It is

    A. especially valuable for designing an end-user interface
    B. generally better suited for larger applications
    C. most useful when there is some uncertainty about requirements or design solutions
    D. as iterative process

20. What is the term for the final step in system reengineering, when the revised specifications are used to generate new, structure program code for a structured and maintainable system? 20.____

    A. Direct cutover B. Reverse engineering
    C. Workflow engineering D. Forward engineering

21. Which of the following are included in an MIS audit? 21.____
    I. Physical facilities
    II. Telecommunications
    III. Control systems
    IV. Manual procedures
    The CORRECT answer is:

    A. I, IV B. II, III
    C. I, II, III D. I, II, III, IV

22. In the traditional systems life cycle model, which of the following stages occurs EARLIEST? 22.____

    A. Programming B. Design
    C. Installation D. Systems study

23. Which of the following concerns is addressed by front-end CASE (Computer-Assisted Software Engineering) tools? 23.____

    A. Testing B. Analysis
    C. Maintenance D. Coding

24. In an individual MIS, the most commonly used analytical application is a 24.____

    A. statistical program B. gateway
    C. spreadsheet D. utility

25. Certain kinds of expert systems use the property of inheritance to organize and classify knowledge when the knowledge base is composed of easily identifiable chunks or objects of interrelated characteristics. These systems are known specifically as 25.____

    A. political models B. rule bases
    C. formal control tools D. semantic nets

KEY (CORRECT ANSWERS)

1. D
2. C
3. B
4. B
5. C

6. D
7. A
8. A
9. A
10. B

11. C
12. B
13. C
14. C
15. B

16. C
17. D
18. D
19. B
20. D

21. D
22. D
23. B
24. C
25. D

TEST 3

DIRECTIONS: Each question or incomplete statement is followed by several suggested answers or completions. Select the one that BEST answers the question or completes the statement. *PRINT THE LETTER OF THE CORRECT ANSWER IN THE SPACE AT THE RIGHT.*

1. Of an organization's total MIS budget, the majority can be expected to be spent on 1.____

    A. training
    B. programming
    C. operations
    D. administration

2. Each of the following is an element of the installation stage in the traditional model of a systems life cycle EXCEPT 2.____

    A. testing
    B. programming
    C. conversion
    D. training

3. For network applications in which some processing must be centralized and some can be performed locally, which of the following configurations is most appropriate? 3.____

    A. Bus B. Ring C. Star D. Token ring

4. In systems development, the main difference between strategic analysis and enterprise analysis is that 4.____

    A. enterprise analysis makes use of the personal interview
    B. enterprise analysis produces a smaller data set
    C. strategic analysis is used exclusively in profit concerns
    D. strategic analysis tends to have a broader focus

5. Each of the following is a type of source data automation technology EXCEPT 5.____

    A. magnetic ink character recognition (MICR)
    B. touch screen
    C. bar code
    D. optical character recognition (OCR)

6. The main DISADVANTAGE associated with the parallel strategy of information system conversion is that 6.____

    A. run and personnel costs are extremely high
    B. it presents many difficulties in the area of documentation
    C. it provides no fallback in case of trouble
    D. it does not provide a clear picture of how the system will eventually operate throughout the entire organization

7. Which of the following types of systems is most appropriate for solving unstructured problems? 7.____

    A. Expert system
    B. Executive support system (ESS)
    C. Management information system (MIS)
    D. Decision support system (DSS)

8. In terms of information ethics, what is the term for the existence of laws that permit individuals to recover damages done to them by actors, systems, or organizations?

   A. Liability
   B. Subrogation
   C. Accountability
   D. Due process

9. Descriptions that focus on the dynamic aspects of a system's structure, or on change, evolution, and processes in general, are described as

   A. charismatic
   B. synchronic
   C. motile
   D. diachronic

10. One of the features of object-oriented programming is that all objects in a certain group have all the characteristics of that group. This feature is defined as

    A. base
    B. legitimacy
    C. class
    D. multiplexing

11. The most prominent data manipulation language in use today is

    A. Intellect
    B. Easytrieve
    C. APL
    D. SQL

12. Feasibility studies involved in systems analysis tend to focus on three specific areas. _____ feasibility is NOT one of these.

    A. Technical
    B. Operational
    C. Cultural
    D. Economic

13. A computer may sometimes handle programs more efficiently by dividing them into small fixed-or variable-length portions, with only a small portion stored in primary memory at one time. This is known as

    A. multitasking
    B. caching
    C. allocation
    D. virtual storage

14. Of the following applications, end-user computing is MOST appropriate for the development of

    A. scheduling systems for optimal production
    B. tracking daily trades of securities
    C. systems for handling air traffic
    D. systems for the development of three-dimensional graphics

15. In a hierarchical database, what is the term for the specialized data element attached to a record that shows the absolute or relative address of another record?

    A. Tickler   B. Index   C. Register   D. Pointer

16. For which of the following types of databases is the direct file access method most appropriate?

    A. Bank statements
    B. Payroll
    C. On-line hotel reservations
    D. Government benefits program

17. A _____ structured project with _____ technology requirements would most likely involve the lowest degree of risk to an organization.

- A. small, highly; low
- B. small, flexibly; high
- C. large, flexibly; high
- D. large, highly; low

18. Historically, under federal law creators of intellectual property were protected against copying by others for a period of

- A. 10 years
- B. 17 years
- C. 28 years
- D. the creator's natural life

19. Most modern secondary storage devices operate at speeds measured in

- A. nanoseconds
- B. milliseconds
- C. microseconds
- D. seconds

20. Which of the following signifies the international standard for transmitting voice, video, and data to support a wide range of service over the public telephone lines?

- A. HTML
- B. ISDN
- C. TCP/IP
- D. ASCII

21. An important limitation associated with executive support systems today is that they

- A. use data from different systems designed for very different purposes
- B. have a narrow range of easy-to-use desktop analytical tools
- C. are used almost exclusively by executives
- D. do an inadequate job of filtering data

22. Each of the following is an element of the systems study stage in the traditional model of a systems life cycle EXCEPT

- A. identifying objectives to be attained by a solution
- B. determining whether the organization has a problem that can be solved with a system
- C. analyzing problems with existing systems
- D. describing alternative solutions

23. The commercial software product *Lotus Notes* is an example of

- A. intelligent agent software
- B. groupware
- C. a star network
- D. electronic data interchange (EDI)

24. Weaknesses in a system's _____ controls may create errors or failures in new or modified systems.

- A. data file security
- B. implementation
- C. physical hardware
- D. software

25. Which of the following is a term used to describe the ability to move from summary data to more specific levels of detail? 25.____

   A. Drill down
   C. Downsizing
   B. Forward chaining
   D. Semantic networking

KEY (CORRECT ANSWERS)

1. C
2. B
3. C
4. D
5. B

6. A
7. B
8. A
9. D
10. C

11. D
12. C
13. D
14. D
15. D

16. C
17. A
18. C
19. B
20. B

21. A
22. B
23. B
24. B
25. A

EXAMINATION SECTION
TEST 1

DIRECTIONS: Each question or incomplete statement is followed by several suggested answers or completions. Select the one that BEST answers the question or completes the statement. *PRINT THE LETTER OF THE CORRECT ANSWER IN THE SPACE AT THE RIGHT.*

1. New projects are generally evaluated on three feasibility criteria-technical feasibility, economic feasibility and operational feasibility. Which of the questions below relates MOST closely to the determination of operational feasibility?   1.____

    A. Will it be necessary to hire additional programmers and operators for the proposed system?
    B. Will the operation of this system yield benefits in excess of its cost?
    C. Is the computer system expected to be operating satisfactorily by the time that the project is completed?
    D. Once the system is operating on the computer, will managers and their subordinates accept it?

2. As a result of widespread computerization of business procedures, there have been an increasing number of instances where it has been alleged that computerization represents a real threat to personal privacy.   2.____
Which one of the following is NOT a major contributing factor to this problem?

    A. Use of common identifiers such as the social security number makes it possible to relate increasing amounts of information about an individual
    B. Previously separate information is related as a result of integration of previously separate programs
    C. Operating systems cause increased conformity to standards established outside of the organization
    D. Increasing amounts of information are frequently required as computer programs become more complicated or comprehensive

3. Which of the following represents one of the most common examples of *spooling*?   3.____

    A. Loading multiple web pages at once
    B. Entering large amounts of data into a spreadsheet application
    C. Saving a number of files to be accessed by another user at a later time
    D. Printing a number of jobs while working in another application

4. The following items represent considerations in organizing the personnel of an EDP department.   4.____
Which of these items is NOT directly related to the form of the organization?

    A. Span of control—the number of people that can be effectively supervised by a manager
    B. Separating planning and operating functions
    C. The model of the computer being used
    D. The stage of the development of the data processing installation

5. Which of the following activities would take place FIRST in the establishment of a new EDP department?

   A. Selection of an EDP manager
   B. Establishment of a systems analysis and design group
   C. Establishment of a programming group
   D. Determination of day-to-day machine operating activities

6. Each of the items shown below are difficulties faced in the operation of an EDP department.
   Which of these difficulties can be MOST directly related to organizational problems?

   A. Excessive machine downtime
   B. A high ratio of rerun time to productive time
   C. Deterioration of external relationships
   D. Contraction of the EDP budget

7. Which of the following techniques CANNOT be used by the programmer to add reliability to the operations taking place within the program?

   A. Record label checking—comparing the label on a disk or tape with a predetermined standard contained within the program
   B. Record counts—comparing the number of records processed with some independently determined standard
   C. Suspense accounts—posting invalid items to a suspense account in order to retain all data requiring investigation in a single place
   D. Turnaround documents—generating machine-sensible data for use in clerical processes that will ultimately result in data to be entered into the computer

8. In most cases, a request for computer services should originate from

   A. the computer analyst's department
   B. upper-level management
   C. the users of the requested system
   D. lower management

9. Which of the following factors is probably NOT relevant to an analysis determining the economic feasibility of replacing keypunch verification with programmed checks? The

   A. cost of executing the portion of the program containing the checks
   B. value of sales lost as a result of undetected errors
   C. cost punched cards eliminated
   D. cost of verifier operators eliminated

10. Which of the following statements is TRUE regarding the grandfather-father-son technique for protecting data files?

    A. Whenever possible, a different computer should be used for updating each updating cycle

B. Operating employees should be rotated so that no employee has primary responsibility for any two successive updating cycles
C. This technique permits regeneration of files even when an error is discovered in one updating cycle
D. This technique provides satisfactory regeneration capability only when it is not accompanied by other operating controls

11. Which of the following techniques can be used to provide file backup and recovery for direct access files in a real time system? 11.____

    A. There are no techniques that can be used in such a system
    B. Periodic dumps combined with maintenance of an up-to-date transaction tape
    C. Periodic circularization of users to get verification of file content
    D. Duplexing all communications controllers

12. The PRIMARY function of a modem in a data communication system is 12.____

    A. accessing data from core storage
    B. making computer and telephone signals compatible
    C. converting from ASCII to EBCDIC code
    D. generating signals needed to test the telephone lines

13. A multiplexor is generally used in a data communications system to 13.____

    A. generate identification bits for data
    B. interface between the operating system and the applications program
    C. permit several terminals to share the use of a single transmission line
    D. provide an audit trail

14. Which of the following factors is NOT a major consideration when developing a multivendor system (i.e., a system using plug-to-plug compatible equipment)? 14.____

    A. Compatibility of the equipment with the existing electrical equipment in the computer room
    B. Relative cost of various components
    C. Ability and willingness of separate maintenance groups to work together
    D. Financial stability of various suppliers

15. Which of the following statements about hardware monitor usage in a multiprogramming computer is generally INCORRECT? They 15.____

    A. must be physically connected to the computer system
    B. generate output that must be further analyzed before meaningful conclusions can be reached
    C. can tell you which program is degrading the system
    D. permit determination of Boolean combinations of systems activities

16. Which of the following statements BEST describes *spooling?* 16.____

    A. The method used to increase the transfer rates of magnetic tapes
    B. A method used to provide increased throughput by improved overlapping input-output and processing operations

C. A method for linking two or more computers together into a network
D. A method for balancing the use of auxiliary storage by rotating usage around the available units

17. Which one of the following is generally presented as a PRIMARY advantage associated with the use of a hardware monitor?

    A. It causes no system degradation
    B. Identifies poorly written programs
    C. Permits modeling of newly announced but as yet unavailable systems
    D. Can be used in complex systems with no prior training

17.____

18. An *audit trail* is essential to the development of a smoothly operating EDP system. Which statement below MOST adequately defines an audit trail?

    A. An ability to trace transactions from their origin to their final use and vice versa
    B. A set of cross-indexed documentation
    C. Organizing the physical flow of activities in an efficient manner
    D. Having a CPA (or some other independent, qualified professional) audit the organization's records periodically

18.____

19. Which statement below BEST describes *thrashing* in the operation of a virtual computer system?

    A. Failure of a disk as a result of excessive vibration
    B. Eliminating operator errors by use of an edit run
    C. Excessive swapping of program segments between auxiliary memory and core
    D. An error condition caused by a non-ending loop in the operating system

19.____

20. Which statement below BEST describes a capability associated with virtual storage?

    A. It is possible to program as if more core is available than exists in the system
    B. All computers are now automatically compatible
    C. Only tapes and disks can be used for storage
    D. The programmer can write efficient programs while completely ignoring the nature of the computer system being used

20.____

KEY (CORRECT ANSWERS)

1. D
2. C
3. D
4. C
5. A

6. C
7. D
8. C
9. C
10. C

11. B
12. B
13. C
14. A
15. C

16. B
17. A
18. A
19. C
20. A

EXAMINATION SECTION
TEST 1

DIRECTIONS: Each question or incomplete statement is followed by several suggested answers or completions. Select the one that BEST answers the question or completes the statement. *PRINT THE LETTER OF THE CORRECT ANSWER IN THE SPACE AT THE RIGHT.*

1. The speed disparity between adjacent devices can cause problems with an interface. These problems are usually resolved by temporarily storing input in a(n)

    A. channel
    B. control unit
    C. register
    D. buffer

    1.____

2. A typical computer spends most of its time

    A. compiling
    B. waiting for input or output
    C. executing instructions
    D. interpreting commands

    2.____

3. What is the basic input device on a small computer?

    A. Keyboard   B. Cursor   C. Mouse   D. Processor

    3.____

4. When two hardware devices want to communicate, they will FIRST exchange _____ signals.

    A. interrupt   B. protocol   C. interface   D. boot

    4.____

5. Which of the following is retrieved and executed by the processor?

    A. Instructions
    B. Clock pulses
    C. Information
    D. Data

    5.____

6. What type of architecture is used by most microcomputers?

    A. Standard
    B. Serial
    C. Single-bus
    D. Multiple-bus

    6.____

7. Typically, _____ is NOT a problem associated with a computer's main memory.

    A. cost
    B. volatility
    C. capacity
    D. speed

    7.____

8. Which of the following types of memory management is the SIMPLEST?

    A. Sector-oriented
    B. Dynamic
    C. Block-oriented
    D. Fixed partition

    8.____

9. What is the term for the time during which a disk drive is brought up to operating speed and the access device is positioned?

    A. E-time
    B. Rotational delay
    C. Seek time
    D. Access time

    9.____

10. What type of code is written by programmers?

    A. Load module
    B. Source
    C. Object
    D. Operating

11. A _____ is the basic output device on a small computer.

    A. printer
    B. keyboard
    C. display screen
    D. hard disk

12. Which of the following serves to manage a computer's resources?

    A. User
    B. Operating system
    C. Programmer
    D. Software

13. A computer processes data into

    A. information
    B. pulses
    C. code
    D. facts

14. What is the term for the entity used to link external devices to a small computer system?

    A. Interface
    B. Network
    C. Plug-in
    D. Modem

15. For a transaction processing application, a _____ file organization should be selected.

    A. sequential
    B. indexed
    C. direct
    D. random

16. Which element of a microcomputer directly controls input and output?

    A. Buffer
    B. Processor
    C. Bus
    D. Control unit

17. A computer's data and program instructions are stored in

    A. memory
    B. the video buffer
    C. a program
    D. an output port

18. What is the term for the metal framework around which most microcomputers are constructed?

    A. Mainframe
    B. Hard disk
    C. Motherboard
    D. Expansion slot

19. The read/write head of a computer's disk drive is contained on the

    A. magnetic drum
    B. data element
    C. token
    D. access mechanism

20. A(n) _____ is used to link a small computer's secondary storage device to the system.

    A. control unit
    B. interface board
    C. register
    D. buffer

21. What processor management technique is used on most timesharing network systems?

    A. Time-slicing
    B. Command sorting
    C. Apportionment
    D. Interrupt processing

22. Which of the following procedures is used to copy data from a slow-speed device to a high-speed device for eventual input to a program? 22.____

   A. Queuing
   B. Spooling
   C. Buffing
   D. Scheduling

23. A location in memory is located by its 23.____

   A. section   B. register   C. address   D. decoder

24. _____ data is represented by a wave. 24.____

   A. Microwave   B. Digital   C. Binary   D. Analog

25. A programmer defines the logical structure of a problem by using a(n) 25.____

   A. assembler
   B. compiler
   C. interpreter
   D. nonprocedural language

KEY (CORRECT ANSWERS)

1.	D	11.	C
2.	B	12.	B
3.	A	13.	A
4.	B	14.	A
5.	A	15.	C
6.	C	16.	B
7.	D	17.	A
8.	D	18.	C
9.	C	19.	D
10.	B	20.	B

21. A
22. B
23. C
24. D
25. D

TEST 2

DIRECTIONS: Each question or incomplete statement is followed by several suggested answers or completions. Select the one that BEST answers the question or completes the statement. *PRINT THE LETTER OF THE CORRECT ANSWER IN THE SPACE AT THE RIGHT.*

1. Data is converted from digital to analog form through the process of
   - A. demodulation
   - B. teleporting
   - C. cross-modulation
   - D. modulation

2. Which of the following represents the simplest data structure?
   - A. Record
   - B. File
   - C. List
   - D. Directory

3. The term for a set of parallel wires used to transmit data, commands, or power is
   - A. bus
   - B. cabling
   - C. line
   - D. twisted pair

4. _____ limit the number of peripherals that can be linked to a microcomputer system.
   - A. Channels
   - B. Bus lines
   - C. Buffers
   - D. Slots

5. A data structure in which memory is allocated as a series of numbered cells is a(n)
   - A. array
   - B. block
   - C. record
   - D. register

6. On a disk, each program's name and location can be located on the
   - A. index
   - B. address
   - C. label
   - D. register

7. Onto which of the following structures is a processing chip stored?
   - A. Board
   - B. Plate
   - C. Bus
   - D. Disk

8. Two or more independent processors can share the same memory under a system known as
   - A. time-sharing
   - B. FAT binaries
   - C. multitasking
   - D. multiprocessing

9. A _____ is the basic storage unit around which a microcomputer system is designed.
   - A. bit
   - B. block
   - C. word
   - D. byte

10. A user communicates with an operating system by means of a(n)
    - A. interface
    - B. peripheral
    - C. command language
    - D. application

11. A _____ is used to convert data from pulse form to wave form and back again.
    - A. channel
    - B. modem
    - C. SCSI port
    - D. bus

12. Data values can be accessed according to their element numbers in a(n)
    - A. list
    - B. register
    - C. record
    - D. array

13. Under a _____ memory management scheme, a program is allocated as much memory as it needs.

    A. sector-oriented
    B. dynamic
    C. block-oriented
    D. fixed partition

14. What is the term for the process of removing errors from a program?

    A. Compiling
    B. Debugging
    C. Troubleshooting
    D. Extraction

15. _____ is the term for the time during which a desired sector of a disk approaches the access device.

    A. Run time
    B. Rotational delay
    C. Seek time
    D. Access time

16. What is the term for the process by which a networked computer selects the terminal it will communicate with?

    A. Compiling
    B. Polling
    C. Interfacing
    D. Selection

17. After compilers and assemblers read a programmer's code, they generate a(n)

    A. object module
    B. nonprocedural language
    C. subroutine
    D. load module

18. Memory that loses its content when the machine's power is turned off is described as

    A. read-only
    B. redundant
    C. dependent
    D. volatile

19. Which module of an operating system sends primitive commands to a disk drive?

    A. Motherboard
    B. IOCS
    C. CPU
    D. Command processor

20. The BASIC measure of data communications speed is

    A. bit rate
    B. baud rate
    C. kilobytes per second
    D. bits per second

21. The term _____ is used to denote a single, meaningful data element, such as a person's telephone number.

    A. field   B. item   C. record   D. file

22. What is the term for the machine-level translation of a programmer's source code?

    A. Load module
    B. Subroutine
    C. Source library
    D. Object module

23. Which part of an instruction directs the actions of the processor?

    A. Pulse
    B. Operation code
    C. Statement
    D. Operand

24. A _____ is used to store programs that enter a multiprogramming system.

    A. tape   B. spool   C. buffer   D. queue

25. _____ is a device used to avoid data dependency and redundancy.

   A. Sequential filing
   B. Continuous backup
   C. Random filing
   D. Database

KEY (CORRECT ANSWERS)

1. A
2. C
3. A
4. D
5. A

6. A
7. A
8. D
9. C
10. C

11. B
12. D
13. B
14. B
15. B

16. B
17. A
18. D
19. B
20. B

21. A
22. D
23. B
24. D
25. D

EXAMINATION SECTION
TEST 1

DIRECTIONS: Each question or incomplete statement is followed by several suggested answers or completions. Select the one that BEST answers the question or completes the statement. *PRINT THE LETTER OF THE CORRECT ANSWER IN THE SPACE AT THE RIGHT.*

1. The PRIMARY purpose of program analysis as it is used in government is to

   A. replace political judgments with rational programs and policies
   B. help decision-makers to sharpen their judgments about program choices
   C. analyze the impact of past programs on the quality of public services
   D. reduce costs by eliminating waste in public programs and services

    1.____

2. While there is no complete method for program analysis that is agreed to by all the experts and is relevant to all types of problems, the MOST important element in program analysis involves the

   A. development of alternatives and the definition of objectives or criteria
   B. collection of information and the construction of a mathematical model
   C. design of experiments and procedures to validate results
   D. collection of expert opinion and the combination of their views

    2.____

3. Electronic data processing is a particularly valuable tool of analysis in situations where the analyst has a processing problem involving

   A. *small* input, *few* operations, and *small* output
   B. *large* input, *many* operations, and *small* output
   C. *large* input, *few* operations, and *large* output
   D. *small* input, *many* operations, and *small* output

    3.____

4. In order for an analyst to use electronic data processing to solve an analytic problem, the problem must be clearly defined.
   The BEST way to prepare material for such definition in electronic data processing is to

   A. discuss the problem with computer programmers in a meeting
   B. prepare a flow diagram outlining the steps in the analysis
   C. write a memorandum with a list of the relevant program issues
   D. write a computer program using FORTRAN, BASIC, or another language

    4.____

5. There is a wide variety in the types of computer memory available and a wide range of information processing tasks. Significant trade-offs exist between size, speed, and cost. In a situation where large capacity and low unit cost are more important than access speed, the BEST memory system is the

   A. magnetic core   B. magnetic drum
   C. magnetic disk   D. transistor (solid state)

    5.____

6. Interactive or conversational programming is important to the program analyst ESPECIALLY for

   A. preparing analyses leading to management information systems
   B. communicating among analysts in different places

    6.____

C. using canned programs in statistical analysis
D. testing trial solutions in rapid sequence

7. Program analysis often calls for recommendation of a choice between competing program possibilities that differ in the timing of major costs.
Analysts using the present value technique by setting an interest or discount rate are in effect arguing that, other things being equal,

A. it is inadvisable to defer the start of projects because of rising costs
B. projects should be completed within a short time period to save money
C. expenditures should be made out of tax revenues to avoid payment of interest
D. postponing expenditures is advantageous at some measurable rate

8. Of the following, the formula which is MOST appropriately used to estimate the net need for a given type of service is that net need equals

A. current clients - anticipated losses + anticipated gains
B. $\dfrac{\text{current supply} + \text{current clients}}{\text{Standard}}$
C. (client population x standard) - current supply
D. current supply - anticipated losses + anticipated gains

9. The purpose of feasibility analysis is to protect the analyst from naive alternatives and, MOST generally, to

A. identify and quantify technological constraints
B. carry out a preliminary stage of analysis
C. anticipate potential blocks to implementation
D. line up the support of political leadership

Questions 10-11.

DIRECTIONS: Answer Questions 10 and 11 on the basis of the following chart. In a hypothetical problem involving four criteria and four alternatives, the following data have been assembled.

	Cost Criterion	Effectiveness Criterion	Timing Criterion	Feasibility Criterion
Alternative A	$500,000	50 units	3 months	probably feasible
Alternative B	$300,000	100 units	6 months	probably feasible
Alternative C	$400,000	50 units	12 months	probably infeasible
Alternative D	$200,000	75 units	3 months	probably infeasible

10. On the basis of the above data, it appears that the one alternative which is dominated by another alternative is Alternative

A. A   B. B   C. C   D. D

11. If the feasibility constraint is absolute and fixed, then the critical trade-off is between   11._____

    A. lower cost on the one hand and faster timing and higher effectiveness on the other
    B. lower cost and higher effectiveness on one hand and faster timing on the other
    C. lower cost and faster timing on the one hand and higher effectiveness on the other
    D. lower cost on the one hand and higher effectiveness on the other

12. A classification of an agency's activities in a program structure is MOST useful if it highlights   12._____

    A. trade-offs that might not otherwise be considered
    B. ways to improve the efficiency of each activity
    C. the true organizational structure of an agency
    D. bases for insuring that expenditures stay within limits

13. CPM, like PERT, is a useful tool for scheduling large-scale, complex processes.   13._____
    In CPM, the critical path is the

    A. path composed of important links
    B. path composed of uncertain links
    C. longest path through the network
    D. shortest path through the network

14. Classical evaluative research calls for the use of control groups. However, there are practical difficulties in collecting data on individuals to be used as "controls" in program evaluations.   14._____
    Researchers may attempt to overcome these difficulties by

    A. using control groups that have no choice such as prison inmates or inmates of other public institutions or facilities
    B. developing better measures of the inputs, processes, and outputs relevant to public programs and services
    C. using experimental demonstration projects with participants in the different projects serving as comparison groups for one another
    D. abandoning attempts at formal evaluation in favor of more qualitative approaches employing a journalistic style of analysis

15. During the course of an analysis of the remaining "life" of a certain city's landfill for refuse disposal, there was a great deal of debate about the impact of changing rates of garbage generation on the amount of landfill needed and about what rates of garbage generation to expect over the next decade.   15._____
    Faced with the need to attempt to resolve this debate, an analyst would construct a simple model of the refuse disposal system and

    A. project landfill needs without considering refuse generation in the future
    B. conduct a detailed household survey in order to estimate future garbage generation rates
    C. ask the experts to continue to debate the issue until the argument is won by one view
    D. do a sensitivity analysis to test the impact of alternative assumptions about refuse generation

16. The limitations of traditional surveys have fostered the development and use of panels. A panel is a

    A. group of respondents that serves as a continuous source of survey information
    B. group of advisors expert in the design and implementation of surveys
    C. representative sample of respondents at a single point in time
    D. post-survey discussion group composed of former respondents

17. The difference between sensitivity analysis and risk analysis is that risk analysis

    A. is applicable only to profit and loss situations where the concept of risk is operable
    B. includes an estimate of probabilities of different values of input factors
    C. is applicable to physical problems while sensitivity analysis is applicable to social ones
    D. requires a computer simulation while sensitivity analysis does not

18. A decision tree, although initially applied to business problems, is a graphic device which is useful to public analysts in

    A. scheduling complex processes
    B. doing long-range forecasting
    C. formulating the structure of alternatives
    D. solving production-inventory problems

19. The purpose of a management information system in an agency is to

    A. structure data relevant to managerial decision-making
    B. put all of an agency's data in machine-processing form
    C. simplify the record-keeping operations in an agency
    D. keep an ongoing record of management's activities

20. Assume that an analyst is presented with the following chart for a fire department and supplied also with information indicating a stable size firefighting staff over this time period.

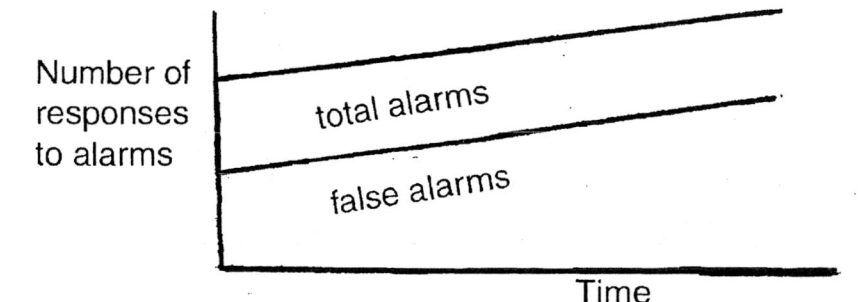

    The analyst could REASONABLY conclude regarding productivity that
    A. productivity over this time period was essentially stable for this firefighting force because the number of responses to real fires during this period was stable, as was the work force
    B. productivity was essentially increasing for this force because the number of total responses was increasing relative to a stable force
    C. productivity was declining because a greater proportion of the total work effort was wasted effort in responding to false alarms
    D. it is impossible to make a judgment about the productivity of the firefighting staff without a judgment about the value of a response to a false alarm

21. In the design of a productivity program for the sanitation department, the BEST measure of productivity would be

    A. tons of refuse collected annually
    B. number of collections made per week
    C. tons of refuse collected per truck shift
    D. number of trucks used per shift

22. The cohort-survival method for estimating future population has been widely employed. In this method,

    A. migration is assumed to be constant over time
    B. net migration within cohorts is assumed to be zero
    C. migration is included as a multiplier factor
    D. net migration within cohorts is assumed to be constant

23. Cost-effectiveness and cost-benefit analysis represent a systematic approach to balancing potential losses against potential gains as a prelude to public action.
    In addition to limitations based on difficulties of measurement and inadequacies in data that are typical of systematic program analysis, cost-benefit analysis suffers from a serious conceptual flaw in that

    A. the definition of benefit or cost does not typically distinguish to whom benefits or costs accrue
    B. a full-scale cost benefit analysis takes too long to do, is too expensive, and needs too much data
    C. it has been shown that such analyses are more suitable for defense or water resources problems
    D. such analyses are not useful in any problem involving capital and operating costs or benefits

24. If you were asked to develop a total cost estimate for one year for a program involving both a capital improvement and operating costs, the BEST way to estimate the capital cost component would be to

    A. divide the estimated cost of the capital improvement by the projected operating costs over the life of the improvement
    B. multiply the annual operating cost by the projected life of the capital improvement
    C. divide the amortized cost of the capital improvement by the projected life of the improvement
    D. multiply the portion of the capital improvement to be completed within the year by the cost of the improvement

25. In comparing the costs of two or more alternative programs, it is important to consider all relevant costs.
    The MOST important principle in defining "relevant cost" is that

    A. only marginal or incremental cost should be considered in the estimate
    B. only recurring costs should be considered for each alternative
    C. estimates should include the sunk costs for each alternative
    D. cost estimates need to be as precise as in budget preparation

6 (#1)

26. Different techniques for projecting future costs may be suitable in different situations. Assume that it is necessary to estimate the future costs of maintaining garbage collection vehicles.
Under which of the following conditions would it be advisable to develop a cost-estimating equation rather than to use unadjusted current data?   26.___

   A. When it is expected that more complex equipment will replace simpler equipment
   B. Whether or not it is expected that the nature of future garbage collection will change
   C. When the current unadjusted data still has to be verified
   D. When the nature of future garbage collection equipment is unknown

27. The following data has been collected on the costs of two pilot programs, each representing a different approach to the same problem.   27.___

	Total cost	Fixed cost	Variable cost	Average unit cost	Number of users
Program A	$45,000	$20,000	$50 per user	$90 per user	500
Program B	$42,000	$ 7,000	$100 per user	$120 per user	350

Assume that the pilot programs are extended city-wide and other factors are constant. Using the above data, what would a cost analyst conclude about the relative costs of the two programs? Program

   A. B would be less costly with fewer than 300 users and Program A would be less costly with more than 300 users
   B. B would be less costly with fewer than 260 users and Program A would be less costly with more than 260 users
   C. A would be less costly without regard to the size of the program
   D. B would be less costly without regard to the size of the program

Questions 28-30.

DIRECTIONS: Answer Questions 28 through 30 on the basis of the following data assembled for a cost-benefit analysis.

	Cost	Benefit
No program	0	0
Alternative W	$ 3,000	$ 6,000
Alternative X	$10,000	$17,000
Alternative Y	$17,000	$25,000
Alternative Z	$30,000	$32,000

28. From the point of view of pushing public expenditure to the point where marginal benefit equals or exceeds marginal cost, the BEST alternative is Alternative   28.___

   A. W   B. X   C. Y   D. Z

29. From the point of view of selecting the alternative with the best cost-benefit ratio, the BEST alternative is Alternative.   29.___

   A. W   B. X   C. Y   D. Z

30. From the point of view of selecting the alternative with the best measure of net benefit, the BEST alternative is Alternative   30.___

   A. W   B. X   C. Y   D. Z

Questions 31-35.

DIRECTIONS: The set of answers listed below applies to Questions 31 through 35. Each answer is a type of statistical test.
A. Analysis of variance
B. Pearson Product-Moment Correlation (r)
C. t-test
D. x^2 test (Chi-squared)

Pick the test which is MOST appropriate to the situation described. An answer may be used more than once.

31. A comparison between two correlated means obtained from a small sample.
The CORRECT answer is:

   A.   B.   C.   D.

32. A comparison of three or more means.
The CORRECT answer is:

   A.   B.   C.   D.

33. A comparison of the divergence of observed frequencies with those expected on the hypothesis of equal probability of occurrence.
The CORRECT answer is:

   A.   B.   C.   D.

34. A comparison of the divergence of observed frequencies with those expected on the hypothesis of a normal distribution.
The CORRECT answer is:

   A.   B.   C.   D.

35. A comparison between two uncorrelated means obtained from small samples.
The CORRECT answer is:

   A.   B.   C.   D.

36. There are many different models for evaluative research.
A time-series design is an example of a _____ experimental design.

   A. field   B. true   C. quasi-   D. pre-

37. In policy research, as in all kinds of research, it is important to develop research hypotheses early.
The MAIN purpose of a research hypothesis is to

   A. include the kind of statistical procedures to be used in the research
   B. provide a ready answer in case data is not available for doing research
   C. serve as a guide to the kind of data that must be collected in order to answer the research question
   D. clarify what is known and what is not known in the research problem

38. While descriptive and causal research are not completely separable, there has been a distinct effort to move in the direction of causal research.
Such an effort is epitomized by the use of

    A. predictive models and measures of deviation from predictions
    B. option and attitudinal surveys in local neighborhoods
    C. community studies and area profiles of localities
    D. individual case histories and group case studies

39. The one of the following which BEST describes a periodic report is that it

    A. provides a record of accomplishments for a given time span and a comparison with similar time spans in the past
    B. covers the progress made in a project that has been postponed
    C. integrates, summarizes, and perhaps interprets published data on technical or scientific material
    D. describes a decision, advocates a policy or action, and presents facts in support of the writer's position

40. The PRIMARY purpose of including pictorial illustrations in a formal report is usually to

    A. amplify information which has been adequately treated verbally
    B. present details that are difficult to describe verbally
    C. provide the reader with a pleasant, momentary distraction
    D. present supplementary information incidental to the main ideas developed in the report.

KEY (CORRECT ANSWERS)

1. B	11. B	21. C	31. C
2. A	12. A	22. B	32. A
3. B	13. C	23. A	33. D
4. B	14. C	24. C	34. D
5. C	15. D	25. A	35. C
6. D	16. A	26. A	36. C
7. D	17. B	27. B	37. C
8. C	18. C	28. C	38. A
9. C	19. A	29. A	39. A
10. C	20. D	30. C	40. B

TEST 2

DIRECTIONS: Each question or incomplete statement is followed by several suggested answers or completions. Select the one that BEST answers the question or completes the statement. *PRINT THE LETTER OF THE CORRECT ANSWER IN THE SPACE AT THE RIGHT.*

1. A measurement procedure is considered to be RELIABLE to the extent that 1.____

    A. independent applications under similar conditions yield consistent results
    B. independent applications under different conditions yield similar results
    C. scores reflect true differences among individuals or situations
    D. scores reflect true differences in the same individual over time

2. Different scales of measurement are distinguished by the feasibility of various empirical operations. 2.____
An ordinal scale of measurement

    A. is not as useful as a ratio or interval scale
    B. is useful in rank-ordering or priority setting
    C. provides the data for addition or subtraction
    D. provides the data for computation of means

3. A widely used approach to sampling is systematic sampling, i.e., selecting every Kth element in a listing. 3.____
Even with a random start, a DISADVANTAGE in this approach is that

    A. the listing used may contain a cyclical pattern
    B. it is too similar to a simple random sample
    C. the system does not insure a probability sample
    D. it yields an unpredictable sample size

4. A rule of thumb sometimes used in sample size selection is to set sample size equal to five percent of the population size. Other things being equal, this rule 4.____

    A. tends to oversample small populations
    B. tends to oversample large populations
    C. provides an accurate rule for sampling
    D. is a relatively inexpensive basis for sampling

5. With regard to a stratified random sample, it may be APPROPRIATE to sample the various strata in different proportions in order to 5.____

    A. approximate the characteristics of a true random sample
    B. establish classes that are internally heterogenous in each case
    C. avoid the necessity of subdividing the cases within each stratum
    D. adequately cover important strata that have small numbers of cases

6. One possible response to the "unknown" or "no answer" category in a tabulation of survey information is to "allocate" the unknown responses, i.e., to estimate the missing data on the basis of other known information about the respondents. 6.____
This technique is APPROPRIATE when the unknown category

A. is very small and is randomly distributed within all subgroups of respondents
B. is very large and is randomly distributed within all subgroups of respondents
C. reflects an interviewing failure and a subgroup in the sample tends to produce more unknowns
D. is a legitimate category and a subgroup in the sample tends to produce more unknowns

7. In presenting cross-tabulated data showing the relation ship between two variables, it is MOST meaningful to compute percentages

    A. in both directions in all instances
    B. of each cell in relation to the grand total
    C. in the direction of the smaller number of cells
    D. in the direction of the causal factor

8. In portraying data based on a sampling operation, it is MOST meaningful and comprehensible to the reader to present

    A. percentages for the sample and the universe
    B. percentages by themselves
    C. percentages and the base figures
    D. numbers by themselves

9. A new bridge spanning a river is expected to carry 60,000 cars a day on a rainy day and 80,000 cars a day on other kinds of days.
    If there is a $1 toll and one chance in four of a rainy day, the expected value of a day's revenue is

    A. $35,000   B. $75,000   C. $95,000   D. $140,000

10. The analyst who is asked to estimate the probability of a relatively rare event occurring cannot use the classical frequency measures of probability but rather should

    A. use a random-numbers table to pick a probability
    B. project historical data into the future
    C. indicate that no probabilistic judgment is possible
    D. make the best possible judgment as to the subjective probability

11. A useful source of census data for computing annual indicators is the

    A. Public Use Sample   B. Continuing Population Survey
    C. Census of Population   D. Census of Governments

12. An analyst presented with a set of household records showing age, ethnicity, income, and family status and wishing to study the inter-relationship of all of these variables simultaneously will probably request

    A. one four-way cross-tabulation
    B. four three-way cross-tabulations
    C. six two-way cross-tabulations
    D. four single tabulations

13. Downward communication, from high management to lower levels in an organization, will often not be fully accepted at the lowest levels of an organization unless high-level management

    A. communicates through several levels of mid-level management, where the message can be properly modified and interpreted
    B. communicates directly with the level of the organization it wishes to reach, bypassing any intermediate levels
    C. first establishes an atmosphere in which upward communication is encouraged and listened to
    D. establishes penalties for non-compliance with its communications

14. A top-level manager sometimes has an inaccurate view of the actual lower-level operations of his agency, particularly of those operations which are not running well.
    Of the following, the MOST frequent cause of this is the

    A. general unconcern of top-level management with the way an agency actually operates
    B. tendency of the people at the lowest level in an agency to lie about their actual performance
    C. unwillingness of top-level management to deal with unfavorable information when it is presented
    D. tendency of mid-level management to edit bad news and unpleasant information from reports directed to top management

15. In the conduct of productivity analyses, work measurement is a USEFUL technique for

    A. substantiating executive decisions
    B. designing a research study
    C. developing performance yardsticks
    D. preparing a manual of procedure

16. Issue analysis is closely identified with the "fire-fighting" function of management. As such, issue analysis is a(n)

    A. systematic assessment over time of an agency's strategic options
    B. annual review of the issues that have come up during the past year
    C. basis for a set of procedures to be followed in an emergency
    D. analysis of a specific policy question often performed in a crisis environment

17. The transportation agency in a large city wishes to study the impact of fare increases on ridership in buses. Rider-ship data for peak hours has been assembled for the same time period for three geographic subareas (A, B and C) with approximately the same socio-economic characteristics, residential density, and distance from the central business district (CBD). Subarea A had experienced a moderate fare increase on its bus line; Subarea B had had no fare increase; and Subarea C had experienced a major fare increase during the time period.
    In the design of this study, the analysis should be framed :

    A. Ridership = f (fare level)
    B. Ridership = f (fare level, distance from CBD)
    C. Fare level = f (ridership)
    D. Ridership = f (fare level, socio-economic characteristics, residential density)

18. What organizational concept is illustrated when a group is organized on an *ad hoc* basis to accomplish a specific goal?

    A. Functional Teamwork
    B. Line/staff
    C. Task Force
    D. Command

19. The concept of "demand" provides an appropriate theoretical basis for estimating the needs for public services or programs where the service will be on a

    A. fee basis and involves life-sustaining necessities
    B. free basis and involves life-sustaining necessities
    C. free basis and does not involve life-sustaining necessities
    D. fee basis and does not involve life-sustaining necessities

20. Analysts should be wary of relying exclusively on traditional service standards (e.g., one acre of playground per 1,000 population).
    Such standards are often DEFICIENT because they tend to overstate

    A. the consumer view and understate behavior and values of producers
    B. the producer view and understate behavior and values of users or consumers
    C. local conditions and understate national conditions
    D. behavioral factors and understate practical effects

21. The BEST measure of the performance of a manpower program would be the

    A. percentage reduction in unemployment by impacted population groups
    B. number of trainees placed in jobs at the beginning of the training program
    C. percentage of students completing a training program
    D. cost per student of the training program and the job placement effort

22. Indices are single figures that measure multi-dimensional concepts.
    The critical judgment in the construction of an index involves

    A. the trade-off between accuracy and simplicity
    B. determination of enough data to do the measurement
    C. avoidance of all possible error
    D. developing a theoretical basis for it

23. Evaluation of public programs is complicated by the reality that programs tend to reflect negotiated compromises among conflicting objectives.
    The absence of clear, unitary objectives PARTICULARLY complicates the

    A. assessment of program input or effort
    B. development of effectiveness criteria
    C. design of new programs to replace the old
    D. diagnosis of a program's processes

24. The basic purpose of the "Super-Agencies" is to

    A. reduce the number of departments and agencies in the city government
    B. reduce the number of high-level administrators
    C. coordinate agencies reporting to the mayor and supervise agencies in related fields
    D. supervise departments and agencies in unrelated fields

25. In most municipal budgeting systems involving capital and operating budgets, the leasing   25.____
or renting of facilities is usually shown in

    A. the operating budget   B. the capital budget
    C. a separate schedule   D. either budget

26. New York City's budgeting procedure is unusual in that budget appropriations are considered in two parts, as follows: 26.____

    A. Capital budget and income budget
    B. Expense budget and income budget
    C. Revenue budget and expense budget
    D. Expense budget and capital budget

27. The "growth rate" referred to in current political and economic discussion refers to   27.____
change from year to year in a country's

    A. gross national product   B. population
    C. available labor force   D. capital goods investment

Questions 28-29.

DIRECTIONS: Questions 28 and 29 are based on the following illustration. Assume that the figures in the chart are cubes.

28. In the illustration above, how many times GREATER is the quantity represented by Figure III than the quantity represented by Figure II?   28.____

    A. 2   B. 4   C. 8   D. 16

29. The illustration above illustrates a progression in quantity BEST described as   29.____

    A. arithmetic   B. geometric   C. discrete   D. linear

Questions 30-35.

DIRECTIONS: Answer Questions 30 through 35 on the basis of the following chart.

In a national study of poverty trends, the following data have been assembled for interpretation.

Persons Below Poverty Level, By Residence

Item	Number (millions) U.S.	Number (millions) Metropolitan Areas	Percent U.S.	Percent Metropolitan Areas
1969				
Total	38.8	17.0	22.0	15.3
Under 25 years	20.0	8.8	25.3	18.1
65 years & over	5.5	2.5	35.2	26.9
Black	9.9	5.0	55.1	42.8
Other	28.3	11.8	18.1	12.0
1979				
Total	24.3	12.3	12.2	9.5
Under 25 years	12.2	6.4	13.2	10.4
65 years & over	4.8	2.3	25.3	20.2
Black	7.2	3.9	32.3	24.4
Other	16.7	8.2	9.5	7.3

30. If no other source of data were available, which of the following groups would you expect to have the HIGHEST rate of poverty?

    A. Others over 65
    B. Others under 65
    C. Blacks over 65
    D. Blacks under 65

31. Between 1969 and 1979, the percentage of poor in the United States who were black

    A. increased from 25.5% to 29.6%
    B. decreased from 55.1% to 32.3%
    C. decreased from 9.9% to 7.2%
    D. stayed the same

32. The data in the second column of the table indicate that, in the metropolitan areas, the number of poor declined by 4.7 million or 36.2% between 1969 and 1979. Yet, the fourth column shows a corresponding decline from 15.3% to 9.5%, or only 5.8%
    This apparent discrepancy reflects the fact that the

    A. metropolitan areas are growing while the number of poor is contracting
    B. two columns in question are based on different sources of information
    C. difference between two percentages is not the same as the percent change in total numbers
    D. tables have inherent errors and must be carefully checked

33. The percentages in each of the last two columns of the table for 1969 and 1979 don't add up to 100%. This is for the reason that

    A. rounding off each entry to the nearest decimal place caused an error in the total such that the total is not equal to 100%
    B. these columns show the percentage of Blacks, aged, etc. who are poor rather than the percentage of poor who are Black, aged, etc.
    C. there was an error in the construction of the table which was not noticed until the table was already in print
    D. there is double counting in the entries in the table; some people are counted more than once

33._____

34. Data such as that presented in the table on persons below poverty level are shown to a single decimal place because

    A. data in every table should always be shown to a single decimal place
    B. it is the minimal number of decimal places needed to distinguish among table entries
    C. there was no room for more decimal places in the table without crowding
    D. the more accurately a figure is shown the better it is for the user

34._____

35. In comparing the poverty of the young (under 25 years) with that of the older population (65 years and over) in 1969 and 1979, one could REASONABLY conclude that

    A. more young people than old people were poor but older people had a higher rate of poverty
    B. more older people than young people were poor but young people had a higher rate of poverty
    C. there is a greater degree of poverty among the younger population than among the older people
    D. young people and old people have the same rate of poverty

35._____

Questions 36-37.

DIRECTIONS: Answer Questions 36 and 37 ONLY on the basis of information given in the passage below.

Two approaches are available in developing criteria for the evaluation of plans. One approach, designated Approach A, is a review and analysis of characteristics that differentiate successful plans from unsuccessful plans. These criteria are descriptive in nature and serve as a checklist against which the plan under consideration may be judged. These characteristics have been observed by many different students of planning, and there is considerable agreement concerning the characteristics necessary for a plan to be successful.

A second approach to the development of criteria for judging plans, designated Approach B, is the determination of the degree to which the plan under consideration is economic. The word "economic" is used here in its broadest sense; i.e., effective in its utilization of resources. In order to determine the economic worth of a plan, it is necessary to use a technique that permits the description of any plan in economic terms and to utilize this technique to the extent that it becomes a "way of thinking" about plans.

8 (#2)

36. According to *Approach B*, the MOST successful plan is generally one which 36.____

   A. costs least to implement
   B. gives most value for resources expended
   C. uses the least expensive resources
   D. utilizes the greatest number of resources

37. According to *Approach A*, a successful plan is one which is 37.____

   A. descriptive in nature
   B. lowest in cost
   C. similar to other successful plans
   D. agreed upon by many students of planning

Questions 38-40.

DIRECTIONS: Answer Questions 38 through 40 ONLY on the basis of information provided in the passage below.

The primary purpose of control reports is to supply information intended to serve as the basis for corrective action if needed. At the same time, the significance of control reports must be kept in proper perspective. Control reports are only a part of the planning-management information system. Control, information includes non-financial as well as financial data that measure performance and isolate variances from standard. Control information also provides feedback so that planning information may be updated and corrected. Whenever possible, control reports should be designed so that they provide feedback for the planning process as well as provide information of immediate value to the control process.

Since the culmination of the control process is the taking of necessary corrective action to bring performance in line with standards, it follows that control information must be directed to the person who is organizationally responsible for taking the required action. Usually the same information, though in a somewhat abbreviated form, is given to the responsible manager's superior. A district sales manager needs a complete daily record of the performance of each of his salesmen; yet, the report forwarded to the regional sales manager summarizes only the performance of each sales district in his region. In preparing reports for higher echelons of management, summary statements and recommendations for action should appear on the first page; substantiating data, usually the information presented to the person directly responsible for the operation, may be included if needed.

38. A control report serves its primary purpose as part of the process which leads DIRECTLY to 38.____

   A. better planning for future action
   B. increasing the performance of district salesmen
   C. the establishment of proper performance standards
   D. taking corrective action when performance is poor

39. The one of the following which would be the BEST description of a control report is that a control report is a form of 39.____

   A. planning   B. communication
   C. direction   D. organization

40. If control reports are to be effective, the one of the following which is LEAST essential to the effectiveness of control reporting is a system of   40._____

    A. communication B. standards
    C. authority D. work simplification

KEY (CORRECT ANSWERS)

1. A	11. B	21. A	31. B
2. B	12. A	22. A	32. C
3. A	13. C	23. B	33. B
4. B	14. D	24. C	34. D
5. D	15. C	25. A	35. A
6. C	16. D	26. D	36. B
7. D	17. A	27. A	37. C
8. C	18. C	28. C	38. D
9. B	19. D	29. B	39. B
10. D	20. B	30. C	40. D

EXAMINATION SECTION
TEST 1

DIRECTIONS: Each question or incomplete statement is followed by several suggested answers or completions. Select the one that BEST answers the question or completes the statement. *PRINT THE LETTER OF THE CORRECT ANSWER IN THE SPACE AT THE RIGHT.*

1. A trainee is working on an important assignment which should be completed immediately, when his supervisor gives him another assignment which he is told to do right away. Of the following, which would be the MOST appropriate reaction for the trainee? The trainee should

    A. show any annoyance he genuinely feels at being interrupted while working on an important assignment
    B. explain his other assignment to the supervisor and then follow the latter's decision on which to do first
    C. tell the supervisor that it decreases efficiency to be removed from a task he is in the middle of
    D. tell the supervisor to give the assignment to someone else

    1.____

2. A trainee may come into contact with employees who do a wide variety of work, including programming experts (programmers, systems analysts, systems managers), administrators who know little about computers, operators of computers and key punch equipment, clerks, and typists. It is the BEST policy, in dealing with these individuals, for the trainee to be

    A. deferential to the programming experts and administrators, and firm with the equipment operators and clerical employees
    B. lenient with the equipment operators and clerical employees, while anticipating a high standard of work from programming experts and administrators
    C. friendly with the programming experts, computer operators, and keypunchers-the computer team-and less close to non-programming administrators and clerical employees
    D. cooperative with all programming experts and administrators, and considerate of equipment operators and clerical employees

    2.____

3. A trainee is about to run his program, when trouble develops with the computer. He is informed that he will almost certainly be able to run his program in about forty minutes. In this circumstance, which of the following would it be MOST appropriate for him to do while he is waiting to use the computer?

    A. Relax with a cup of coffee
    B. Keep up-to-date by reading a newspaper
    C. Work on other assigned tasks
    D. Talk to co-workers if they have time to spare

    3.____

4. A supervisor has explained one operation in a procedure to a trainee and has asked him to perform that operation. The supervisor is unaware that the trainee knows how to do the next operation too.
   In such a situation, the trainee should

    4.____

A. perform the operation assigned and then go on to the next operation
B. do exactly what he was told to do without further comment
C. ask if the supervisor wants him to on to the next operation after he finishes the operation assigned
D. explain tactfully to the supervisor that he should not underestimate a trainee's ability

5. After receiving instructions and guidelines on the data and procedures involved, a trainee submits a computer program to the office requesting it. The office requests certain modifications in the program. After submitting the revised program, the trainee is told that the office has further modified its requirements, and that the program should be revised accordingly.
At this point, it would be BEST for the trainee to

   A. agree to make the required revisions as soon as possible
   B. ask the requesting office for assurances that it will have no further modifications
   C. tell the supervisor in that office how much time has been wasted on needless revisions
   D. complete any other assignments before returning to this one

6. A trainee is asked to rewrite the program of a programmer who has been shifted to other duties. The two of them must confer so that the trainee can get necessary background information. The programmer says that he wants to meet the trainee in person and that his schedule will allow them to meet any weekday only from noon to one o'clock. The trainee is scheduled to go to lunch every day at noon.
The trainee should

   A. tell the programmer to make other arrangements
   B. arrange to change the lunch schedule that day
   C. discuss the program over the phone
   D. have the programmer write him a letter explaining his program

7. A trainee feels that, in order to deal effectively with the two clerks in the unit, he has to use a different approach with each clerk.
The attitude of the trainee is

   A. *unacceptable,* because the two clerks should be treated alike
   B. *unacceptable,* because there is only one good approach in dealing with people
   C. *acceptable,* because the trainee probably has a knack for dealing with various people
   D. *acceptable,* because people with different personalities may have to be treated differently

8. A trainee explained to a typist how to type a certain report. Several hours later, the trainee returned to pick up the finished material. The trainee said, *This looks very good. Thanks a lot.*
The statement made by the trainee was

   A. *poor,* because the typist does not need to be thanked for doing her regular job
   B. *poor,* because the value of praise is decreased when it is given too frequently
   C. *good,* because praise is essential whether or not it is actually deserved
   D. *good,* because the statement will probably encourage the typist to continue doing good work

9. After a newly appointed trainee had worked on a job for a few days, his supervisor asked him if he had any suggestions on how to do the job better.
   Asking a newly appointed trainee for suggestions is

   A. *good*; because it may give the trainee a sense of participation
   B. *bad*; it is a sign of the supervisor's insecurity
   C. *good*; it will show whether the trainee can handle the job
   D. *bad*; any suggestions may be interpreted as dissatisfaction

10. A good supervisor gets things done through his people. This can generally BEST be achieved by

    A. continually emphasizing his authority over subordinates
    B. giving credit to subordinates for work well done
    C. reporting poor performance to top management
    D. treating subordinates as close personal friends

11. In a computer room environment, which of the following is the MOST important thing for a supervisor to encourage?

    A. The development of more than two people to handle every job in the computer room
    B. An atmosphere in which operators talk freely of the problems of management
    C. A cooperative team approach among the operators
    D. A condition where operators report to the supervisor on actions of other operators

12. A basic principle of supervision is that a supervisor CANNOT delegate

    A. authority   B. responsibility
    C. power   D. making assignments

13. Which of the following is generally LEAST important to consider in evaluating the performance of an operator? The

    A. number of jobs that have abnormally terminated during his shift
    B. number and length of jobs run during his shift
    C. degree to which he can work well without close supervision
    D. amount of formal academic education he has

14. To properly train a new computer operator, you should FIRST

    A. teach him the use of peripheral equipment
    B. have a plan for his training
    C. let him watch an experienced operator
    D. have him read the console run book

15. Which of the following is MOST essential for a good training program in an agency computer installation?

    A. A training consultant assigned to the computer room
    B. One trained person operating each piece of equipment
    C. Everyone receiving thorough training on each piece of equipment
    D. Sufficiently trained back-up personnel for each piece of equipment

16. Which of the following is MOST important to stress as you train a new operator?

    A. Your own experience and ability, in order to give him confidence
    B. How to operate equipment in such a way as not to produce problems
    C. The location and use of manuals
    D. The location and use of operation logs

17. A supervisor should be sure that his subordinates understand what is expected of them. Which of the following is MOST likely to produce this understanding?

    A. Establishing work standards and explaining them to subordinates
    B. Praising subordinates when they do outstanding work
    C. Frequently discussing the work load with subordinates
    D. Encouraging subordinates to work harder

18. Of the following, which would be the LEAST appropriate action for you to take while training a new operator? To

    A. give him an explanation of manuals used in the computer room
    B. personally demonstrate the operation of the equipment he will use
    C. have him use equipment while you watch him closely
    D. discuss with him the various makes of equipment on the market

19. Your superior has informed you that he is concerned about the decreased level of production of your section. After a careful study of the problem, you find that not only has the level of production decreased, but also the morale of your subordinates is low.
    In order to best remedy this situation, you should FIRST

    A. establish a new set of office procedures, stressing that they should be strictly followed
    B. inform your subordinates that your superior is displeased with their work, and demand an immediate improvement in their work habits
    C. explain your feelings about the situation to your subordinates and ask for their suggestions on how it can be changed
    D. explain to your superior that due to the low morale of your subordinates, there is nothing you can do

20. In order to find out who handles the work first, how many copies are made, and the nature of the output, it would be BEST to consult a(n)

    A. functional organization chart
    B. work distribution chart
    C. chart narrative
    D. information flow diagram

21. Participation of workers from the user work units in the planning of the changeover from manual to EDP systems is MOST likely to

    A. assure that good management techniques will be used
    B. facilitate the installation of new procedures
    C. end employee dissatisfaction with management
    D. bring problems because of poor methodology

22. When using questionnaires to secure factual information in a preliminary part of systems analysis, it is BEST to

    A. design a questionnaire that is thorough so that follow-up interviewing will not be needed
    B. follow up the questionnaire with interviews on responses that are not clear
    C. limit the questionnaire to four pages and a total of not more than 30 items
    D. use a questionnaire that will also allow the respondent to give his opinion on the questionnaire content and organization

23. Assume that you have been assigned to organize and coordinate the training of EDP personnel who have been assigned to work with new equipment.
    Of the following, the BEST action for you to take FIRST is to

    A. temporarily replace the staff with employees experienced with that equipment
    B. determine the actual and needed skills of the assigned EDP personnel
    C. find out about pertinent courses available from outside sources
    D. prepare a manual describing the new system

24. Of the following, the method that is LEAST useful in securing information about an agency's overall operations during preliminary systems analysis is

    A. sending questionnaires to key people
    B. interviewing workers at their jobs
    C. analyzing computer programs now in use
    D. observing manual operations and paper flow

25. In the course of your research on an existing system, you discover that several response items on a daily report form tend to be omitted.
    Your recommendation should be to

    A. question the use of these items and determine their value and place in the reporting scheme
    B. ignore the omissions because omissions are just as significant as entries
    C. omit these items from any new form if the response level is less than 5%
    D. put these items near the top of any new form so that they cannot be ignored

KEY (CORRECT ANSWERS)

1.	B	11.	C
2.	D	12.	B
3.	C	13.	D
4.	C	14.	B
5.	A	15.	D
6.	B	16.	B
7.	D	17.	A
8.	D	18.	D
9.	A	19.	C
10.	B	20.	D

21. B
22. B
23. B
24. C
25. A

TEST 2

DIRECTIONS: Each question or incomplete statement is followed by several suggested answers or completions. Select the one that BEST answers the question or completes the statement. *PRINT THE LETTER OF THE CORRECT ANSWER IN THE SPACE AT THE RIGHT.*

1. A systems analyst is beginning interviews in an operational area where he is expected to make a complete analysis. At first glance, the operation has poor supervision, poor working conditions, low morale, staff shortages, and general opposition to change. The first interview with the section chief is not very helpful to the analyst in understanding the operation.
Of the following, it would be BEST for the analyst to

   A. bypass the section chief and speak directly to the workers
   B. pressure the section chief into being more open with him
   C. explain to the section chief how the analysis can help him with some of his problems
   D. formulate alternate plans for general systems improvement on the basis of obvious faults in the operation

1._____

2. After having initially trained workers of a user section in their new job tasks, it is BEST for you as a trainer to

   A. turn the group over completely to their regular supervisor for any further training
   B. follow up very closely to see that they are doing the work properly
   C. restrict any further contact with the group to those workers who seem to have the most difficulty
   D. continue your training role and make yourself available as a consultant

2._____

3. Which of the following statements offers the BEST guideline in drawing up schedules for analysis and coding?

   A. If you break down the work assignments into small enough units, you should be able to make good estimates of the time necessary to complete the project.
   B. Put enough good analysts and coders on a project, and you can meet practically any deadline.
   C. In order to avoid the effects of Parkinson's Law (work expands to fill the time allotted), you should usually draw up a tight schedule.
   D. Additional time for unforeseen problems should be added to time estimates when trying to predict a relatively accurate final completion target date.

3._____

4. In the course of instructing a trainee in the operation of a machine, there comes a time when it is best to let the trainee make an initial trial under the instructor's direct supervision.
This step in the learning sequence is usually IMMEDIATELY

   A. *before* the instructor demonstrates the operation of the machine
   B. *before* the instructor explains the purpose of the machine
   C. *after* the instructor demonstrates the operation of the machine
   D. *after* the instructor explains the purpose of the machine

4._____

5. Assume that a new EDP system is being installed for a division. The analyst observes suspicion and indifference in the user's staff toward the new project.
Of the following, what is the BEST course of action to be taken?

    A. Arrange for transfers for the discontented workers
    B. Assign more work to the employees
    C. Develop greater competition among the workers and a stronger interest in management functions
    D. Educate the workers in the purposes and objectives of the project

6. While doing a systems study, an analyst often observes the activities in the area under study to clarify the jobs of the employees and the methods utilized in processing the work of the section.
One general rule *essential* for observing and being accepted as an observer is to

    A. discuss the work being done in the area, giving frank criticism of current methods
    B. tell the employees the details of all possible changes
    C. avoid voicing criticism to the employees being observed
    D. avoid showing interest so as to maintain a formal distance from the employees

7. Downward communication, from high management to lower levels in an organization, will often not be fully accepted at the lowest levels of an organization *unless* high-level management

    A. communicates through several levels of mid-level management, where the message can be properly modified and interpreted
    B. communicates directly with the level of the organization it wishes to reach, bypassing any intermediate levels
    C. first establishes an atmosphere in which upward communication is encouraged and listened to
    D. establishes penalties for non-compliance with its communications

8. A top-level manager sometimes has an inaccurate view of the actual lower-level operations of his agency, particularly of those operations which are not running well. Of the following, the MOST frequent cause of this is the

    A. general unconcern of top-level management with the way an agency actually operates
    B. tendency of the people at the lowest level in an agency to lie about their actual performance
    C. unwillingness of top-level management to deal with unfavorable information when it is presented
    D. tendency of mid-level management to edit bad news and unpleasant information from reports directed to top management

9. In the conduct of productivity analyses, work measurement is a *useful* technique for

    A. substantiating executive decisions
    B. designing a research study
    C. developing performance yardsticks
    D. preparing a manual of procedure

3 (#2)

...dentified with the *firefighting* function of management. As such, 10.____

...ıent over time of an agency's strategic options
 issues that have come up during the past year
 cedures to be followed in an emergency
 policy question often performed in a crisis environment

...ɔt is illustrated when a group is organized on an *ad-hoc* basis 11.____
...ɑl?

    B. Line/Staff
    D. Command

12. Assume that, in the course of making a feasibility study for the installation of an EDP system, older workers show extreme resistance to converting the manual system. The resistance takes the form of far-fetched reasons why EDP will not work in their situations. Of the following, the BEST course of action to take in dealing with these workers is to tell them   12.____

    A. that they are as good as the younger workers and should adapt well to EDP
    B. exactly what changes in their work will be made because of the change to EDP
    C. that their reasons for disliking EDP are ill-founded and that they have nothing to fear
    D. that the methods used in their unit will be adapted to their desires, if possible

13. As a supervisor, you have received a rather complicated set of instructions for a new project which is to begin immediately. Some of the instructions are confusing. Your FIRST step should be to   13.____

    A. attempt to clear up with your supervisor any ambiguities before beginning the project
    B. instruct your staff to get started on the project immediately while you try to clarify the instructions
    C. discuss the matter with other supervisors at your level to find out if they have received clarification
    D. figure out the instructions as best you can and provide firm guidelines for your subordinates on the basis of your own good judgment

14. During the course of your work on the development of a new system, you realize that there is a big difference between what you think is needed and what the head of your agency thinks is needed. The agency head does not have a technical background in computer work.
Your BEST course of action is to   14.____

    A. develop a system based on what the agency head thinks is needed
    B. create a system based on what you think is needed
    C. base your system on what you believe would be an acceptable compromise between the two viewpoints
    D. discuss the differences between the two points of view with the agency head and abide by his decision

15. As part of the unit under your supervision, you have been assigned a recent college graduate who is learning computer systems analysis. Although he has had computer systems and programming courses in college, he appears to be slow in doing the analysis preparatory to designing a subsystem.
The BEST course of action for you to follow *first* in dealing with this worker is to

    A. check the possibility of his reassignment to a unit that has less strenuous work demands
    B. reduce the size of the subsystem assigned to him so that he can finish his work with little assistance
    C. let him work at his own pace, but help him with any parts of the analysis that are especially troublesome
    D. remind him of the need for meeting production demands and threaten to terminate his employment if his production does not improve

16. While working on a system design, a systems analyst is told by the user that certain changes must be made that will affect the system specification.
Of the following, which method would you use to handle these changes?

    A. Establish a formal procedure, including an approval mechanism requiring sign-offs by user and system management
    B. Make changes as the requests are made since there is usually no need to consult management
    C. Refuse to permit changes in specifications that will impact the project schedule
    D. Permit changes in specifications to be handled informally if they do not substantially alter the cost of system implementation

17. The BEST attitude for you to assume in conducting interviews with user staff during the preliminary analysis is to

    A. act superior; their increased respect will cause them to be more open with you
    B. try to gain the respect of the staff by giving them a great deal of technical information on computers
    C. be personal; exchange views on management innovations including the proposed computer installation
    D. get the staff involved in the study; let them know that the information they are supplying is important

18. Observation of work procedures is used for many purposes in the process of systems analysis.
Which of the following represents a FAULTY purpose of observation in an analytic situation?
To

    A. give the analyst an overall view of the flow of routine tasks
    B. identify workers who are performing poorly in a manual operation
    C. confirm information secured in an interview
    D. clarify information secured in written form

19. The input requirements of a new system are such that the work-flow in a clerical division will have to radically change. The supervisor of the division has asked you to help him in the training and instruction of his staff. Your PRIMARY consideration in this task is to

    A. perform it as quickly as possible so as to promote a rapid readjustment
    B. concentrate on what you know best, the input requirements of the EDP system
    C. organize a thorough training course and help the supervisor reorganize the work assignments
    D. concentrate on those staff members who are reacting to the changeover in a negative emotional manner

20. On-the-job training is one of the most common methods used to teach the employees of a user section the skills necessary for job performance in a changeover from a manual system to an EDP system.
    Which of the following is most likely to be a DISADVANTAGE of this type of training?

    A. In most instances, on-the-job training is carried out with little or no planning, causing a lack of focus.
    B. The employee gains experience in the environment in which he will be working.
    C. Employees usually resent this type of training because they must learn from their own mistakes.
    D. After the employee has developed sufficient skills, the trainer must follow up to determine the results of the training.

21. Most of the analysts working under your supervision are consistently submitting subsystems as ready for coding which actually have logical inconsistencies of one sort or another. You have called this to their attention but the problem persists.
    Of the following, the BEST method of improving their performance is to

    A. constantly make them aware of the delays caused by incomplete analysis
    B. correct the deficiencies yourself before submitting subsystems to programmer
    C. encourage the analysts to do more exchanging of flow charts among themselves so that they can find each other's mistakes
    D. reduce your criticism since it can be harmful to team productivity

22. Failure of programmers to document a system *usually* results in

    A. decreased likelihood that programmers involved in system development will be involved in maintaining the system
    B. greater job security for management because the system may not run if their employment is terminated
    C. increased cost of system development
    D. increased cost of system maintenance

23. The one of the following which is most likely to have the GREATEST effect on the computer-related costs of using a data base management system is

    A. the organizational structure of the group using the system
    B. data structure, access patterns, and system parameters such as number and size of buffers
    C. whether or not programs using the system are designed to optimize the use of data dictionaries
    D. the type of computer language used

24. Systems for which programs are data independent, such as those which access data through dictionaries, tend to be

    A. easier to modify as system requirements change with time
    B. more efficient of machine time than programs which access data directly
    C. more likely to lead to severe data security problems
    D. restricted to library and language processing applications

25. In evaluating the economic feasibility of systems which enable on-line access to files that would ordinarily be independently maintained in manual form by a number of groups, it is particularly important to look at the trade-off between the cost of system operation and the reduced

    A. clerical costs in each group
    B. cost of system development
    C. communications costs
    D. cost of supplies

KEY (CORRECT ANSWERS)

1. C		11. C	
2. B		12. B	
3. D		13. A	
4. C		14. D	
5. D		15. C	
6. C		16. A	
7. C		17. D	
8. D		18. B	
9. C		19. C	
10. D		20. A	

21. C
22. D
23. B
24. A
25. A

TABLE OF CONTENTS
LOGICAL DATABASE DESIGN

Page

1. INTRODUCTION 2

    1.1 What Is Logical Database Design? 2

        1.1.1 LDD's Relation to Other Life Cycle Phases . 2
        1.1.2 Characteristics of LDD 6

    1.2 An Ideal Logical Database Design Methodology . 8

        1.2.1 LDD Practices 8
        1.2.2 Data Dictionary System 9

    1.3 Intended Audience for this Guide 10

    1.4 Purpose of this Guide 10

    1.5 Assumptions 11

    1.6 Scope of this Guide 11

    1.7 Structure of this Guide 12

2. THE FRAMEWORK THAT SUPPORTS LDD 14

    2.1 The Role of LDD in the Life Cycle 14

        2.1.1 Needs Analysis 15
        2.1.2 Requirements Analysis 16
        2.1.3 Logical Database Design 17
        2.1.4 Physical Database Design 18

    2.2 Detailed Framework for LDD 19

        2.2.1 LDD Information Requirements 19
        2.2.2 LDD Phases 20
        2.2.3 Strategies for LDD Development 23
        2.2.4 Summary of LDD Features 25

3. PROJECT ORGANIZATION 26

    3.1 Functional Roles Needed for LDD 26

    3.2 Training Required for LDD 28

    3.3 Project Planning and Management Requirements . 29

4. LOCAL INFORMATION-FLOW MODELING 30

    4.1 Information Used to Develop the LIM 31

    4.2 Functions of the LIM 34

    4.3 Procedure for Developing the LIM 34

        4.3.1 Review Need for Analysis 36
        4.3.2 Determine Subsystems 37
        4.3.3 Plan Development of the LIM 39
        4.3.4 Develop LIM 40
        4.3.5 Develop Workload With Respect to LIMs 44

5. GLOBAL INFORMATION-FLOW MODELING 47

    5.1 Information Used to Develop the GIM 48

    5.2 Functions of the GIM 49

    5.3 Procedure for Developing the GIM 49

        5.3.1 Verify the LIMs 51
        5.3.2 Consolidate LIMs 52
        5.3.3 Refine Boundary of Automated Information
              System (AIS) 54
        5.3.4 Produce GIM 57

6. CONCEPTUAL SCHEMA DESIGN 58

    6.1 Information Used to Develop the CS 59

    6.2 Functions of the CS 59

    6.3 Procedure for Developing the CS 60

        6.3.1 List Entities and Identifiers 62
        6.3.2 Generate Relationships among Entities 64
        6.3.3 Add Connectivity to Relationships 69
        6.3.4 Add Attributes to Entities 72
        6.3.5 Develop Additional Data Characteristics .. 74
        6.3.6 Normalize the Collection 75

7. EXTERNAL SCHEMA MODELING 77

    7.1 Information Used to Develop the ES 77

    7.2 Functions of the ES 77

    7.3 Procedure for Developing the ES 78

```
            7.3.1 Extract an ES from the CS ................. 80
            7.3.2 Develop Workload With Respect to ESs ...... 82
            7.3.3 Add Local Constraints to the ES .......... 84
8.   CONCLUSIONS ........................................... 85
9.   ACKNOWLEDGMENTS ....................................... 86
10.  REFERENCES AND SELECTED READINGS ..................... 87
```

LIST OF FIGURES

FIGURES	DESCRIPTION	PAGE
1	Information Systems Life Cycle	5
2	Diagram of the Four LDD Phases	22
3	Local Information-Flow Modeling (LIM) Procedure	35
4	Example of a LIM	41
5	Global Information-Flow Modeling (GIM) Procedure	50
6	Example of a GIM	56
7	Conceptual Schema (CS) Design Procedure	61
8	Example of an E-R Diagram	66
9	Alternate Notation for an E-R Diagram	67
10	Replacing a Relationship with an Entity	68
11	Example of an E-R Diagram with Connectivity	71
12	Example of an E-R-A Diagram	73
13	External Schema (ES) Modeling Procedure	79

LIST OF ABBREVIATIONS

AA	Application Administrator
AIS	Automated Information System
BSP	Business Systems Planning
CS	Conceptual Schema
DA	Data Administrator
DBA	Database Administrator
DBMS	Database Management System
DD	Data Dictionary
DDA	Data Dictionary Administrator
DDS	Data Dictionary System
EKNF	Elementary Key Normal Form
E-R	Entity-Relationship
E-R-A	Entity-Relationship-Attribute
ES	External Schema
GIM	Global Information-flow Model
IRDS	Information Resource Dictionary System
LDD	Logical Database Design
LIM	Local Information-flow Model
PERT	Program Evaluation and Review Technique
QA	Quality Assurance

LOGICAL DATABASE DESIGN

Logical Database Design. The methodology includes four phases: Local Information-flow Modeling, Global Information-flow Modeling, Conceptual Schema Design, and External Schema Modeling. These phases are intended to make maximum use of available information and user expertise, including the use of a previous Needs Analysis, and to prepare a firm foundation for physical database design and system implementation. The methodology recommends analysis from different points of view--organization, function, and event-- in order to ensure that the logical database design accurately reflects the requirements of the entire population of future users. The methodology also recommends computer support from a data dictionary system, in order to conveniently and accurately handle the volume and complexity of design documentation and analysis. The report places the methodology in the context of the complete system life cycle. An appendix of illustrations shows examples of how the four phases of the methodology can be implemented.

Key words: data dictionary system; data dictionary system standard; data management; data model; database design; database management system, DBMS; Entity-Relationship-Attribute Model; Information Resource Dictionary System, IRDS; logical database design.

1. INTRODUCTION

1.1 What Is Logical Database Design?

Logical Database Design (LDD) is the process of determining the fundamental data structure needed to support an organization's information resource. LDD provides a structure that determines the way that data is collected, stored, and protected from undesired access. Since data collection, storage, and protection are costly, and since restructuring data generally requires expensive revisions to programs, it is important that the LDD be of high quality. This guide describes procedures that lead to the development of a high quality LDD.

A high quality LDD will be: (1) internally consistent, to reduce the chances of contradictory results from the information system; (2) complete, to ensure that known information requirements can be satisfied and known constraints can be enforced; and (3) robust, to allow adaptation of the data structure in response to foreseeable changes in the information requirements. To fulfill these considerations, a good LDD should be independent of any particular application, so that all applications can be satisfied, and independent of any particular hardware or software environment, so that the data structure can be supported in any environment. A good LDD will ensure that modularity, efficiency, consistency, and integrity are supported in the data structure underlying the databases of the information system.

1.1.1 LDD's Relation to Other Life Cycle Phases.

LDD is closely related to the life cycle phases of Needs Analysis, Requirements Analysis, and Physical Database Design. Needs analysis and requirements analysis provide the information requirements needed to perform LDD. LDD produces data models and schemas for use in physical database design. The Physical Database Design phase receives the data structures prepared during LDD and adapts them to the specific hardware and software environment to form the internal schema of each database.

Figure 1 shows LDD's place in the life cycle and depicts the functional and data activities that can be performed in parallel. LDD can be performed in parallel to the phases of Requirements Analysis, Systems Specification, and Systems Design. The synchronized performance of these phases will assist in providing the information needed for a good LDD and will result in speeding the systems development process.

By taking a brief overview of the development of an information system, we can see how LDD is used. The life cycle of an information system should consist of the following phases:

1. Needs Analysis

    Also known as Enterprise Analysis, this phase is conducted before other work on the systems development project begins. Its purpose is to establish the context and boundaries of the systems development effort, and provide the focus, scope, priorities, and initial requirements for the target system.

2. Requirements Analysis

    The results of the Needs Analysis are carried further in this phase, which provides both the functional and the data requirements for the system under development. Requirements analysis is performed in parallel to the LDD and Systems Specification phases. Prototyping may be performed during this phase to refine requirements.

3. Systems Specification

    During this phase, the functional information provided by requirements analysis is used to produce specifications for: input and output reports that are both external and internal to the system; the functions, processes, and procedures of operational subsystems; and decision support capabilities.

4. Logical Database Design

    This phase is performed concurrently with the phases of Requirements Analysis, Systems Specification, and Systems Design. During this phase, the data requirements provided by the Needs Analysis and Requirements Analysis phases are used to perform the following iterative data modeling and design activities:

A. Local and Global Information-flow Modeling

The following are defined: data flows throughout the system; information models for each application (i.e., local) and for the entire system (i.e., global); and, data classifications, requirements, and sources for the subsystems including those for decision support. The LDD data modeling activities correspond to the functional specification activities of to the Systems Specification phase.

B. Conceptual and External Schemas

The following are defined: data structures for system-wide (i.e., conceptual) and application-oriented (i.e., external) views of the system; user views of the databases including those providing decision support capabilities; and logical database schema designs and constraints. LDD schema design activities correspond to the functional design activities of the Systems Design phase.

5. Systems Design

This phase delineates: the functional control flows using the data flows from LDD; high level and detailed system architectures; the software structure design; and the module external design (i.e., the design for interfaces among modules of code).

6. Physical Database Design

This phase produces physical data flows and the detailed internal schema for the specific hardware, software, and database implementations to be used, in order to balance maximum data storage efficiency, data retrieval performance, and data update performance. Physical database design is performed in parallel to the Implementation phase.

7. Implementation

This phase produces: logic definition for programs; module design; internal data definitions; coding; testing and debugging; acceptance testing; and conversion from the old system to the new one.

INFORMATION SYSTEMS LIFE CYCLE

FUNCTIONAL ACTIVITIES

DATA ACTIVITIES

- Needs Analysis
- Requirements Analysis
- Systems Specification
- **LOGICAL DATABASE DESIGN**
  - Local and Global Information Modeling
  - Conceptual and External Schema Design
- Systems Design
- Implementation
- Physical Database Design
- Operation and Maintenance

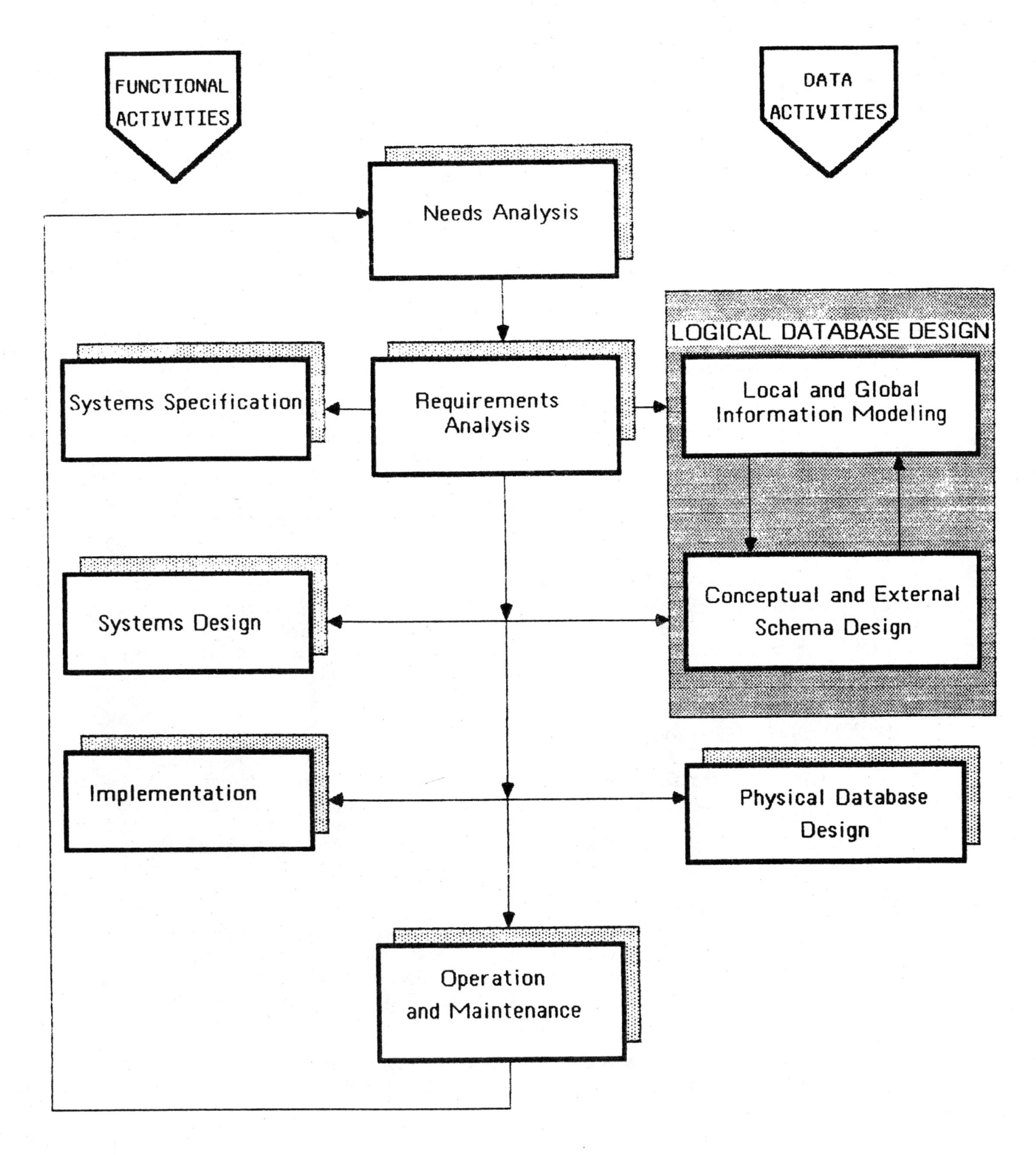

FIGURE 1

8. Operation and Maintenance

   During this phase the information system performs to serve the users' information needs and to collect data about the system's ongoing operation. Programmers and analysts continue to debug the system and modify it to support changing users' needs. Database designers continue to maintain database effectiveness and efficiency during system modifications and data changes. When modifications to the system are no longer adequate to support user needs, the current system should evolve to a new target system and the cycle will begin again.

As this description of the information system's life cycle shows, LDD plays a major role in development. LDD greatly enhances the performance of the Quality Assurance (QA) process, which would be ongoing from the Systems Specification and LDD phases through the Operation and Maintenance phase. Because LDD emphasizes the iterative approach, QA will have many opportunities to check the results of one iteration against the results of other iterations. Since LDD is performed in parallel to the Requirements Analysis, Systems Specification, and Systems Design phases, QA will be able to compare both the interim and final results of concurrent phases to resolve any difficulties sooner than through the traditional approach. The automated Data Dictionary System (DDS), described in Section 1.2.2, should be used during Requirements Analysis and LDD to provide immediate, shared access to data requirements and database designs, and to support the QA process.

1.1.2 Characteristics of LDD.

The potential benefits of LDD to the development life cycle can only be gained, however, through a good quality LDD. For LDD to perform its role well, the results of the logical design process must have certain characteristics. A LDD should be:

o Independent of the hardware and software environment, so that the design can be implemented in a variety of environments and so the design will remain relevant even if the hardware and software selected to support the information system eventually change.

o Independent of the implementation data model or the Database Management System (DBMS) in use, so that the design will apply to any present or future data model or data management system, which would not necessarily be a DBMS.

o Comprehensive in representing present and future applications so that all known, anticipated, and probable needs can be included or considered in the design, to avoid costly system alterations in the future.

o Able to satisfy the information requirements of the entire organization, encompassing all possible applications rather than being limited to one or two; this way the information system will have the capacity to be an organizational resource, not just the resource of one department or application area.

A good LDD should also fulfill a set of precise technical goals to provide a firm foundation for:

o Maintainability and reusability, achieved through the use of modularity in the database design.

o Robustness, allowing both the design and the system to be adaptable to hardware and software changes.

o Security, controlled through compartmentalization in the database design which will limit specified types of data access to designated personnel or organizational units.

o Update and storage efficiency, achieved through controlled redundancy that limits the number of places where the same data will be stored.

o Retrieval efficiency, so that data can be organized to be readily accessible by system users.

o Consistency and integrity, achieved through several measures including data integrity constraints and controlled redundancy.

If done correctly, logical database design for a complex information system is a massive undertaking. The short-term cost of LDD is great, but the long-term benefits of better information and greater flexibility provide substantial savings over the system's life cycle.

1.2 An Ideal Logical Database Design Methodology

A methodology is an organized system of practices and procedures applied to a branch of knowledge to assist in the pursuit of that knowledge, which in this case is database design. In other words, a LDD methodology is a planned approach to database design that assists in database development in support of an information system.

1.2.1 LDD Practices.

This guide describes a methodology that includes the preferred practices and procedures characterizing the development of a good quality LDD and a successful information system. Although normalization is often considered the primary activity of LDD, normalization is only one of many procedures performed in LDD. Normalization is a valuable but limited tool in that it only considers functional data dependencies. Other procedures should be used in conjunction with normalization for a coherent database design. An ideal LDD methodology should be supported by:

1. A LDD guide, such as the one provided in this document, that describes clearly defined steps for analysts and designers to follow in order to produce a good LDD.

2. Analytical methods, such as the ones described in this guide, to assist in the detection of redundancies, incompleteness, and possible errors in the conceptual and functional data modeling. Some of these methods include: (a) a hierarchical, iterative approach to organizational or functional concept development; (b) differentiation of various points of view in information development, such as organizational components, higher and lower level functions, and event, control, and decision structures; and (c) normalization procedures.

3. A series of specified checkpoints for progress reviews by designers and management, and for information exchange meetings with the personnel of LDD's parallel phases, Requirements Analysis, Systems Specification, and Systems Design.

4. A mode of notation (i.e., graphic or symbolic) to describe and build a detailed conceptual model of the data and functions under study.

5. A specification language (e.g., the language used by a Data Dictionary System) to specify information requirements and the LDD design in a consistent, unambiguous manner.

6. An automated tool such as a Data Dictionary System, capable of supporting the documentation and analysis of LDD complexity, especially for large systems development projects. This tool should be used to assist in: (a) describing the conceptual model; (b) describing the data needed to support the functions of the conceptual model; (c) performing completeness and consistency checking of the conceptual model and the data needed to support the functions of the conceptual model [AFIF84].

1.2.2 Data Dictionary System.

A Data Dictionary System (DDS) is a computer software system used to record, store, protect, and analyze descriptions of an organization's information resources, including data and programs. It provides analysts, designers, and managers with convenient, controlled access to the summary and detailed descriptions needed to plan, design, implement, operate, and modify their information systems. The DDS also provides end-users with the data descriptions that they need to formulate ad hoc queries. Equally important, it provides a common language, or framework, for establishing and enforcing standards and controls throughout an organization.

The data dictionary (DD) is the data that is organized and managed by the Data Dictionary System. The DD is a resource that will be of great value long after a logical database design is completed. The data dictionary can provide support for information about all aspects of system development to be stored, updated, and accessed throughout the system's life cycle.

The term Information Resource Dictionary System (IRDS) is beginning to replace the term Data Dictionary System due to recognition of the flexibility and power of the software [ANSI84, FIPS80, KONI84]. This paper uses the terms Data Dictionary System (DDS) and data dictionary (DD) to conform to the current practice of software vendors.

1.3 Intended Audience for this Guide

This guide is intended primarily to provide information and guidance to: Data Administrators (DAs) and Database Administrators (DBAs) in leading their LDD projects; Applications Administrators (AAs) and application specialists in the types of data and data validation that LDD will require; and, end-users and systems analysts in how they can best contribute to the LDD project to maximize its benefits.

1.4 Purpose of this Guide

This guide provides a coherent plan of action that will allow management and database designers to direct and perform the database design successfully. The LDD plan offered here is sufficiently general to be compatible with existing tools and techniques in use for database design. By defining a methodology that provides a more stable view of the relationships among data items, this guide can be used to increase the effectiveness of an information system over its life cycle.

When the LDD approach described here is used, particularly if used with the assistance of a Data Dictionary System, an increase in clear communication can result among the end-users, systems analysts, designers, and the applications programmers who will actually code and implement the system. By providing a detailed and unambiguous description of the system's information requirements in relation to the users' perspectives, LDD offers a bridge between the end-users and the physical database designers and applications programmers.

This guide describes a methodology to be used in optimizing the flexibility and integrity of an information system. Flexibility will be ensured through the identification of the least changing characteristics of the system, which give a stable foundation upon which to build the information system. Data integrity will be optimized through the centralized control, completeness, and consistency that a quality LDD will provide. The information system that results from these LDD procedures will perform better over the system's life cycle because it will address current and probable future needs more completely and will allow requirements changes to be incorporated more effectively.

1.5 Assumptions

Several assumptions have been made in the preparation of this guide about the types of information systems in which LDD will be used. Because LDD is a non-trivial process to be undertaken when a need for it exists, it is assumed that:

o The information system's databases will be sizable and complex to support multiple applications, may have no single dominant application, and will probably contain tens or hundreds of data collections and relationships, and thousands of data elements. DBMS support is not assumed, although it is usually desirable.

o The information system and its databases are intended for use over a long period of time so that the benefits to the life cycle costs will justify the investment of time, money, and effort in LDD.

o The data requirements of the information system will be significant and include the use of ad hoc queries where the precision of the database structure will prove important.

1.6 Scope of this Guide

This guide is limited in scope to the LDD phase. The interaction of LDD with the immediately preceding and subsequent life cycle phases is mentioned, since these determine LDD's information resources and products. Because LDD works from the results of the preceding Needs Analysis and concurrent Requirements Analysis phases, and prepares a foundation for the subsequent Physical Database Design phase, these phases will be described briefly.

1.7 Structure of this Guide

Chapter 2 addresses the relationship between LDD and the phases of Needs Analysis, Requirements Analysis, and Physical Database Design. The major phases of the LDD approach are further discussed along with the types of analysis strategies that will be needed to accompany LDD. Figure 2, in Section 2.2.2, illustrates the interaction of the four phases of the LDD methodology to assist the reader in visualizing the LDD process.

In Chapter 3, the organizational aspects of the LDD project are described, including the key roles in LDD development, the training required for the personnel in these roles, and the part played by management in planning for and monitoring the LDD process.

The following chapters, 4 through 7, define the four phases of the LDD approach in detail. Chapters 4 through 7 are identically structured so that each chapter has three sections: (1) the first section of each phase discusses the information used by that phase, (2) the second section discusses the general functions of that phase, and (3) the third section discusses the procedure for accomplishing that phase. The third section of each phase includes a diagram of the steps within that phase, followed by a subsection on each step. Each step is followed by a summary chart.

Chapter 4 discusses Local Information-flow Modeling and describes three modes of analysis corresponding to the target system's (1) organizational components, (2) functions, and (3) the events to which the target information system will respond. These three analysis modes are examined in relation to data flow and data structure design techniques.

Chapter 5 addresses Global Information-flow Modeling and emphasizes the need to balance the perspectives of data flow and data structure in the development of a design that will favor both equally. The Conceptual Schema Design is described in Chapter 6 in relation to the use of Entity-Relationship-Attribute (E-R-A) data modeling diagrams and normalization techniques. Chapter 7 defines External Schema Modeling (i.e., subschema modeling) as it reflects the data structure and data flow from the end-user's perspective in the development of workload specifications for physical database design.

A glossary of acronyms used in this guide is included at the beginning of the document for reference. An appendix of examples has been included at the end of the document to illustrate the types of graphics that will be used and analysis that will occur during the four phases of LDD.

2. THE FRAMEWORK THAT SUPPORTS LDD

LDD plays an important part in the life cycle of the information system. This chapter describes: (1) the relationship between the database design and the functioning of the information system; (2) the interactions between LDD and the Needs Analysis, Requirements Analysis, and Physical Database Design phases; (3) the information requirements needed to perform LDD; (4) the phases within LDD; and (5) strategies for LDD development and their impact.

2.1 The Role of LDD in the Life Cycle

LDD defines the data structure that supports the databases of an information system. The database system and the information system are inextricably linked, but they are different.

An information system is one or more multi-purpose computer systems that may be supported by a network through which many types of users, perhaps in different locations, update, query, and provide data to the system in order to have current information available on a variety of topics. Decision support capabilities may be incorporated in the information system's structure to assist end-users in the decision-making process.

A database is a component of an information system and may contain a variety of general and detailed information that is made available to the information system's end-users through queries. The information system's ability to respond to user's queries is directly related to logical database design.

The design of the information system's databases will determine the ways in which the information system will function. If the information system will be required to answer ad hoc queries, the data structures within the databases should be modeled to provide maximum flexibility in data accessibility and retrieval. If the system will be required to respond quickly to certain predefined queries, then the structural modeling should be constructed to support rapid retrieval performance, which will generally require indexes or redundant data. If the time and expense needed to update the data in the system are of paramount importance, then ease in locating and changing data values should be stressed in the database design. If the storage cost of large databases is a primary consideration, then the minimization of physical redundancy should be emphasized in the database design.

Usually a combination of such requirements exist for an information system, with conflicting implications for the design of the underlying databases. These requirements and their implications for the databases that support the information system are defined during the LDD phase, and their conflicts are resolved during the Physical Database Design phase.

The structure of the logical design of the database plays a crucial role in determining the capabilities and performance of an information system. A good physical database design cannot be developed without adequate preparation. A good logical database design prepares the groundwork for a quality physical database design and a successful system implementation.

The phases of Needs Analysis, Requirements Analysis, Logical Database Design, and Physical Database Design are closely linked. The ability to perform the subsequent phases is determined by the performance of the previous and parallel phases. Each of these phases must be performed well for the resulting database to represent the desired system accurately. These phases are described below.

2.1.1 Needs Analysis.

As we have seen in Chapter 1, a Needs Analysis describes the primary needs a new information system should fulfill. Without this formal expression of the organization's perception of its needs, the analysts and designers will have to work from their own assumptions of the information system's purposes. Their assumptions could unknowingly conflict with the organization's vaguely described or unstated purposes. The resulting lack of clarity in direction would be costly.

A specific Needs Analysis methodology should be adopted and used by an organization previous to undertaking any extensive systems development project. The use of a well-defined methodology assures that most, if not all, of the important questions about the purpose of the proposed system will have been asked and answered at the end of the Needs Analysis phase. One of the most familiar and extensively used Needs Analysis methodologies available at this time is IBM's Business Systems Planning (BSP) approach [MART82].

In the Needs Analysis methodology adopted, the following minimum set of questions should be posed:

1. What organizational problems require a solution that the target information system could effect?

2. What new or improved information is needed to perform what types of functions?

3. What are the boundaries and interfaces of the target system?

4. What possible improvements in information availability could be expected from the target information system? The following are goals of many system development projects:

    o Greater accuracy of information.
    o Improved timeliness.
    o Better end-user interfaces.
    o Improved privacy and security.
    o Rapid access to distant information centers by information sources and end-users.

Once a Needs Analysis methodology has been adopted and these types of questions have been answered in detail, the purposes and plans for the systems development project can be made available to the systems development personnel. If the Needs Analysis has been performed well and a comprehensive methodology has been used, sufficient information has probably been collected for LDD to begin. Close coordination with the Requirements Analysis phase is needed for LDD to continue.

2.1.2 Requirements Analysis.

The requirements analysis effort will verify and supplement the results of the Needs Analysis phase. Since LDD and Systems Specification are directly supported by the concurrent Requirements Analysis phase, it is critical that the procedures and performance of requirements analysis be planned carefully to coordinate with these other phases.

The Requirements Analysis phase will involve two types of analysis: (1) analysis of the types of data and data flows needed within the organization; and (2) analysis of the functions performed within the organization which will require the use of this data. The purpose of requirements analysis is to provide data requirements to support the LDD phase, and functional requirements to support the Systems Specification phase.

Requirements analysts verify which functions and subsystems will remain external to the system and require interfaces. By defining the information products of external subsystems or systems that are inputs to the target system, and by defining the information products of the target system that are used by external subsystems or systems, the analysts can designate the high level input/output transformations of information that must take place within the target system. The specific functions and subfunctions performed within the target system are logically organized and described. Further, the analysts define the known constraints on accuracy, timeliness, and other performance requirements, which will be further defined in LDD. Once general requirements have been described, further refinements of the requirements are developed. Prototyping may be used in conjunction with the LDD and Systems Specification phases to refine and model requirements.

As requirements are defined, the information may be stored in the form of a data dictionary to be manipulated by a Data Dictionary System. The use of a DDS will provide automated support for the storage, analysis and querying of data, for the definition and presentation of technical and management reports, and for the simultaneous access of requirements information for use in concurrent phases. Requirements information stored in a data dictionary can be supplemented with information from LDD and other phases, and can be maintained for on-line use throughout the system's life cycle.

2.1.3 Logical Database Design.

The LDD designers decide which data must be stored and maintained to support the functions and subfunctions of the target system. By abstracting from the functions to the data structures, the designer defines the data objects to be modeled and decides which properties and constraints are relevant in modeling these objects. The Conceptual Schema is the primary product of LDD.

The Entity-Relationship-Attribute modeling technique has been chosen to define the LDD data structure (see Chapter 6). Organizations that prefer other equivalent data modeling techniques may easily adapt this LDD methodology to those techniques.

An important consideration for LDD is to ensure that all information required from the LDD phase is developed and provided to the Physical Database Design phase at the appropriate time. This information required from LDD includes the volume of data, the priority and frequency of the logical access paths to be implemented in the physical database, and constraints on performance, integrity, security, and privacy.

2.1.4 Physical Database Design.

The first step of the Physical Database Design phase is to select the appropriate data model (e.g., relational, network, or hierarchical) and the data management system to support it. This selection may, unfortunately, be dictated by the software that the organization is currently using, or by the availability of software for hardware that has already been procured. Preferably, the data model and the data management system will be selected to match the requirements defined by the LDD Conceptual Schema and the workload. A useful reference in the selection process is [GALL84].

The second step, once the selection has been made, is to translate the Entity-Relationship-Attribute model from the Conceptual Schema into the selected data model. This translation is a rather simple matter for the relational model: entities become tables, relationships are implemented by means of foreign keys, and attributes become columns. The network model translation is not much more difficult: entities become records, relationships become sets or repeating groups, attributes become data items, and attributes are omitted from a member record if they are in the owner. The hierarchical model is difficult: entities become records, attributes become data items, but relationships may become either true hierarchical relationships or logical children. These translations are discussed in detail in [CHEN82] and papers referenced therein.

The next step is to develop a detailed physical data structure, including the development of indexes and other access paths, detailed record structures (perhaps combining the logical records to reduce physical accesses), loading factors, and so on. Detailed methodologies are discussed in [CARL80, CARL81, MARC78].

2.2 Detailed Framework for LDD

The information requirements needed for the performance of LDD are described in Section 2.2.1. Although LDD has previously been presented as a single phase within the information system life cycle, in Section 2.2.2 LDD will now be subdivided into four simpler phases to be performed iteratively. Strategies for analysis and the information requirements of these phases will be described in detail in Section 2.2.3.

2.2.1 LDD Information Requirements.

In addition to information obtained from Needs Analysis, LDD designers will need other information to be collected and analyzed during the Requirements Analysis phase, conducted in parallel to LDD and Systems Specification. The following information must be available to LDD designers:

- Predefined constraints on the system, such as the use of existing hardware or software, the need to convert an existing system, and the scope of the projected information system.

- Project constraints, such as the amount of time, money and personnel allocated by the organization for the development project.

- Processing requirements, such as the type of functions that the information system will be expected to perform, and the general application areas that it will be expected to support.

- Organizational, functional and data subsets, such as departments, types of actions, and types of information that the target system will be expected to supply or support.

- Performance requirements, such as maximum retrieval and update times.

- Capacity requirements, such as the number of data objects within the target system, and storage restrictions if the limitations of existing hardware are applicable.

o Data integrity requirements, such as the control needed over redundant data, and the need for automated integrity checks during data input and update, including edit and validation rules.

o Security and privacy requirements, such as the need for encryption for some types of data, or the limitation of access for certain types of data to specific personnel.

o Reliability and maintainability requirements that define the need for the continuous functioning of the system.

o Distributed processing and data requirements, such as the need for network connections among databases in multiple locations, or the need for shared or replicated data in multiple locations.

2.2.2 LDD Phases.

As we have seen from Chapter 1, LDD generally involves information modeling and database design that are largely hardware and software independent. LDD focuses attention on the subsystems that generate the information comprising the target system. Throughout the phases of LDD, each subsystem is examined and described in terms of: (1) the organizational components, (2) the application areas or functions, and (3) the events, which occur within or affect that subsystem. The number and type of these subsystems to be analyzed during each phase of LDD will depend on the type of analysis strategy selected, as described in Section 2.2.3.

LDD consists of four distinct phases during which all the subsystems within the system, the data flows, data structures, and user views of the databases are described. These phases are performed iteratively and in sequence until the LDD is completed. The phases of LDD are the subject of this paper and are described more fully beginning at Chapter 4. In brief, the four phases of LDD are:

1. Local Information-flow Modeling

    During this phase, data flows are modeled for individual subsystems within the target system, including each organizational component, function, and event. Subsystems are modeled one at a time. A data flow is the information that is exchanged, or "flows," within and between subsystems. Data is defined at a general rather than specific level, in terms of general formats or packages (e.g., all the data contained within a particular type of report). The products of this phase are Local Information-flow Models (LIMs).

2. Global Information-flow Modeling

During this phase, individual data flows are combined and global data flows are modeled for collections of individual subsystems (i.e., organizational components, applications, or events) viewed as a whole. Data will continue to be viewed at the format or package level. The products of this phase are Global Information-flow Models (GIMs).

3. Conceptual Schema Design

During this phase, the data within the data flows, defined in the previous phases, is abstracted from the packages in which it resides, and defined in terms of its functional use. The data is described in terms of: (a) entities, the basic data components; (b) relationships, the ways in which entities are associated with each other or share characteristics; and (c) attributes, the data that describes the data entities. Entity-Relationship-Attribute (E-R-A) diagrams may be used as an analysis method. The E-R-A abstraction provides the basis for a conceptual data structure. The products of this phase are Conceptual Schemas (CSs).

4. External Schema Modeling

During this phase, the conceptual schema is adapted to conform to the needs of the application areas within the information system. By modeling the data from the user's perspective, the designer is able to verify the Conceptual Schema and derive a structured user's view of the data. The products of this phase are External Schemas (ESs) and are also known as subschemas.

Figure 2 depicts the iterative relationship of the four LDD phases. The vertical line through the center indicates a division between the phases on the left that are oriented

DIAGRAM OF THE FOUR LDD PHASES

FROM
NEEDS ANALYSIS
AND
REQUIREMENTS ANALYSIS

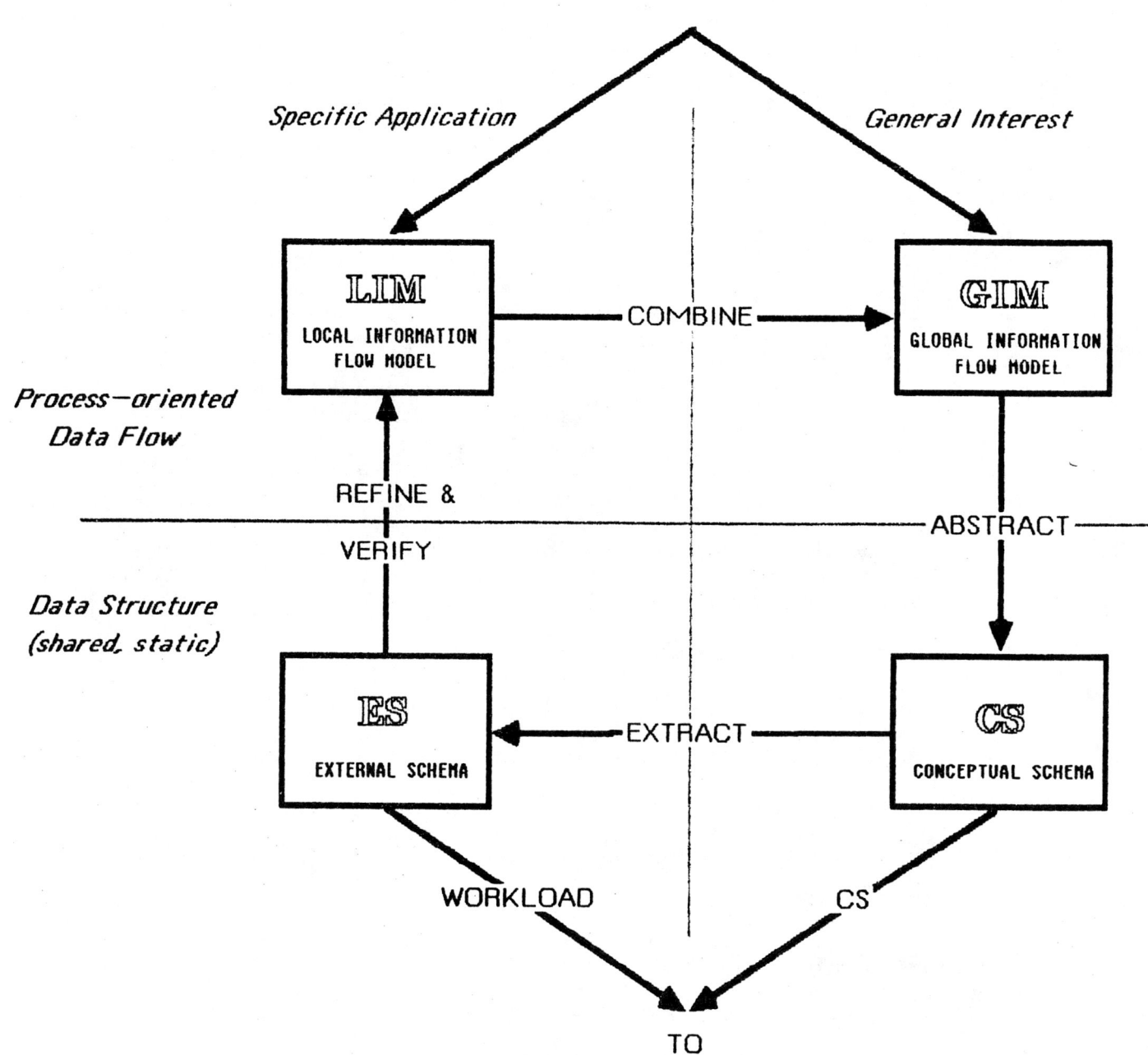

Specific Application — *General Interest*

LIM — LOCAL INFORMATION FLOW MODEL — COMBINE → **GIM** — GLOBAL INFORMATION FLOW MODEL

Process-oriented Data Flow

REFINE & VERIFY

ABSTRACT

Data Structure (shared, static)

ES — EXTERNAL SCHEMA ← EXTRACT — **CS** — CONCEPTUAL SCHEMA

WORKLOAD — CS

TO
PHYSICAL DATABASE DESIGN
(INTERNAL SCHEMA)

FIGURE 2

toward a specific application (e.g., toward one organizational component, function, or event), and those phases on the right that are oriented toward organizing these specific applications into areas of general interest.

The horizontal line across the diagram indicates a division between the upper phases that are oriented toward the performance of functions and the dynamic data flow among these functions, and the lower phases that are oriented toward relatively static, shared data structures.

At the top of the diagram, Needs Analysis and Requirements Analysis indicates that these phases provide information to LDD. The results of Needs Analysis may be sufficient to begin the initial iterations of the LIM and GIM phases, particularly if the Business Systems Planning (BSP) methodology has been used. Subsequent iterations will require further information from the Requirements Analysis phase.

The diagram in Figure 2 should be read clockwise, beginning at Local Information-flow Modeling (LIM), where data flows are modeled. In Global Information-flow Modeling (GIM), the individual data flows from LIM are combined into global data flows. These are abstracted to the underlying shared entities, relationships and attributes in the Conceptual Schema (CS). Parts of the CS are then extracted to form each External Schema (ES), which is a particular user's view of the shared data. At this point, each ES is then compared with the appropriate, previously developed LIM, to ensure that the data required by the LIM has been included in the ES view. When errors are detected in this comparison, the ES, and possibly the CS, will require modification. The workload data that was originally developed for the LIM is translated into operations on data in the ES. Finally, the workload data and the CS are passed on to the next life cycle phase, Physical Database Design, for the development of the internal schema.

2.2.3 Strategies for LDD Development.

Several analysis strategies are possible in approaching LDD. The choice of the strategy will depend on the type of system to be developed and the definition of the data that will need to be integrated in its design. The scope of the data can be described as horizontal and the level of detail as vertical. The system can be viewed horizontally in the breadth of functions that the information system will support. If the system will provide many functions to many departments or locations, then the system and its data will have a broad, horizontal scope. If the system performs few functions but performs them in great detail, then the system and its data will have a depth of detail. A large system will generally include both a breadth of scope and a depth of detail. Three possible strategies for approaching the logical design phases are described, with their ramifications for system development success. Refer to Figure 2 in following the sequence of LDD procedures for the following strategies. The three strategies for approaching LDD are:

1. Breadth First.

   In this strategy, a large number of Local Information-flow Models (LIMs) will be developed at first, but in limited detail. The LIMs will then be consolidated into one Global Information-flow Model (GIM) with a broad scope but limited detail. One or more Conceptual Schemas (CSs) will be developed with broad scope but limited detail. The External Schemas (ESs) extracted from the CS will provide quality control and structure for the next iteration of LIM. The LDD phases will be repeated for the various subsystems, adding greater detail for each LIM, until the data element level is reached. This strategy is analogous to top-down system design.

   Impact: This strategy is appropriate for the development of very large, very complex information systems, where a great depth and breadth of data must be integrated through the development process.

2. Depth First.

   In this strategy, a small number of LIMs will be developed through iterations of the LDD phases to the data element level. The LIMs will be consolidated into a GIM having depth of detail but a limited horizontal scope. A small number of ESs will be developed, again with depth of detail but limited scope. Further iterations of the entire process are developed until the desired horizontal scope is attained.

   Impact: This strategy is inappropriate for the development of an information system that requires the integration of design components of considerable scope and many levels of detail. The use of this strategy may result in the need to redesign the system to effect integration. This strategy is appropriate only for the development of throw-away or expendable training or prototype projects, such as a prototype system used to verify a development concept, or an experimental system used to train personnel in other systems development concepts or in Data Dictionary System use.

3. Critical Factors First.

In this strategy, a large number of LIMs are developed, including details for the critical aspects of the target system (e.g., critical functional requirements, critical performance characteristics, proof of concept, etc.). The LIMs will be consolidated into a GIM with broad scope but uneven detail. One or more CSs will be developed with the same broad scope but uneven levels of detail. The process will be repeated with increasing levels of detail for each LIM, with subsystems analyzed in order of priority, until the data element level is reached. The critical subsystems will be processed through the LDD cycle first, and the non-critical subsystems will follow later.

Impact: This strategy is appropriate for the development of a very large system if the critical factors of the target system can be identified and accepted. It is also appropriate for prototype development and for evolutionary development, where some functions will be implemented first and other functions will follow.

2.2.4 Summary of LDD Features.

The four phases of LDD use a variety of symbologies to assist in analysis. These include the use of bubble diagrams in the analysis of data flows, Entity-Relationship-Attribute (E-R-A) diagrams in CS development, normalization analyses where applicable, and Data Dictionary System (DDS) contents and automated analysis reports throughout LDD.

The outputs of LDD's phases are: Local Information-flow Models (LIMs) and Global Information-flow Models (GIMs) that model data flows for the organizational components, functions, and events; Conceptual Schemas (CSs) that provide an E-R-A model, or another type of data model, for use by programmers and designers; and External Schemas (ESs) that present an application-oriented user view for use within the organization as a representation of the data to be included in the target system.

3. PROJECT ORGANIZATION

For LDD to be performed successfully, plans should be made to support the information requirements of LDD and to incorporate LDD roles into the organization. In this chapter, LDD functional roles, training, and project planning needs are described.

3.1 Functional Roles Needed for LDD

The following functional roles are described in terms of the development of LDD. A role may be performed by many people, or one person may perform several roles, depending on the complexity of the database. Some LDD roles may overlap with roles to be performed in Requirements Analysis and other phases. The roles required for LDD are the following:

o Application Administrators (AAs) who will work with designers and analysts to define and validate the data and functions. One or more AAs may be needed according to the size of the system and the complexity of the application areas. AAs will work with a number of application specialists.

o Application Specialists who are knowledgeable about the application data being modeled, or about the application functions that use the data, or about both. The application specialists will assist the designers and analysts in preparing an accurate LDD.

o Data Administrator (DA) who will facilitate the LDD and systems development process by ensuring consistency in data definition, and overseeing the data management, data integrity, and data security functions performed in LDD development. The DA will continue to perform this role in regulating these facets of the information system once it is completed, and so will also use the LDD once it is developed. The DA may have a sizable staff, depending on the complexity of the data resource and the time available to perform LDD and other tasks. The DA staff may include the Database Administrator and the Data Dictionary Administrator. The DA staff will work closely with the AAs.

o Database Administrator (DBA) who will control the database and the DBMS, facilitate the LDD and systems development process, assist in data maintenance, and use the LDD as it is developed. The DBA is concerned primarily with technical aspects of the database, in contrast to the DA, who is more concerned with information policy and interacts with management and users. The DBA will continue in this role once the information system is operational. The DBA may have a small staff to support this function. This function will continue throughout the life cycle of the target system.

o Data Dictionary Administrator (DDA) who will oversee the operation of the Data Dictionary System (DDS), and assist in the data maintenance process for LDD. The DDA may be supported by a staff, including a Librarian and possibly data entry personnel. Data entry may also be performed directly by designers and analysts in the course of their work. The DDA function should continue throughout the life cycle of the target system, to continue to maintain documentation about the system.

o Data Dictionary Librarian who will maintain the data in the data dictionary (DD), and support the LDD and systems development effort.

o Database Designers/Analysts who will develop the information requirements, logical database diagrams, models and schemas. They will be expert in database design, familiar with the DDS, and become familiar with the application areas. They will perform the functions that are the focus of this report. Database designers will be needed throughout the life cycle of the information system, to maintain high performance and efficiency as the database changes through time.

o Project Managers who will direct the LDD and systems development projects. They will be familiar with the application areas, computer systems, systems development practices, and become familiar with LDD procedures.

o End-users of the DDS and the information system under development who will access and update information in the databases, and who will generate reports and decisions from this information. End-users will include personnel from all organizational levels and will perform the following roles:

- Data Entry and Update

- Data Retrieval

- Data Analysis

- Data Management and Control

- Project Management

- Upper Management

3.2 Training Required for LDD

The personnel involved in the LDD phase of development, particularly AAs and Application Specialists, will require training so that they will be able to work with database designers as a team. Some personnel will already be knowledgeable in these areas, but many will need to be trained. Project management should arrange to have LDD personnel trained in:

o The purpose and general procedures of LDD.

o The points of view to be represented within the system (i.e., organizational components, functions, and events).

o Use of the symbology, such as how to construct and interpret E-R-A and bubble diagrams.

o Use of the Data Dictionary System or other automated tool.

End-users who review the LDD may require any of three levels of training in the use of the Data Dictionary System, depending on the extent of each end-user's responsibility:

o Reading knowledge of LDD reports that are generated via the DDS, to be able to recognize when the report indicates a modeling error.

o Interpretive capability to understand LDD reports generated via the DDS, to be able to recognize what is wrong in a report that indicates a modeling error.

o Expert knowledge of the DDS procedures and an understanding of the products of LDD, to be able to correct errors in modeling detected in DDS reports.

3.3 Project Planning and Management Requirements

The systems development Project Manager and the LDD Manager should plan for and control the systems development project so that a high quality LDD results. In addition to the activities of traditional management roles, managers in these positions must determine that several procedures have been adopted before the project begins.

The Project Manager must be sure that good methodologies have been selected or developed for the Needs Analysis, Requirements Analysis, LDD, and other phases. In addition, it is necessary to determine that these methodologies are coordinated according to a schedule so that the results of previous and parallel phases are available for use by other phases. The schedule should also include various types of training for personnel working on parallel phases. Further, the Project Manager must decide on a strategy for LDD development that will support the breadth of scope and depth of detail to be encountered in analyzing the target system.

The Logical Database Design Manager will fill a similar role for the LDD phase. The LDD Manager will: (1) select a good LDD methodology and analysis strategy suitable to the type of system under development; (2) coordinate LDD training with the managers for parallel phases; (3) coordinate LDD activities with the Requirements Analysis Manager, so that information will be available for LDD to conform to appropriate schedules; (4) define checkpoints to review the progress of the LDD work; (5) determine the types and characteristics of the DDS documentation and analysis reports to be generated to support the LDD phases; and (6) manage the synthesis and integration of information from many sources within the organization to support LDD.

4. LOCAL INFORMATION-FLOW MODELING

A Local Information-flow Model (LIM) is a description of the movement of data collections such as reports, forms, memos, messages, transactions, and files to, from, and within a particular focal point. The focal point may be an organizational component (e.g., the personnel department), a function or application (e.g., payroll processing), or an event (e.g., a milestone in the budget cycle). The first iteration of this phase will produce a single LIM summarizing the inputs and outputs of the entire organization served by the database being designed. During subsequent iterations multiple LIMs will be produced, each describing a part of the next higher-level LIM. The level of detail may be very high (e.g., very general types of data going into or out of an entire organization), intermediate (e.g., reports and other data going into, out of, or processed within an office), or very low (e.g., transformation of an employee number into an employee name), depending on the number of iterations through the four phases of logical database design.

There are two reasons for choosing this approach:

1. Complexity is controlled at every stage of the iteration by restricting the scope of each LIM. Interviews with users can concentrate on the most critical aspects of the user's organization, function, or event, with the assurance that a higher-level context has already been developed and that details can be filled in later. The interviewer need not be overwhelmed with trying to understand everything all at once. Note that a top-down approach is advisable--starting from data elements and working up is more likely to end in a disastrous lack of direction and an abundance of confusion.

2. The different aspects--organization, function, and event--represent the fact that organizational structures are important, but they do not give a complete model of information processing. Functions and responsibilities are shared by sequential or simultaneous access to and transformation of data. All aspects may be required to give a true picture of database requirements. Note that manual functions should be analyzed if there is a significant chance that they will be automated during the life of the database.

The general objective is for a LIM to represent whatever an application specialist knows about his or her job and organization. The LIM does not represent details about how information is captured or derived before it reaches the application specialist or how it is used or processed after it leaves her or him.

The emphasis of the LIM should be on business functions and events--that is, data, operations, and products that are basic to achieving organizational objectives--rather than on any particular technology for implementing those functions. One reason for this particular emphasis is the fact that technology changes much more rapidly than the business functions (the need for payroll is constant, but the policies and technologies implementing it are changeable). A database should be relatively stable and retain its value over a long period of time--the time and cost of data collection and organization are too great to permit the database to be considered anything less than a major capital investment. Another reason for the emphasis on business functions is that these are familiar and well-understood by the data users, who are the people responsible for achieving organizational objectives. The abstract concepts of data modeling, introduced in the phase concerned with the development of the Conceptual Schema, are generally not meaningful to the user unless there is some familiar context of business functions. One way of viewing the LIM is that it is a means for relating the abstract External Schema (a part of the Conceptual Schema) to a concrete business context.

4.1 Information Used to Develop the LIM

Information that is relevant to the development of the LIM may be obtained through examination of documents or through interviews, or, preferably, through interviews based on thorough preparation via documents. The following information is generally needed:

1. The nature, objectives, structure, and scope of the subsystem must all be analyzed to ensure compatible LIMs. Both the present and the future should be considered. Non-routine operations, or operations that are performed infrequently, may be particularly important--for example, end-of-year accounting operations may have unique but critical requirements. Interactions with customers, vendors, and other parts

of the external environment may be very important.

2. Existing automated systems and other available hardware, software, and data resources should be studied to determine how they interact with the subsystem being studied; the emphasis should be on the queries, reports, and transactions that are actually relevant rather than on what is currently produced. It is important to maintain continuity with the present while still ensuring sufficient flexibility for long term growth of the information resource. Existing systems may already have replaced certain functions and as such should themselves be "interviewed." This can be difficult since existing systems may be poorly structured and documented. However, existing systems have already solved problems -- what are those problems? Existing systems may be enforcing policies that the people are no longer aware of -- what are those policies? Existing systems may also be creating data that everyone takes for granted -- how are existing systems combining files, applying algorithms, etc.?

3. The subsystem's perspective on decisions must be analyzed. The position titles and descriptions held by decision-makers, the business models that they use, the information that they require, and the relationships that they have with other decision-makers must all be analyzed. Senior management views (strategic planning), middle management views (control and tactical policy), and applications views (operations) are all required to give balance to the total collection of LIMs. Historical and "what if" data are particularly important in analyzing the data flow of higher-level decision makers.

4. Real-world rules and policies should be studied. Geographic location requirements are particularly important (e.g., there is little point in designing a highly integrated central database if the policy is to maintain local control of data). Policies on data retention and archiving may also be important (e.g., archiving may constitute a major information subsystem). Security, privacy, integrity, and error handling policies (including policies and procedures for recovery from both data processing and organizational mistakes) may have major effects on the data structures (for example, classified and unclassified data may have to be stored separately).

5. A catalog of reports and forms needed for routine tasks is clearly relevant to the LIM. Collections of reports and forms are relevant to high-level LIMs, individual reports and forms are relevant to intermediate-level LIMs, and parts of reports and forms are relevant to low-level LIMs. The timeliness and quality of the reports and forms should be recorded. Reports that have outlived their usefulness are irrelevant to LDD.

6. Collections of informal data are also very important. This data can include files or folders of memos and letters (e.g., Freedom of Information Act requests, and customer complaints in writing), notes on telephone conversations (e.g., payroll inquiries), and databases on personal computers.

7. Formal reference data collections such as FIPS codes, ZIP codes, pay scale tables, and address or telephone directories are relevant.

8. "Log" books or lists may be used to assign unique numbers, organize office functions, record significant events, or otherwise coordinate activities.

9. Other regular sources of information, such as telephone contacts, should be carefully studied, since these may be very relevant to getting the job done.

10. Information from the higher-level GIM and the higher-level LIM which is being subdivided provide context for developing more detailed LIMs in successive iterations of the LDD cycle. Once LDD has begun, the examination of this information will be the first step in providing a LIM.

11. Quantitative information on volume of data and frequency of processing for all of the above. This information will be used to help develop an estimate of the database workload.

Since each LIM is a refinement of the previous iteration of the design cycle, the LIM is constrained by the previous higher-level LIM and External Schema. If deeper analysis uncovers an error at the higher level, then that higher-level should be corrected before proceeding further. Otherwise, other lower-level LIMs, based on the erroneous LIM and External Schema, may contain errors or be inconsistent with each other.

4.2 Functions of the LIM

The primary function of the LIM is to serve as part of the Global Information-flow Model (GIM). Other functions of the LIM are:

1. The LIM provides a guide for the development of further details. Each iteration is based on a decomposition of a previously developed LIM, unless the focus is switched from an organizational component to a function or event, in which case the new LIMs are based on combinations of previously developed LIMs.

2. The LIM may be used as a guide to planning the development of a new application program or system, modifying an old application program or system, or modifying the organizational structure. In each case, the LIM is analyzed to see whether the flow of data is efficient and effective; changes are suggested if unused reports are being produced, if similar functions are being performed unnecessarily, if functions that should be performed by a computer system are being performed manually, or if the data flow can be reduced by combining organizational components that sequentially process the same data.

3. The LIM is also used to collect information concerning the database workload. This information is eventually used to optimize and evaluate the physical database design.

4.3 Procedure for Developing the LIM

Figure 3 shows the five sequential steps in the development of the LIM. The steps are described in the following paragraphs.

LOCAL INFORMATION-FLOW MODELING (LIM) PROCEDURE

STEP 4.3.1 — REVIEW NEEDS

STEP 4.3.2 — DETERMINE SUBSYSTEMS

STEP 4.3.3 — PLAN DEVELOPMENT OF THE LIMs

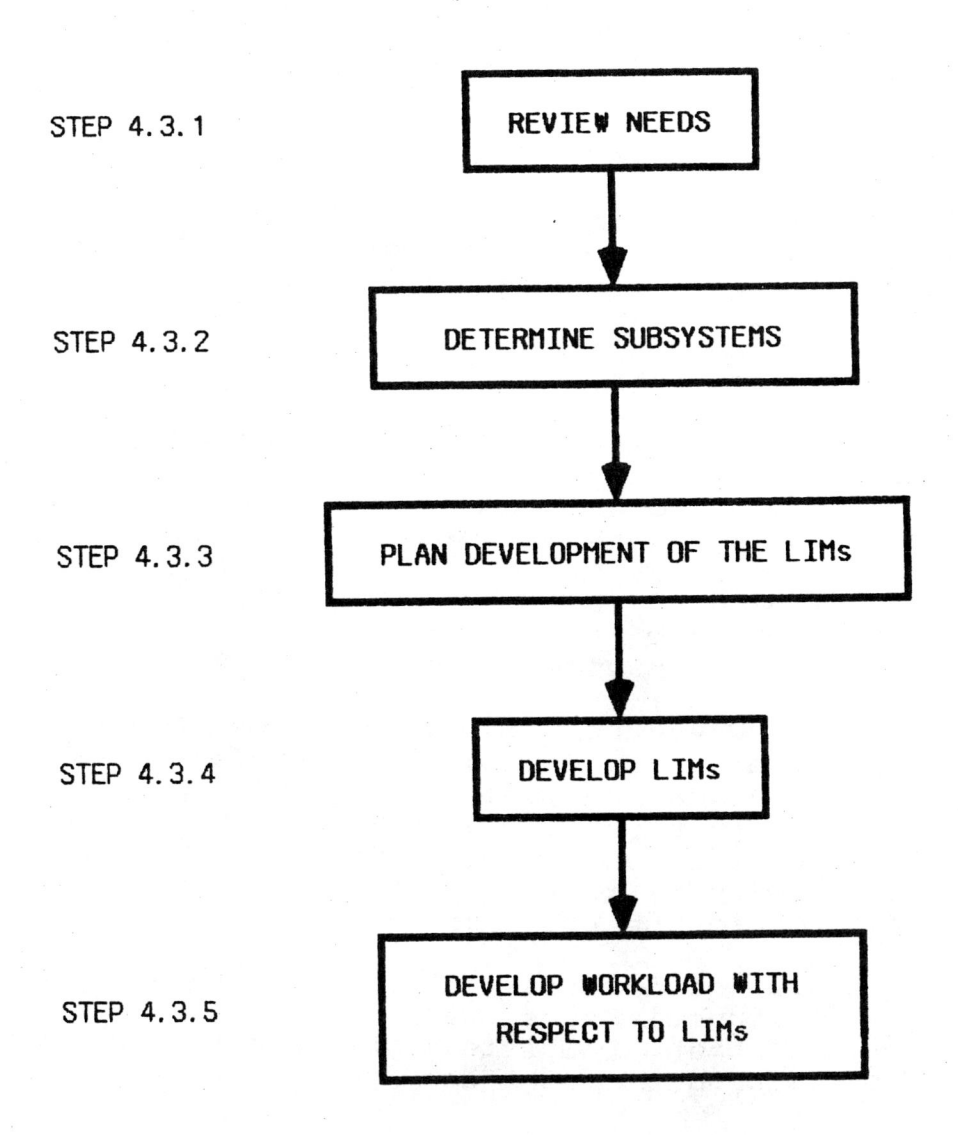

STEP 4.3.4 — DEVELOP LIMs

STEP 4.3.5 — DEVELOP WORKLOAD WITH RESPECT TO LIMs

FIGURE 3

4.3.1 Review Need for Analysis.

The primary function of this step is to determine whether the organizational component, function, or event under consideration should be subdivided for further analysis, or whether it has already been analyzed sufficiently.

The first iteration of the logical database design methodology will begin with a preliminary determination of boundaries--that is, which organizational components, functions, and events require interaction with the proposed database. Next, it is necessary to determine the best method for subdividing the design problem--by organizational components, by functions, or by events. Generally, the first few subdivisions will be along organizational boundaries. These boundaries are usually well-defined, familiar, and non-threatening to the application specialists. They serve very well in identifying broad classes of data, major functions and events, and data flows.

Organizational decomposition may be insufficient, however, for the detailed development of data structures which are shared among different organizational components. Later iterations should concentrate on subdividing the functions and events that have been identified during the study of organizational subdivisions; such functions and events must provide data to the database and use data from it, so are directly relevant to the structure of the database.

Since functions and events frequently cross organizational boundaries, their analysis may suggest the need for reorganization to eliminate duplicate or unnecessary jobs, and will almost certainly require cooperation among application specialists from different organizational components. Consequently, such analysis is very delicate and should not be attempted too early in the LDD process.

Eventually it will be determined that there is no need to subdivide any more functions or events; the logical database design process is then "complete," although maintenance of the LIMs and other products must continue indefinitely.

```
-----------------------------------------------------------
| Step 4.3.1    Review Need for Analysis                  |
|                                                         |
| Function:      To determine whether more detail is      |
|                required                                 |
|                                                         |
| Output:        Determination of whether to subdivide a  |
|                subsystem                                |
|                                                         |
| Team Members:  User - AA, DA                            |
|                Developer - AA, DA                       |
|                                                         |
| Tools:         Use DD to report on previous work        |
|                                                         |
| Guidelines:    Decision involves both technical and     |
|                management issues                        |
-----------------------------------------------------------
```

4.3.2 Determine Subsystems.

Once a decision has been made to subdivide an organizational component, function, or event, the next step is to determine the appropriate subdivisions. Two situations may be distinguished:

1. The subdivision involves a further refinement of an organizational component, function, or event. This is the normal case in business systems analysis, so various methodologies from business systems planning, organizational analysis, and software engineering may be applied. Either function-oriented methodologies [DEMA78, GANE79, MYER78, ROSS77] or data-oriented methodologies [JACK83, ORRK82] may be used as measures of the relative merit of different decompositions.

2. The subdivision involves a switch from one type of analysis to another. For example, the previous iteration of subdivision was based on organizational components, but this iteration is to be based on functions. In this case, the primary activity is composition, rather than decomposition--the various aspects of a function that appear in different organizational components must first be joined together to form a coherent statement of the whole function, and

then functional decomposition can proceed at later iterations. Clearly, it is extremely important that data flow has been carefully documented during previous iterations; data flow is the primary clue to the common basis for different organizational perspectives on a single function. The effect of a Data Dictionary System is to allow the DA to combine an organizational hierarchy, a functional hierarchy, and an event hierarchy into a consistent network which can be supported by the database structure.

In either case, the result will be a list of well-defined subsystems--organizational components, functions, or events-- of the LIM being analyzed. The subsequent steps will determine how each subsystem interacts with the data flowing into or out of that LIM, and the data flowing from or to the other subsystems.

```
-------------------------------------------------------------
  Step 4.3.2    Determine Subsystems

  Function:      Determination of how to subdivide a
                 subsystem

  Output:        List of lower-level subsystems

  Team Members:  User - AA, DA
                 Developer - AA, DA

  Symbology:     Organization charts, data-flow or
                 event diagrams

  Tools:         Use DD to represent organizational
                 components, functions, or events

  Guidelines:    Care is required -- poorly chosen
                 subsystems will have overly complex
                 interfaces
-------------------------------------------------------------
```

4.3.3 Plan Development of the LIM.

This step involves the development of a detailed plan for this iteration of the analysis. The plan may include priorities, so that decomposition will consider critical factors first. Two strategies are possible:

1. Each step in the subdivision spawns a set of independent plans. Detailed work may proceed in parallel, given a sufficiently large staff, with the results coordinated primarily through the data dictionary. The advantage of this approach is that planning is minimized. The disadvantage is that quality control of the data dictionary becomes extremely critical during and after execution of the plan. Synonyms and homonyms for functions and data must be detected and resolved quickly or different analysis paths will unknowingly overlap, resulting in confusion and duplication of effort. The philosophy of this strategy is to move quickly and solve problems later (possibly during the development of the GIM).

2. Each step in the subdivision involves the development of a single, coordinated plan. Detailed work is coordinated in advance, so that problems of synonyms, homonyms, and duplicated effort are minimized. The advantage of this approach is that overall control of the effort is maintained. The obvious disadvantage is that this approach requires extremely knowledgeable DA and AA staff to formulate, monitor, and control the execution of the plan. Also, more work must be done serially rather than in parallel.

In either case, it is necessary to develop a detailed project management plan, with milestones, time and cost estimates, and assignments for application specialists as well as for AA and DA personnel.

```
-------------------------------------------------------
| Step 4.3.3      Plan Development of the LIM
|
| Function:       Develop project management plan for
|                 this subsystem
|
| Output:         Milestones, time and cost estimates
|
| Team Members:   User - AA, DA
|                 Developer - AA, DA, Managers
|
| Symbology:      Project management charts
|
| Tools:          Use DD to represent project management
|                 data and boundaries
|
| Guidelines:     Assignments must be very specific
-------------------------------------------------------
```

4.3.4 Develop LIM.

Various system analysis and design methodologies may be used in conjunction with a data dictionary to document the data flows that are developed. Either function-oriented methodologies [DEMA78, GANE79, MYER78, ROSS77] or data-oriented methodologies [JACK83, ORRK82] are suitable. Whereas previous steps have involved consultation with management, this step and the following are best accomplished by short interviews (no more than two hours per iteration) with application specialists. Reference material and the LIM developed during the previous iteration are used to prepare for the interview and to verify the analyst's interpretation of the application specialist's statements. All materials may be made available to the application specialists in advance of the interview. (Note that discrepancies revealed during an interview should prompt further questions rather than challenges--the interview should not be threatening.) Graphical simplicity is very desirable, so that untrained users can judge the correctness of the LIMs that are relevant to them.

Useful types of diagrams include the following:

1. An organization chart can be used to show the hierarchical relationships among organizational LIMs.

2. A "bubble" diagram with an organizational focal point connected to other organizations by data flows can be used to represent an organizational LIM, as in the following:

EXAMPLE OF A LOCAL INFORMATION-FLOW MODEL

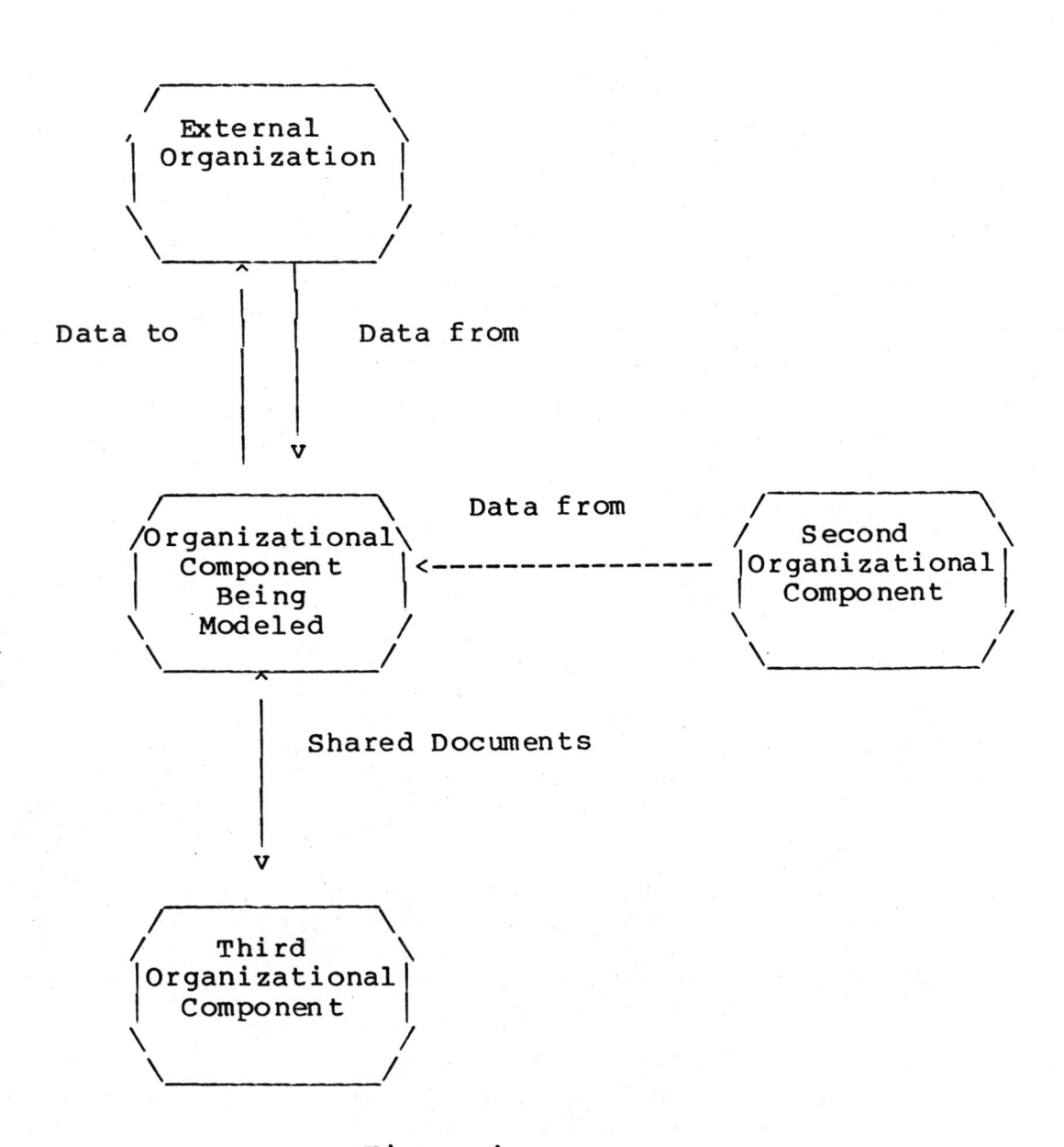

```
            ┌─────────────┐
            │  External   │
            │Organization │
            └─────────────┘
               ^     │
       Data to │     │ Data from
               │     v
  ┌──────────────┐   Data from   ┌──────────────┐
  │Organizational│<──────────────│   Second     │
  │  Component   │               │Organizational│
  │    Being     │               │  Component   │
  │   Modeled    │               └──────────────┘
  └──────────────┘
         ^
         │ Shared Documents
         v
  ┌──────────────┐
  │    Third     │
  │Organizational│
  │  Component   │
  └──────────────┘
```

Figure 4

-41-

3. A functional hierarchy can be used to show the hierarchical relationships among the functional LIMs.

4. A data-flow diagram [DEMA78, GANE79, MYER78] or action diagram [ROSS77] can be used to show inputs, outputs, subfunctions, and data flows among the subfunctions of a functional LIM. (Note that this type of diagram shows two levels of the LIM hierarchy.)

5. A Gantt chart can be used to show the temporal relationships among events.

6. A PERT chart can be used to show the relationships, especially time dependencies, among functions and events.

7. A state-vector diagram [JACK83] or a decision table can be used to show additional details of functions and events.

The data dictionary is used to record detailed information that would only confuse a diagram; automated analysis of program code, job control language, and audit trails may provide much of the detail. The selectivity of data dictionary queries and reports helps to make the details comprehensible. Diagrams should be produced automatically from the data dictionary. Also, graphic input could be a means of populating the data dictionary when this capability becomes automated in the future.

A special but important example of data flow is storage and retrieval of information by an organizational component, function, or event; the storage medium is treated like another organizational component, function, or event.

Data flow is used to determine the formal consistency and completeness of the analysis--for example, whether each data flow has a source and a sink (either may be some internal storage medium). The use of a data dictionary is extremely important in this situation to ensure that all of the various aspects of the function are considered. The views of all users who interact with a function must be reflected in that function.

The description of data flows should generally include one level of decomposition. For example, if the data flows in a top-level functional analysis are collections of reports, then each data description in the data dictionary should include a list of the component reports. At a lower level, if the data flows are reports, then their descriptions should include subdivisions of the reports--selected columns, or rows between subtotals, or the subtotals themselves, for example. At a very detailed level, the data descriptions would be data elements.

Information which is useful in understanding the relative importance of the functions and in planning the next iteration of this phase includes the following:

1. Staff time, in work-years or other convenient unit, expended on performing the function.

2. The number of staff personnel performing the function.

3. The number of locations where the function is performed.

4. Whether there is a single step that consumes 80% or more of the time spent on the function.

Step 4.3.4   Develop LIMs

Function: Provide guidance to the development
                of the GIM and CS

Output: LIMs

Team Members: User - AA, DA
                Developer - AA, DBA

Symbology: Use bubbles to represent organizational
                components, events, functions, or
                external interfaces. Use lines to
                represent data flows.

Tools: Use DD to represent subsystems
                and interfaces

Guidelines: Graphical simplicity is desirable
                Use selectivity of DD reports
                Should be easy for users to understand
                and critique

4.3.5 Develop Workload With Respect to LIMs.

The primary function of this step is to develop a preliminary description of the workload: the frequency, sequence, and selectivity with which functions use or produce data, and the volume of stored data [JEFF82, SUST84]. The workload will be used during the development of the External Schemas to determine whether the Conceptual Schema can support the LIM, and what paths must be taken through the Conceptual Schema to obtain the data required by the LIM. It will also be used to determine whether certain functions should be automated. The workload must be used during the development of the Internal Schema (physical database design) to determine appropriate physical record structures, record placement in areas, access methods, loading factors, indexes, and other parameters. Accordingly, this step must be performed during the most detailed iteration of functional analysis; it may be performed at earlier steps to provide additional quality control for the LIMs and Conceptual Schema.

At this phase, the workload is described in terms of data collections that may be very different from the logical records that will eventually constitute the final Conceptual Schema. In particular, the level at this phase may be very high (e.g., data objects like "employee," "project," and "part" rather than data elements like "employee-first-name," "estimated-project-cost," and "part-quantity-in-warehouse") and the grouping of data may be quite arbitrary (e.g., "employee" may include data about skills, projects, and organizations associated with the employee). Eventually these data objects will be restructured to form a database, so it is important to be able to map this preliminary workload into appropriate paths through that database.

The information to be collected and stored in the data dictionary should include the following:

1. The volume (number of instances) of each data collection (e.g., the number of employees, projects, and parts).

2. The priority of the function (e.g., "an airline reservation must be confirmed within 20 seconds" and "a marketing analysis on advance reservations must be available within 2 hours of a request").

3. The frequency of execution of the function.

4. The sequence with which data collections are accessed by the function, and the source of the data from input or database (e.g., start with "employee," then access "project," then access "project-manager" to determine who "manages" a given employee).

5. The parts of each data collection that are used to decide whether a given instance of that data collection is relevant (e.g., "employee-name" identifies the required "employee" data).

6. For each of the parts of data collection, the number of relevant instances (e.g., "1").

7. For each relevant data collection accessed by the function, the parts that are needed for retrieval by the function (e.g., "employee-project" is the only retrieved part of the "employee" data). If applicable, the preferred order is desirable (e.g., the "employee-project" data is to be sorted by "project-number").

8. The parts of each relevant data collection that are needed for update by the function (e.g., "employee-hours" is the only updated part of the "employee" data).

9. At each point where the function branches, the fraction of the time each branch is taken (e.g., 90% of the time "employee-project" will be non-null, so "project" will be accessed, and 10% of the time it will be null so the path will terminate).

Step 4.5.3 Develop Workload with Respect to LIMs

Function: Develop preliminary specifications for physical design

Output: LIMs with volume, frequency, sequence, and selectivity

Team Members: User - AA, DBA
                 Developer - AA, DBA and Analysts

Symbology: LIM diagrams

Tools: Use DD to store workload information to be used for physical design

Guidelines: Keep the scope limited to a single application

---

5. GLOBAL INFORMATION-FLOW MODELING

A Global Information-flow Model (GIM) is basically an interconnected collection of all of the Local Information-flow Models (LIMs). Its structure is quite complex: it combines up to three hierarchies of LIMs (a hierarchy based on organizational components, another based on functions, and possibly another based on events); these must be interconnected in terms of data flow, which itself may be a complex network of data objects, as well as other interrelationships such as organizational authority and responsibility. A Data Dictionary System (DDS) is strongly recommended to manage the GIM. In an extremely complex situation, where even a DDS is unable to present the mass of information in a meaningful way, multiple GIMs may be developed, each representing a major subsystem loosely connected to the other GIMs. Note, in particular, that the GIM, like the LIM, must generally represent both automated and manual data, and both current and planned functions.

The major task involved in developing the GIM is simply adding the new details represented by each new LIM. The new LIMs must be verified for consistency with higher-level LIMs, names must be reconciled with existing names, and the different perspectives (organization, function, and event) must be interrelated. These are basically responsibilities of the DA with assistance from the AAs in detecting and resolving potential problems in performance, cost, reliability, security, and the like. The DA should not require direct access to the users.

The GIM may be represented in various forms according to the methodology chosen. A diagram may consist of ovals or rectangles representing the subsystems, and labelled lines representing the data flows. This is a simple source-sink model which is very useful for communicating with users. Other representations of the GIM include many different types of matrices showing the interactions of organizational components, functions, events, and data objects with each other [MART82]. A data dictionary is recommended for the primary means of representation, from which diagrams and matrices can be produced selectively and automatically. Also, the data dictionary is quite suitable for representing details that would be very confusing in a diagram or matrix, such as the Local Information-flow Models (LIMs) and their relationships with the GIM, the relationships between names in the GIM and in the LIMs, and details of database workload.

Some methodologies dispense with the GIM [NAVA82] and begin the design of the Conceptual Schema with a small number of applications, then add more applications, continually integrating the new applications with the old Conceptual Schema. This has the advantage of facilitating quick development of a prototype, but has the disadvantage of possible major revisions of the Conceptual Schema [JEFF82]. The safer procedure is to develop a GIM with careful control of detail, so that the level of effort is reasonable yet the GIM provides sufficient detail to guide the development of a relatively stable Conceptual Schema. This procedure is also likely to uncover important new interrelationships among LIMs, such as unexpected interrelationships among organizational components, and dependencies within them.

Note the similarity of the Local Information-flow Model and Global Information-flow Model development to Business Systems Planning (BSP) [MART82], which is also based on data flow. The primary difference, which is extremely important, is that each iteration of the Local Information-flow Model and Global Information-flow Model is followed by the development of the Conceptual Schema and External Schemas in the procedures described in this paper. This cyclical and iterative approach balances the data flow perspective with the data structure perspective, so that neither will be emphasized at the expense of the other. BSP, however, emphasizes the data flow perspective almost to the exclusion of the data structure perspective; high level data objects are identified, but their relationships and detailed structures must be developed by another methodology.

5.1 Information Used to Develop the GIM

Information that is relevant to the development of the GIM is obtained primarily from the previous iteration of the GIM and the newly developed LIMs. Other types of information are similar to those used to develop the LIM, except that they are at a higher organizational level.

1. The nature, objectives, and scope of the organization must be analyzed to ensure a compatible GIM.

2. The organizational perspective on decisions must be determined.

3. Organizational rules and policies must be analyzed.

4. Reports and forms must be examined.

5. Available resources must be determined.

5.2 Functions of the GIM

The primary function of the GIM is to guide the development of the Conceptual Schema. Other functions of the GIM are:

1. The GIM provides context for the development of the next iteration of the LIMs.

2. The GIM, like the LIMs, may assist in management planning to increase efficiency; the GIM provides a wider perspective on reducing data flow through changes in functions and organizational structures.

3. The GIM may also be used to design the interfaces among separate, loosely connected Conceptual Schemas, as may be appropriate among several large systems or a distributed database system.

5.3 Procedure for Developing the GIM

Figure 5 shows the four sequential steps in the development of the GIM. The steps are described in the following paragraphs.

GLOBAL INFORMATION-FLOW MODELING (GIM) PROCEDURE

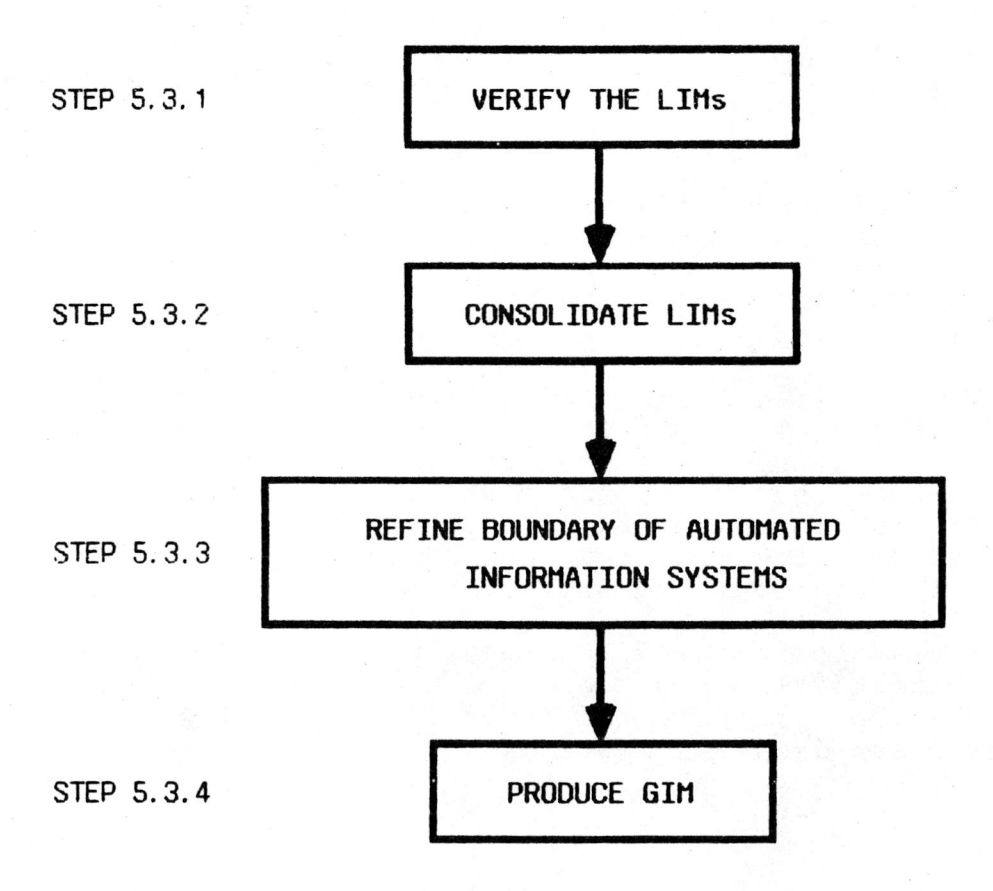

STEP 5.3.1	VERIFY THE LIMs
STEP 5.3.2	CONSOLIDATE LIMs
STEP 5.3.3	REFINE BOUNDARY OF AUTOMATED INFORMATION SYSTEMS
STEP 5.3.4	PRODUCE GIM

FIGURE 5

5.3.1 Verify the LIMs.

The LIMs are organized into a hierachy of organizational components, a separate but interrelated hierarchy of functions, and, possibly, a separate but interrelated hierachy of events. The function of this step is to verify that each new LIM is consistent with the objectives and constraints of the next higher level LIM in its hierarchy. Any inconsistencies require modification of either the lower-level LIM or the higher-level LIM. In the latter case, modifications may propagate all the way up the hierarchy and possibly affect the other hierarchies as well: such modifications may also propagate to the GIM, Conceptual Schema, and External Schemas. The following are the major considerations:

1. The data flow of a LIM must be consistent with that of its higher-level LIM. Each data object at the lower level should either appear at the higher level, or be a part of a higher-level data object, or have both source and sink within the lower-level LIMs. For example, assume that the higher level is a department, and the lower level consists of the branches within it. Data received by one branch from an outside source must be traceable to a departmental data source, but data sent to another branch might not appear at the departmental level.

2. Similarly, the data flow of the higher-level LIM must not be greater than the data flow of the LIMs that comprise it.

3. More generally, the scope of a lower-level LIM must be consistent with the scope of the higher-level LIM, where scope includes such non-data considerations as timing, resources, general objectives, and interrelationships with other hierarchies. For example, the branch should not have more time to perform a task than is available to the department, and should not perform functions that are not assigned to the department.

4. Similarly, the scope of the higher-level LIM must not be greater than the scope of the LIMs that comprise it.

5. If workloads have been developed, the workload of a LIM must be consistent with that of its higher-level LIM. Data volumes should be consistent. Each path through the lower-level data must either be entirely contained within the lower-level LIM or must be traceable to a path in the higher-level data. Priority, frequency, timing dependencies, and numbers of instances should be consistent.

6. Similarly, all of the paths in the higher-level LIM must appear in the lower-level LIM.

Step 5.3.1 Verify the LIMs

Function: To verify that each new LIM is consistent with the objectives and constraints of the next higher level

Output: LIMs organized in a hierarchy of organizational components, functions, or events

Team Members: User - AA, DA
                 Developer - AA, DA

Symbology: LIM diagram

Tools: Use DD to change entries and determine effects of change

Guidelines: Verify LIMs from top down

5.3.2 Consolidate LIMs.

The function of this step is to resolve synonyms that arise when different subsystems use different names for the same data flow and homonyms that arise when different subsystems use the same name for different data flows. Once detected, synonyms and homonyms are relatively easy to resolve. One of the synonyms is chosen for the GIM name, while the others are retained in the data dictionary as alternate names for the appropriate LIMs. For example, "part#" could be the preferred, global name, while "part-

-52-

number" could be used within the context of a particular function, and be represented in the data dictionary as an alternate name. Only one object can be assigned the homonym for its GIM name; each of the other objects is assigned a new, unique name, and the homonym is assigned as an alternate name. For example, if "price" refers to both retail and wholesale price, then "price" could be used globally to refer to retail price, or locally within a particular function to refer to wholesale price; "wholesale-price" could be used to refer to wholesale price globally. Alternatively, "retail-price" and "wholesale-price" could be used globally, and "price" only locally.

Detection of synonyms is largely a manual process, but there are some clues that can be provided by the DDS or other computerized tool:

1. The primary means for detecting possible synonyms is data flow analysis, which can be performed by the DDS--for example, the DDS may be able to produce groups of data objects that have identical sources and sinks, which would indicate that the group members could be the same data object with different names in different subsystems.

2. Name analyses, such as keyword in context, are useful for suggesting possible synonyms.

3. Data element analysis may also help in suggesting possible synonyms by identifying data elements that have similar characteristics, such as their COBOL pictures or legal values.

Detection of homonyms should be primarily a process performed by the DDS--the DDS should reject any attempt to add conflicting characteristics to any data object. Situations in which two distinct objects have the same names and all other characteristics must be detected manually; however, if each object has a meaningful textual description, it is relatively simple to compare descriptions to determine whether they should be combined, or should be given separate names. Homonyms that are not resolved at this step may be resolved at a later step or later iteration of this step when more characteristics are known and therefore there is more likelihood of a conflict being detected by the DDS. Resolution at this step is a convenience but not a necessity.

```
-------------------------------------------------------
  Step 5.3.2    Consolidate LIMs

  Function:      Resolution of synonyms and honomyms

  Output:        One uniform model

  Team Members:  User - DA
                 Developer - DA

  Symbology:     Bubbles and lines

  Tools:         Use DD to store alternate names
                 Use name analyses such as keyword in
                 context to detect synonyms

  Guidelines:    Standardize names in GIM
                 Use local synonyms whenever appropriate
                 in LIMs
-------------------------------------------------------
```

5.3.3 Refine Boundary of Automated Information System (AIS).

The function of this step is to refine the boundary of the automated information system that is being designed. This may reduce the scope of the logical database design and therefore reduce the effort expended in subsequent phases. Note that the final boundary will generally be three dimensional: organizational components, functions, and events. They must all be included in or excluded from the logical database design.

The criteria for drawing the boundary are primarily based on upper management goals as applied by the DA with possible technical advice from the DBA.

The boundary may be represented on a data flow diagram by a line, in a subsystem/data matrix by highlighting subsystems within the boundary or omitting subsystems outside the boundary, and in the data dictionary by a keyword or by relationships between a specific system and the subsystems within the boundary.

Step 5.3.3   Refine Boundary of Automated Information
             System (AIS)

Function: Reduce scope and refine the boundaries
              of the AIS

Output: Models of the AIS

Team Members: User - DA and upper level managers
              Developer - DA and DBA

Symbology: Bubbles and lines

Tools: Use DD to represent specific system and
              subsystems within the boundary

Guidelines: Criteria for refining boundary are
              based on upper management goals

EXAMPLE OF A GLOBAL INFORMATION-FLOW MODEL

```
         ┌─────────────┐         ┌─────────────┐
         │Organizational│        │Organizational│
         │ Component    │<-------│ Component    │
         │ Dependent    │        │ Independent  │
         │  on AIS      │        │   of AIS     │
         └─────────────┘         └─────────────┘
                ^ │
                │ │
    ┌───────────┼─┼──────────────────────────────────┐
    │           │ v                                  │
    │                                                │
┌─────────────┐    ┌─────────────┐    ┌─────────────┐
│Organizational│   │Organizational│   │Organizational│
│ Component    │-->│ Component    │<--│ Component    │
│Providing Data│   │ Interacting  │   │ Interacting  │
│  to AIS      │   │  with AIS    │   │  with AIS    │
└─────────────┘    └─────────────┘    └─────────────┘
    │                   ^                            │
    │                   │               Automated    │
    │                   │              Information   │
Boundary----->          v                System      │
    │                                     (AIS)      │
    │              ┌─────────────┐                   │
    │              │Organizational│                  │
    │              │ Component    │                  │
    │              │ Interacting  │                  │
    │              │  with AIS    │                  │
    │              └─────────────┘                   │
    └────────────────────────────────────────────────┘
```

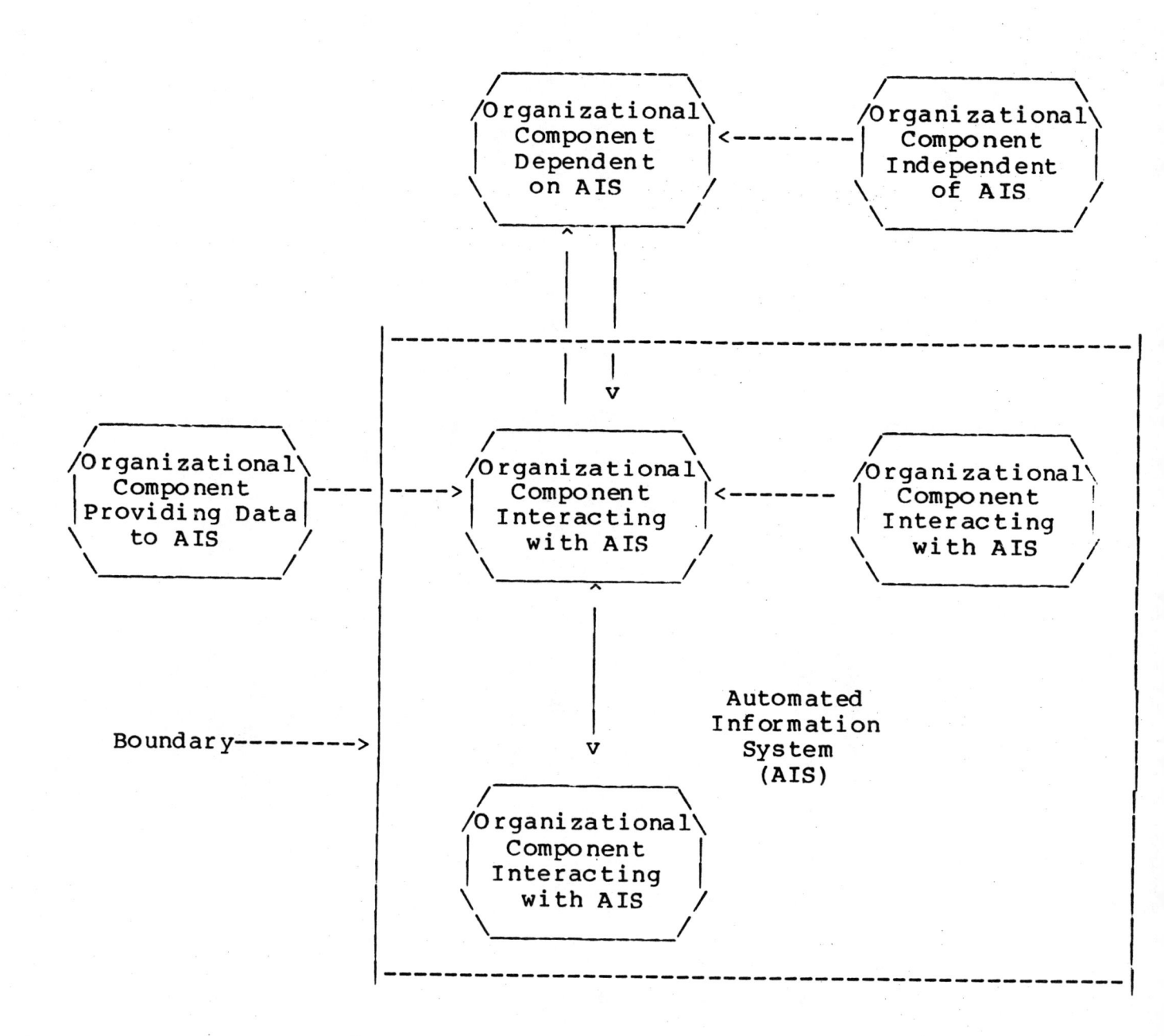

Figure 6

-56-

5.3.4 Produce GIM.

The function of this step is to provide additional quality assurance and documentation for the GIM. Use of a data dictionary is recommended. Details of how the data dictionary represents the GIM, what quality assurance reports are provided, and what documentation is to be produced must be determined by each organization to suit its own capabilities.

```
-------------------------------------------------------------

Step 5.3.4    Produce GIM

Function:      Provide final review and documentation
               for the GIM

Output:        Specification of components of GIM

Team Members:  User - DA and DBA
               Developer - DA and DBA

Symbology:     Bubbles and lines

Tools:         Use DD for corrections

Guidelines:    Quality assurance must be provided
               by application experts

-------------------------------------------------------------
```

6. CONCEPTUAL SCHEMA DESIGN

A Conceptual Schema (CS) is a description of the logical (hardware- and software-independent) structure of the data required by an organization. The phases concerned with development of the Local Information-flow Models (LIMs) and Global Information-flow Model (GIM) concentrated on the interactions between data and organizations, functions, or events; the structure and meaning of the data were not analyzed beyond the relatively simple resolution of synonyms and homonyms. This phase concentrates on the deep exploration of structure and meaning in terms of three important concepts: entity, relationship, and attribute. These concepts correspond very closely to the natural language constructs of noun, verb, and adjective. The following paragraphs, which define these concepts and provide brief examples, may be omitted by readers familiar with the Entity-Relationship-Attribute Model [CHEN80, CHEN81, CHEN82].

1. An entity is a type of real-world object or concept. For example, "employee," "project," and "position description" may be entities of interest to an organization. Note that only "employee" is a physical object--"project" and "position description" are both concepts. To appreciate the difference, consider that a "position description" may be recorded on a piece of paper. If the paper is copied or reproduced electronically in a database, the medium is changed, but the concept--the position description--is still the same. Therefore, the entity of interest is the message, not the medium.

2. A relationship is a type of association or correspondence among entities. For example, "works on" may be a relationship between "employee" and "project." An instance of a relationship is a fact or assertion--e.g., the phrase ´"12345" "works on" "design"´ could express the fact that the "employee" identified by the "employee number" "12345" is associated with the "project" entity identified by the "project-name" "design" through the relationship "works on." This example involves two entities and two instances of entities. A relationship may involve only one entity. For example, ´"design" "precedes" "implementation"´ is a relationship involving two instances of the entity "life-cycle phase." A relationship may also involve more than two entities-- e.g., ´"12345"

"works on" "design" "using" "Entity-Relationship-Attribute Approach" is an instance of a relationship ("works on" ... "using") among three entities ("employee," "project," and "technique").

3. An attribute is a property or characteristic which describes an entity or relationship. For example, the "employee" entity may have attributes such as "birth date," "marital status," and "annual salary," while the "works on" relationship may have attributes such as "hours per week," or "hours to date." Every entity must have an attribute or collection of attributes that distinguishes among entity instances (e.g., an "employee number" identifies a particular "employee"). A relationship may be without attributes, since each instance is identified by the entities that it associates (e.g., the relationship instance "design" "precedes" "implementation" is uniquely identified by "design" and "implementation," in that order).

6.1 Information Used to Develop the CS

Most of the information that is relevant to the development of the CS is provided indirectly by the GIM. Entities are the subjects of the data flows that were identified by the GIM, but they are generally not the data flows themselves. For example, a personnel report is not an entity unless there is system for tracking the production or distribution of the report, in which case each instance of the report might be identified by a control number. The subjects of the personnel report, e.g., "employee" and "project," would be entities.

6.2 Functions of the CS

The primary function of the CS is to provide a single logical structure for the database. Other functions include:

1. The CS provides input to the External Schema Design Phase.

2. The CS provides guidance in the choice of a data model (e.g., either a hierarchical, network, or relational data model may most easily represent the CS).

3. The CS provides guidance in the choice of a DBMS (e.g., a DBMS that easily represents the CS).

4. The CS provides guidance in the development and evaluation of the physical database design (the CS provides the definition of the logical data structure that the physical database must support).

The output of this phase may include the following:

1. For each entity of fundamental interest to the organization, its name, identifier (key), other attributes, synonyms, textual description, and relationships with other entities.

2. Entity-Relationship-Attribute diagrams [CHEN82].

3. Security, privacy, and integrity constraints.

4. Normalized relations [BEER79, BERN76, ZANI82].

6.3 Procedure for Developing the CS

Figure 7 shows the six steps in the development of the CS. The last step may reveal redundancies that will suggest repeating some or all of the preceding steps. The steps are described in the following paragraphs.

CONCEPTUAL SCHEMA (CS) DESIGN PROCEDURE

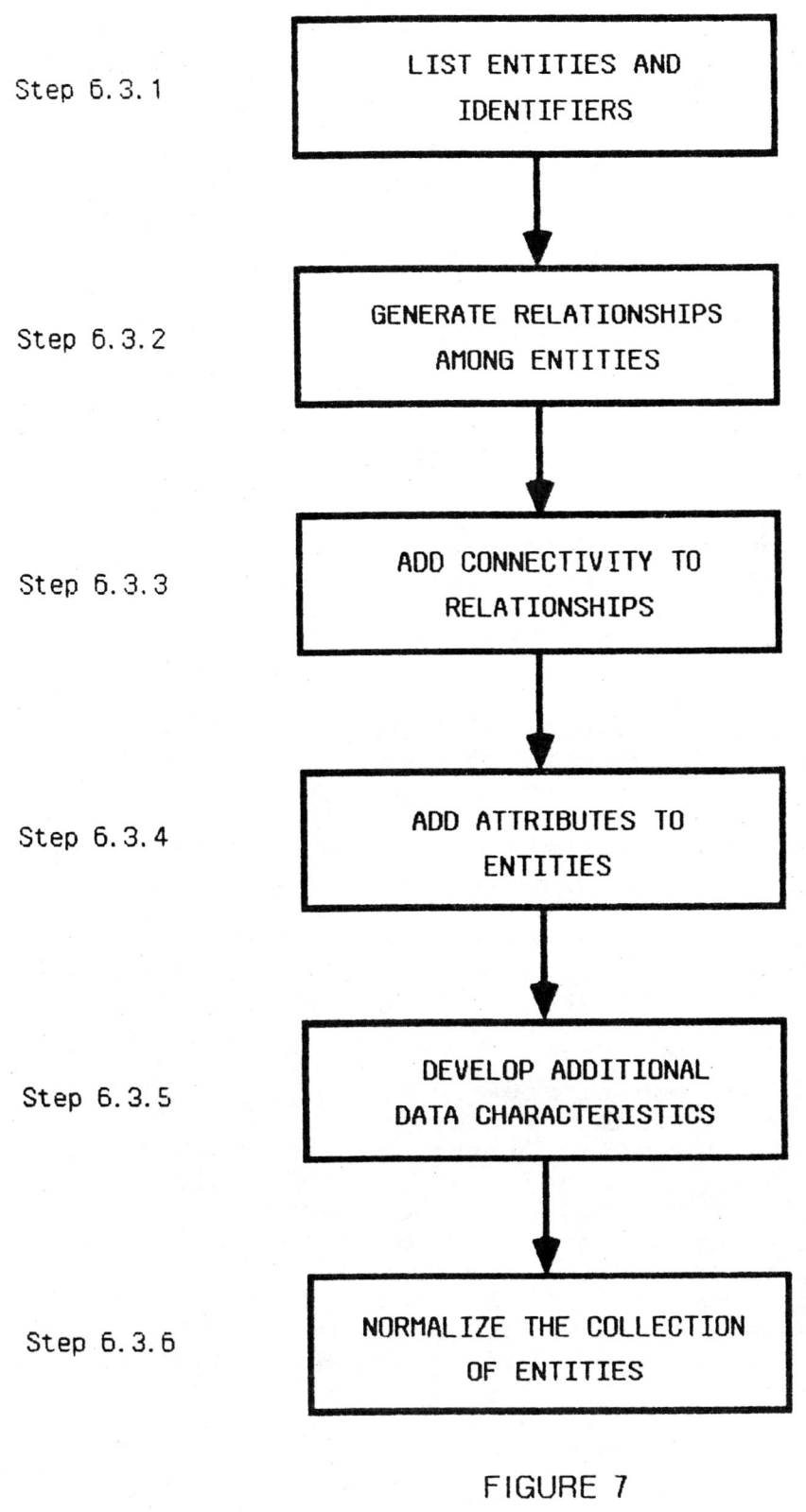

Step 6.3.1	LIST ENTITIES AND IDENTIFIERS
Step 6.3.2	GENERATE RELATIONSHIPS AMONG ENTITIES
Step 6.3.3	ADD CONNECTIVITY TO RELATIONSHIPS
Step 6.3.4	ADD ATTRIBUTES TO ENTITIES
Step 6.3.5	DEVELOP ADDITIONAL DATA CHARACTERISTICS
Step 6.3.6	NORMALIZE THE COLLECTION OF ENTITIES

FIGURE 7

6.3.1 List Entities and Identifiers.

The primary function of this step is to develop a list of entities that must be represented in the CS. Because of the inherent complexity of the real world that the CS models, this is considerably more difficult than one might assume. Some reasonable guidelines are presented below and discussed in the following paragraphs.

1. A data flow may suggest one or more entities.

2. An entity must have a meaningful name and description.

3. An entity must have an identifier.

In general, entities are the subjects of the GIM data flows; an entry in a report or form is usually an attribute which can identify or describe an entity. For example, an assignment matrix could have "project#" as the column heading, "employee-number" as the row title, and an "X" or blank as an indicator of assignment. The matrix itself is not an entity in most cases, but the "project#" and "employee-number" identify entities.

An entity should have a meaningful name consisting of a noun or noun phrase. If there is no obvious choice for the name of a proposed entity, then it is likely that it is not an entity. In addition, the entity must have an extended description that addresses topics such as the lifetime of an entity instance (e.g., is a "dependent" removed from the database when an "employee" resigns?) and criteria for inclusion (e.g., does "employee" include both hourly and salaried personnel?). For additional guidance, refer to [ATRE80, CHEN82, CURT82, KAHN79, ROUS81, SHEP76, SMIT78, SUST83, TEOR82].

An entity must have one or more identifiers (or keys). Each identifier is an attribute or combination of attributes which distinguishes among entity instances. For example, "employee-number," "project-name," and "PD#" could be the identifiers of "employee," "project," and "position description." The identifier of an entity may be composed of identifiers of other entities. For example, the identifier of "assignment" could be composed of the combination of the attributes "employee-number" and "project-name." Note that neither single attribute would uniquely identify a particular "assignment." Note also that "assignment" could equally well be identified by "SS#" and "project#," or even by a unique "assignment-number"--the important fact at this point is that an identifier can be found, so that "assignment" is a legitimate entity.

Analysis of the preceding example demonstrates that care must be exercised in finding an identifier and defining an entity:

- o If the "employee" is released from the "project," is a record of the "assignment" retained?

- o If so, how can such an assignment be distinguished from a current assignment?

- o If the "employee" is returned to the "project," is the "assignment" still the same?

This analysis may indicate that the "employee-number" and "project-name" cannot constitute the identifier. Another attribute, such as "assignment-starting-date-and-time," may be needed for uniqueness. Another possibility is the "assignment-number;" the rules for handling multiple assignments could then be represented by the algorithm for determining the "assignment-number." For example, if the first "assignment-number" is 1, and each succeeding "assignment-number" is increased by 1, then multiple assignments of a given "employee" to a given "assignment" can always be distinguished.

Entities may be determined "top-down" by abstracting from the data flows and the GIM, or "bottom-up" by synthesizing from identifiers and their attributes [SHEP76]. The latter approach is greatly simplified by the use of a computer-based normalization program, as described in step 6.3.6. However, "top-down" is recommended because it forces the developer to concentrate on the semantic characteristics of the data; normalization can then be used to confirm the design.

```
-------------------------------------------------------
Step 6.3.1   List entities and identifiers

Function:       Abstract data flows to determine
                entities

Output:         List of entities with descriptions
                and identifier

Team Members:   User - DA and DBA
                Developer - DA and DBA

Symbology:      Text

Tools:          Use DD to enter entities and identifier

Guidelines:     Be careful in defining an entity
                and finding the identifier for it
                Determine entities top-down
-------------------------------------------------------
```

6.3.2 Generate Relationships among Entities.

The primary function of this step is to examine individual entities to see whether they can be subdivided into simpler, related entities, and to examine collections of entities to see whether they are related components of a more complex entity. A general guideline is to look at entities that share components. For example, "employee" and "assignment" share "employee-number;" obviously, there is a relationship between them. The data dictionary can be of great help in comparing entity structures.

The following are examples of common types of relationships [SUST83]:

1. Membership--a collection of similar secondary entities constitute another, primary, entity. The fiscal years in a five-year plan, the quarters in a fiscal year, or the cities in a state are examples of membership relationships. The relationship between the secondary and primary can be expressed by "in," "of," or "is a member of." The identifier of the primary may be required to identify each secondary; for example, a city name may be ambiguous unless the state is identified. The primary entity would

-64-

include properties common to all the secondary entities, while the secondary entities would have unique properties.

2. Aggregation--a collection of dissimilar secondary entities describes another, primary, entity. Generally all primary entities are related to similar collections of secondary entities. For example, each "employee" is described by the aggregation of "address," "salary-history," "education," etc., which are themselves entities. The relationship between the secondary and primary can be expressed by the phrase "is a property of" or "is a part of." The existence of a secondary entity is usually dependent on the existence of the primary entity.

3. Generalization--each of a collection of similar secondary entities can be considered to represent a special case of another, primary, entity. Different primary entities may be related to different types of secondary entities. For example, "salaried-employee" and "hourly-employee" are each roles of the primary entity "employee." The relationship between the secondary and primary can be expressed by the phrases "is a" or "is a type of." The existence of each secondary entity may be dependent on the existence of the primary entity; for example, every "salaried-employee" or "hourly-employee" must also be an "employee." The primary entity would include properties common to all the secondary entities, while the secondary entities would have unique properties.

These relationships correspond to the programming constructs of iteration (looping through the members of a collection), sequence (manipulating one after another of the aggregated properties), and selection (determining whether a particular role is played by the entity). All of these relationships can be developed bottom-up (from a given collection of secondary entities to the primary), to produce a simplified high-level structure, or top-down (from a primary to a collection of secondaries), to add more detail.

Another type of relationship which is occasionally useful is the following:

4. Precedence--the existence of one entity in the database must precede the existence of another entity in the database. For example, a "proposed-budget" must precede an "approved-budget;" once an "approved-budget" has been entered, however, its existence is independent of the "proposed-budget."

Other, more specialized relationships are discussed in [SUST83].

Diagrams are recommended as a convenient way of communicating with the application specialists. Examples are given below.

EXAMPLE OF AN ENTITY-RELATIONSHIP DIAGRAM

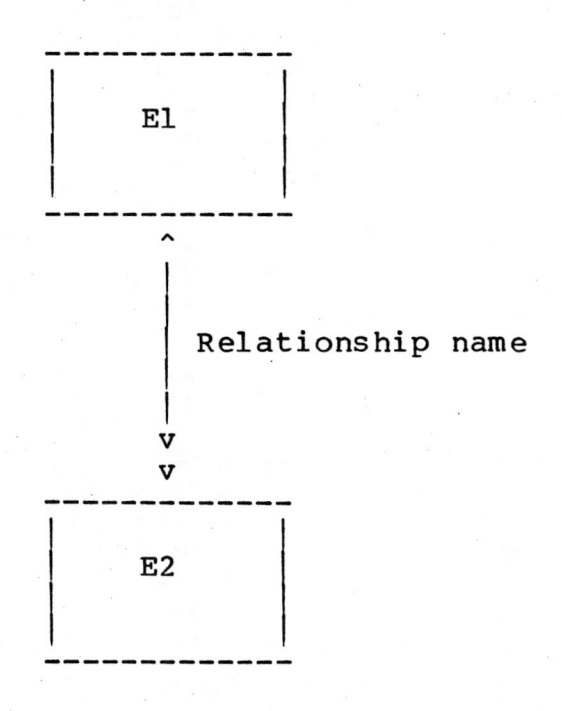

```
   ------------
  |            |
  |     E1     |
  |            |
   ------------
        ^
        |
        |  Relationship name
        |
        v
        v
   ------------
  |            |
  |     E2     |
  |            |
   ------------
```

Figure 8

This example states that entity "E1" has a relationship with another entity "E2." The single and double arrows indicate that an instance of "E1" may be associated with many instances of "E2," while each instance of "E2" is associated with one instance of "E1."

ALTERNATE NOTATION FOR AN ENTITY-RELATIONSHIP DIAGRAM

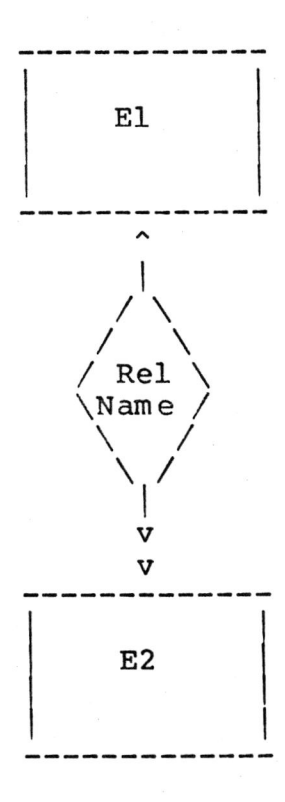

```
           -------------
          |             |
          |     E1      |
          |             |
           -------------
                ^
                |
              / . \
             /     \
            / Rel   \
            \ Name  /
             \     /
              \ . /
                |
                v
                v
           -------------
          |             |
          |     E2      |
          |             |
           -------------
```

Figure 9

The alternate notation is somewhat more cumbersome but it does have the advantage of emphasizing the importance of relationships, and is readily extended to include relationships among more than two entities and relationships with attributes.

In general, the simplicity of labeled lines is preferred. A relationship among more than two entities should usually be transformed into an entity which has simple relationships with those entities. For example,

REPLACING A RELATIONSHIP WITH AN ENTITY

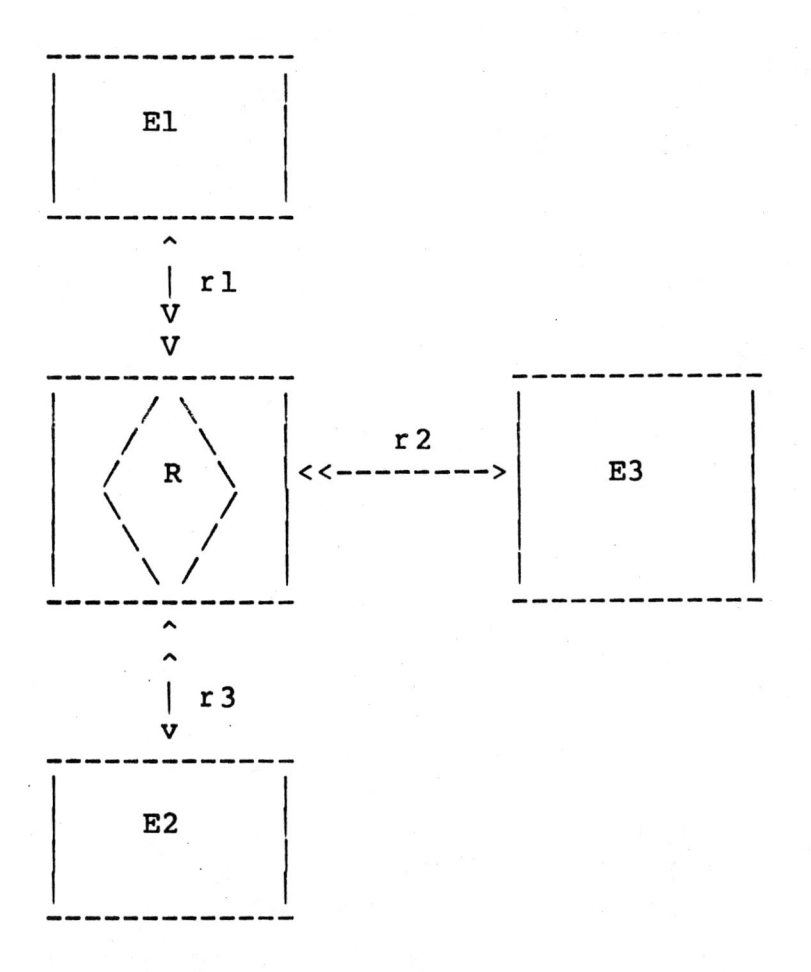

```
            -----------------
           |                 |
           |       E1        |
           |                 |
            -----------------
                   ^
                   | r1
                   V
                   V
            -----------------              -----------------
           |      / \        |            |                 |
           |    /     \      |     r2     |                 |
           |   <   R   >     |<<--------->|       E3        |
           |    \     /      |            |                 |
           |      \ /        |            |                 |
            -----------------              -----------------
                   ^
                   ^
                   | r3
                   V
            -----------------
           |                 |
           |       E2        |
           |                 |
            -----------------
```

Figure 10

The complex relationship R has been replaced by an entity; the diamond within the rectangle indicates that R may be an entity on one diagram and a relationship on a less detailed diagram. New relationships, r1, r2, and r3 must be added unless they are obvious. The fact that an "employee" uses a particular "skill" on a particular "project" would be represented by such a diagram; E1, E2, and E3 would represent "employee," "skill," and "project," while R could be a relationship or an entity identified by the "employee," "skill," and "project" identifiers.

```
-------------------------------------------------------
  Step 6.3.2   Generate relationships among entities

  Function:       Revise entities

  Output:         Entities and relationships

  Team Members:   User - DA and DBA
                  Developer - DA and DBA

  Symbology:      Entity-Relationship diagrams

  Tools:          Add relationships to DD

  Guidelines:     Look for common types of
                  relationships
-------------------------------------------------------
```

6.3.3 Add Connectivity to Relationships.

The primary function of this step is to suggest new entities or ways in which entities can be combined. A secondary function is to provide quantitative data useful to physical database design.

Connectivity describes a relationship between two entities-- how many instances of one entity are associated with how many instances of the other entity. For example, if an "employee" can have only one "manager," but a "manager" can manage many employees, then the relationship "manages" is "1 to many." If a reasonably good number can be given for the "many," that may assist in physical database design. However, the most important situations for logical database design are the following:

o Most relationships will have connectivity "1 to many" or "many to 1."

o If the connectivity is "1 to 1," then the two entities should be combined, provided that the result can be given a meaningful name and description. For example, if a "project" always has exactly one "manager," and a "manager" always has exactly one "project," then the two entities can be combined.

(Note the use of the word "always." In the real world it is likely that there will be periods of transition when a "manager" has no "project," or more than one "project," or a "project" has no "manager." In reality, then, the connectivity might be "0,1 to 0,1,2," and the entities should not be combined.)

o If the connectivity is "1 to 0,1" then this often indicates generalization. For example, the relationship between "employee" and "salaried-employee" is "1 to 0,1," since the "employee" could be an "hourly-employee." The "salaried-employee" entity cannot exist unless the "employee" entity exists.

o If the connectivity is "many to many" (or numbers indicating a similar situation), then the relationship should be replaced by an entity. For example, if there is a "many to many" relationship between "employee" and "manager" (i.e., matrix management), then a new entity, such as "assignment of employee to manager" should be created, and the "many to many" relationship replaced by two "1 to many" relationships. This leads to more entities but simplifies relationships and also simplifies the mapping of the logical database design into a conventional data model.

An example of a diagram with connectivity is shown below.

EXAMPLE OF AN ENTITY-RELATIONSHIP DIAGRAM WITH CONNECTIVITY

```
         ---------------
        |               |
        |      E1       |
        |               |
         ---------------
               ^ 1
               |
               |
               |
               v
               v many
         ---------------
        |               |
        |      E2       |
        |               |
         ---------------
```

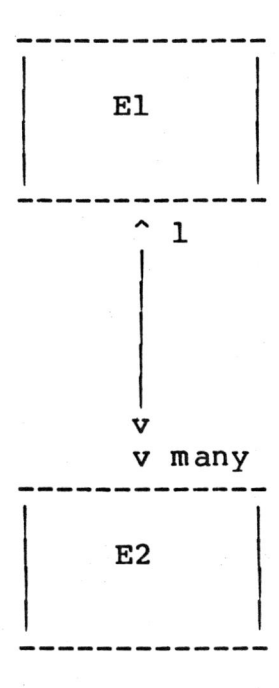

Figure 11

```
-------------------------------------------------------------
|                                                           |
| Step 6.3.3   Add connectivity to relationships            |
|                                                           |
| Function:      Determine connectivity and provide         |
|                quantitative data to physical              |
|                database design                            |
|                                                           |
| Output:        Annotated relationships                    |
|                                                           |
| Team Members:  User - DA and DBA                          |
|                Developer - DA and DBA                     |
|                                                           |
| Symbology:     Extended E-R diagrams                      |
|                                                           |
| Tools:         Add connectivity information to DD         |
|                                                           |
| Guidelines:    Eliminate 1 to 1 and many to many          |
|                relationships                              |
|                                                           |
-------------------------------------------------------------
```

6.3.4 Add Attributes to Entities.

The primary function of this step is to add detail to the entity descriptions in the data dictionary and diagrams. Two strategies are possible:

1. If there is a collection of known attributes (e.g., data elements), then this step can be performed "bottom-up." Each attribute is assigned to an entity (or entities) which identifies a unique instance of that attribute. If no entity is appropriate, one is created, relationships are developed, and so on.

2. This step can be performed "top-down" by examining each entity to determine appropriate descriptors. This procedure is recommended during high-level iterations, when attributes are data collections rather than data elements.

The attributes are represented in the data dictionary by being "contained in" an entity [FIPS80], and in the diagrams by some notation such as that in the following example, where "A1" is the attribute:

EXAMPLE OF AN ENTITY-RELATIONSHIP-ATTRIBUTE DIAGRAM

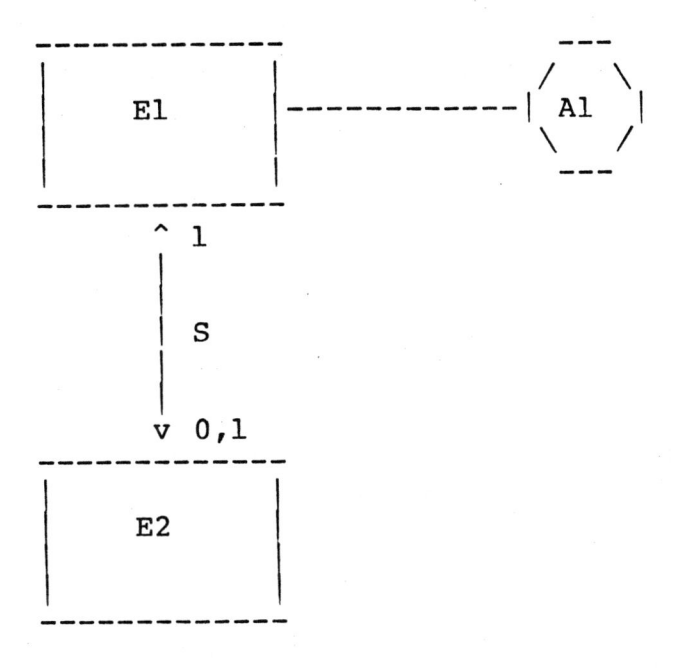

```
    ------------                    ---
   |            |                  /   \
   |    E1      |-----------------|  A1 |
   |            |                  \   /
   |            |                    ---
    ------------
         ^ 1
         |
         | S
         |
         v 0,1
    ------------
   |            |
   |    E2      |
   |            |
   |            |
    ------------
```

Figure 12

The relationship S could be an agreed-upon symbol to indicate that E2 is a subtype of the entity E1.

Another function of this step is to simplify the CS by eliminating unnecessary entities. The rule for doing this is very simple:

o If an entity is single-valued in every relationship with other entities, then it can be eliminated by moving its attributes (including the identifier) into those entities.

For example, suppose that "hourly-pay-scale" is an entity with the attribute and identifier "dollar-amount," and its only relationships are "many to 1" from "salaried-employee" and "hourly-employee" to "hourly-pay-scale." Then "dollar-amount" should be assigned to "salaried-employee" and "hourly-employee," and "hourly-pay-scale" should be eliminated. The justification is simple: "dollar-amount" is single-valued in every relationship, so it acts like a descriptor--i.e., an attribute.

```
-----------------------------------------------------------
 Step 6.3.4    Add attributes to entities

 Function:      Add attributes to the entity
                descriptions

 Output:        E-R-A diagrams

 Team Members:  User - DA and DBA
                Developer - DA and DBA

 Symbology:     E-R-A diagrams

 Tools:         Add attributes to DD

 Guidelines:    Simplify by eliminating unnecessary
                entities
-----------------------------------------------------------
```

6.3.5 Develop Additional Data Characteristics.

The function of this step is to add additional constraints, such as security and integrity, to the entity and relationship descriptions in the data dictionary. These constraints are important but are not easily represented on a diagram; the recommendation is to keep the diagrams simple by representing these constraints only in the data dictionary.

```
-----------------------------------------------------------------
| Step 6.3.5    Develop additional data characteristics
|
| Function:      Add security, integrity, and other
|                constraints
|
| Output:        E-R-A diagrams and updated DD
|                with detailed description of data
|
| Team Members:  User - DA and DBA
|                Developer - DA and DBA
|
| Symbology:     E-R-A diagrams
|
| Tools:         Add constraints to DD
|
| Guidelines:    Keep the diagrams simple
-----------------------------------------------------------------
```

6.3.6 Normalize the Collection .

The primary function of this step is to ensure that the collection of entities is optimal in the following sense:

1. Each non-key attribute is identified only by the simplest possible identifiers. For example, "supplier-address" should not be in a "supplier-part" entity (identified by the combination of "supplier-name" and "part-number") if "supplier-address" is uniquely identified by "supplier-name" alone.

2. Redundant non-key attributes are eliminated. For example, if the "branch" entity contains "division#" and "department#," and the "division" entity (identified by "division#") also contains "department#," then "department#" can be eliminated from "branch." The "department#" can be determined from the unique "division" entity identified in the "branch," so "department#" is redundant in "branch."

3. Entities with the same identifier are combined.

4. Entities with equivalent identifiers (identifiers that identify each other) are combined.

The first two conditions, plus the condition that attributes are single-valued (which was required in step 6.3.4), are sufficient to ensure that the entities are in Third Normal Form [BERN76]. The third and fourth conditions ensure that the entities are in the more rigorous Elementary Key Normal Form (EKNF) [ZANI82], which minimizes the total number of entities. A computer algorithm to obtain EKNF is described in [BEER79, BERN76]; the proofs of correctness and minimality are complex, but the algorithm itself is quite simple.

Commercially available programs perform various levels of normalization [MART77]. A good program should interface to a data dictionary to obtain identifiers and the attributes that they identify, and should provide EKNF as well as various reports, traces, and diagrams. The objective of the preceding steps of this phase is to do such a good job of identifier analysis that the normalization program will produce exactly the entities that are input to it. Experience indicates that discrepancies between the input and output entities are often caused by more serious and subtle errors than those found by the normalization program; the program exposes errors, but its "corrections" are sometimes difficult to understand, and should not be accepted without thorough analysis. A normalization program should definitely not be used as a substitute for careful thought.

Step 6.3.6 Normalize the collection of entities

Function: Remove redundancies and detect errors

Output: Normalized entities

Team Members: User - System analyst and DBA
               Developer - DA and DBA

Tools: Normalization program

Guidelines: Careful manual analysis as well as use
               of the automated tools

---

7. EXTERNAL SCHEMA MODELING

An External Schema (ES) is a subschema (part) of a Conceptual Schema (CS) that is relevant to a Local Information-flow Model (LIM). A LIM, in turn, represents the information requirements of a user, group of users, application program, or application system. An ES includes all entities, relationships, and attributes needed by the LIM. Local names are possible--for example, the Conceptual Schema may have an entity called "employee-number" which is "emp-no" in the personnel ES. An ES reflects the way information is used by an individual task or decision.

7.1 Information Used to Develop the ES

The primary sources of information needed to develop an ES are the CS and the relevant LIM as represented in the data dictionary. If the LIM is inadequate in scope or detail, then it should be expanded using additional information from the sources listed in section 4.1.

7.2 Functions of the ES

The primary function of an ES is to help users and programmers interact with the database by presenting a simplified view of the database in terms which are familiar to them. An ES has the following secondary functions:

1. Detailed iterations of the ES provide one of the inputs to physical database design--they describe the workload, originally developed in terms of LIMs, in terms of the CS.

2. An ES is a piece of the CS which can be assigned privacy and security locks during physical database design and implementation phases.

3. An ES provides quality control of the CS--if the ES cannot be constructed from the CS, then the CS is incomplete. Also, if there are portions of the CS which are not required by any ES, then those portions

are unnecessary or are information sources that are not being utilized by any LIMs. During the early iterations of the logical database design process the ESs will be useful only for comparing high-level descriptions of very general categories of data (e.g., data needed for the support of management decisions), since the relevant LIMs will be based on an organizational perspective and will not have much detail. In addition, the LIMs may not indicate what information is to be in the database and what is to be provided by some other source. During later iterations, the ESs will provide a much more accurate means for ensuring CS quality.

7.3 Procedure for Developing the ES

Figure 13 shows the three sequential steps in the development of the ES. The steps are described in the following paragraphs.

EXTERNAL SCHEMA (ES) MODELING PROCEDURE

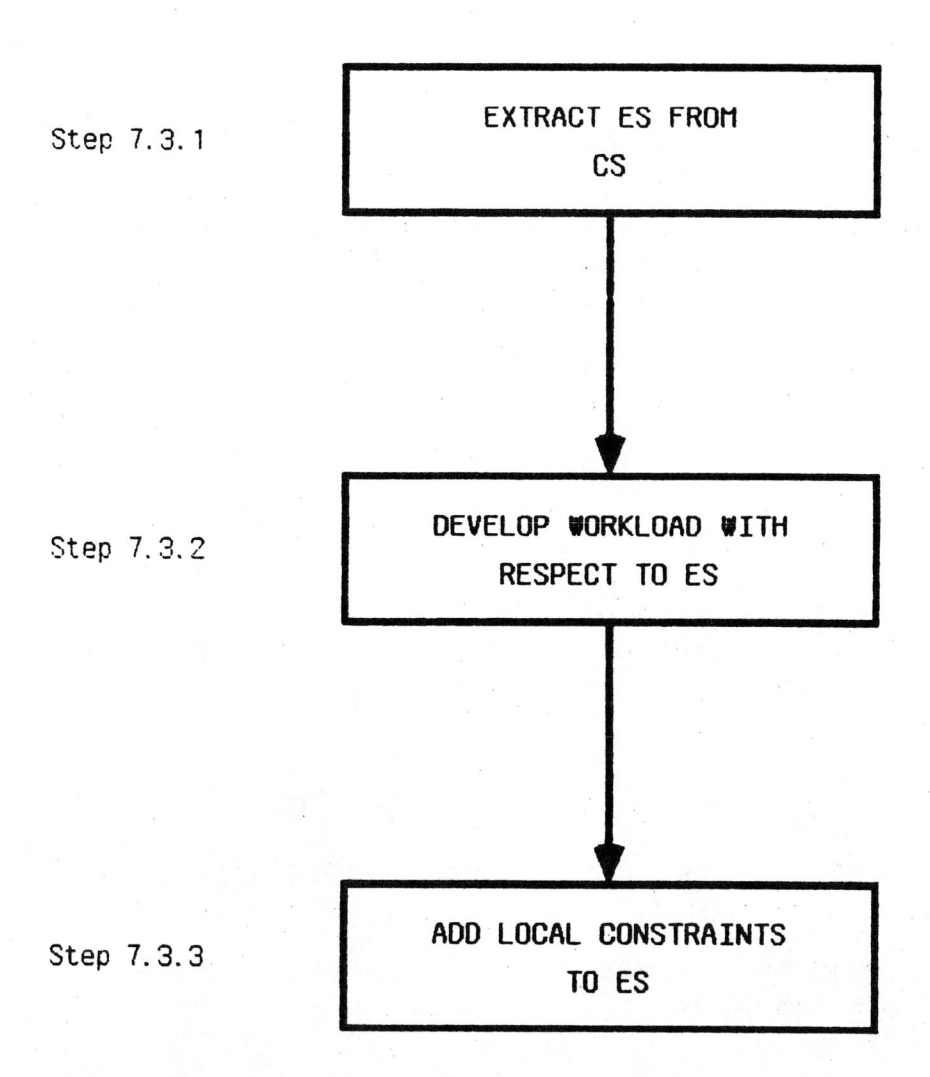

Step 7.3.1 — EXTRACT ES FROM CS

Step 7.3.2 — DEVELOP WORKLOAD WITH RESPECT TO ES

Step 7.3.3 — ADD LOCAL CONSTRAINTS TO ES

FIGURE 13

7.3.1 Extract an ES from the CS.

The primary function of this step is to decide what parts of the CS are required by a particular LIM. First, data flows must be classified into those requiring data from the database and those that are independent of the database [JEFF82]. The data collection may be obtained from or stored in a private file or other non-database location if any of the following are true:

1. The data collection is of interest to only a single user or application and therefore need not be shared.

2. The data collection is transitory, as in a temporary working file, and would not exist long enough to be relevant to other users or applications.

3. The data collection is incomplete or inconsistent, as in a partially completed update, or consists only of references or keys to other data, as in a file of references to data of particular interest to decision support.

In general, a data collection should be obtained from or stored into the database if all of the following are true:

1. The data collection is of interest to many users or applications and should therefore be shared.

2. The data collection is sufficiently long-lived to have many uses.

3. The data collection represents a consistent, complete view of the real world.

There are then two situations that can be distinguished:

o This LIM is not a part of any LIM for which an ES has already been constructed. For example, this LIM might be a top-level organization, function, or event. In this case, the ES will consist of high-level entities, relationships, and attributes from the CS. If a Data Dictionary System (DDS) is available, it should be employed to extract only high-level data objects. These objects will then be manually compared with the data flows of the LIM to determine what parts of the CS are needed by the LIM.

o Alternatively, this LIM is a part of a higher-level LIM for which an ES has already been constructed. For example, this LIM may be a part of a function for which there is an ES. In this case, the ES is based on the higher-level ES. The DDS should be used to extract the data objects relevant to the higher-level ES, and the lower-level data objects which are contained within them. The resulting collection of data objects must then be compared with the data flows of the LIM to verify that all data required by the LIM is in the higher-level ES, or is a part of some data object in the higher-level ES (the DDS can greatly reduce the effort involved in this comparison). If not, the higher-level ES must be extended to include the missing data. The lower-level ES will then consist of the relevant parts of the higher-level ES plus additional entities, relationships, and attributes required by the more detailed level of analysis.

The final result of this step is a diagram of selected parts of the CS plus additional entries in the data dictionary to relate the selected data to the LIM.

```
-----------------------------------------------------------
| Step 7.3.1    Extract an ES from the CS                 |
|                                                         |
| Function:      Decompose CS based upon the              |
|                particular LIM                           |
|                                                         |
| Output:        Decomposed E-R-A diagram                 |
|                                                         |
| Team Members:  User - Programmers, analysts, and DBA    |
|                Developer - DA and DBA                   |
|                                                         |
| Symbology:     E-R-A diagrams                           |
|                                                         |
| Tools:         Use DD to relate data to LIM             |
|                                                         |
| Guidelines:    Verify the extracted ES with LIM         |
-----------------------------------------------------------
```

7.3.2 Develop Workload With Respect to ESs.

The primary function of this step is to translate the workload, originally developed in terms of data flow in the LIM, into data access and update in the ES. The preceding step determined what parts of the database, if any, are required for each data flow, while step 4.3.5 determined the frequency, sequence, and selectivity with which each function uses and updates data. Therefore, this step involves two alternatives for each data collection in the LIM workload sequence:

o   If the data collection is not database data, then nothing need be done.

o   If the data collection is database data, then an appropriate access path must be determined. That is, given the data available at that point in the sequence, what entities and relationships must be accessed to arrive at the required entities? If a path cannot be found, there is an error, which must be corrected by modifying the LIM (e.g., by revising the workload), modifying the partially completed ES (e.g., by changing the distribution of database and non-database data), or modifying the CS (e.g., by adding a new relationship). If a path can be found, it is added into the workload sequence for the ES.

The resulting database workload should be represented in the data dictionary by a sequence of programs or modules interacting with the database objects. Three kinds of interactions with entities must be represented:

- Data use--an entity instance is accessed because various attributes are needed for some computation, report, or control purpose.

- Data update--an entity instance is added or modified.

- Data access--an entity instance is part of a path but has no directly relevant attributes. The entity might be removed from the path, with an improvement in database performance, if the Internal Schema has an appropriate relationship to bypass the entity.

As noted in step number 4.3.5, there are two types of interactions with attributes:

- Entity retrieval--an attribute is needed to determine whether an entity instance is needed by the function.

- Attribute selection--an attribute instance is required for a computation, report, control, or update purpose.

There is one type of interaction with relationships:

- Path component--the relationship is part of a path. Note that the direction is important.

The paths may also be represented graphically by an overlay on an ES or CS diagram [MART84, MCCL84, SUST84]. This provides a simple representation that can be easily understood and verified by application specialists, but is not a substitute for the data dictionary.

```
-----------------------------------------------------
| Step 7.3.2    Develop workload with respect to ES |
|                                                   |
| Function:     Specifications for physical design  |
|                                                   |
| Output:       Workload specifications             |
|                                                   |
| Team Members: User - Programmers, analysts, and DBA|
|               Developer - Analysts, DA and DBA    |
|                                                   |
| Symbology:    E-R-A diagram with path overlay     |
|                                                   |
| Tools:        Update DD to add workload information|
|                                                   |
| Guidelines:   Identify access path to avoid errors|
-----------------------------------------------------
```

7.3.3 Add Local Constraints to the ES.

The purpose of this step is to add any unique constraints imposed on or by the LIM. Examples of such constraints include security and privacy restrictions, local rules for edit and validation, and local integrity constraints.

```
-----------------------------------------------------
| Step 7.3.3    Add local constraints to the ES     |
|                                                   |
| Function:     Add local constraints to each ES    |
|                                                   |
| Output:       Updated E-R-A diagrams and updated DD|
|                                                   |
| Team Members: User - Programmers, analysts, and DBA|
|               Developer - DA and DBA              |
|                                                   |
| Symbology:    E-R-A diagrams                      |
|                                                   |
| Tools:        Update DD to add constraints        |
|                                                   |
| Guidelines:   Identify unique constraints imposed |
|               on or by the LIM                    |
-----------------------------------------------------
```

8. CONCLUSIONS

This report presents a Logical Database Design methodology with the following characteristics:

- o There are four phases: Local Information-flow Modeling, Global Information-flow Modeling, Conceptual Schema Design, and External Schema Modeling.

- o The phases are executed iteratively to control complexity and to provide a means for verifying the results of the different phases against one another.

- o Analysis is performed from different points of view (organization, function, and event) in order to ensure that the logical database design accurately reflects all reasonable information requirements of the organization.

- o The methodology recommends computer support from a Data Dictionary System, in order to conveniently and accurately handle the volume and complexity of design documentation and analysis, and to provide ready access to work already accomplished.

- o Logical database design is integrated into the complete system life cycle.

The purpose of this methodology is to assist in the design of very large and complex information systems, where the effects of poor logical database structures can result in expensive, time-consuming system development efforts whose end results are ineffective and inefficient. The methodology emphasizes both the need for speed, so that the design will be completed in time to be useful, and the need for quality control, to ensure that the design is consistent, complete, and satisfies the eventual users.

APPENDIX A

Agency Financial Management System

INTRODUCTION

A Federal agency is designing a financial management system. None of the applications systems offered by software vendors seem to gracefully accommodate the agency's code structure and its cost accounting procedures for its reimbursable divisions. As a matter of fact, although the individuals on the team surveying these packages are each expert in a particular subject area, they lack a good overview of what their agency's requirements are, or should be.

A primary objective of the design effort is to gain an organizational perspective of the agency's financial data. The logical database design can then be used to develop a system (either in-house or on contract), purchase a system (once requirements are understood) or specify modifications which would be needed if a system were purchased from a vendor or obtained from another agency.

An important consideration in the logical database design project is that the agency's appropriation from Congress constitutes only 63% of the operating budget. Additional income is provided by contracts with other government agencies and the sale of goods and services to the public sector. The financial management system must be able to charge back costs to customers. Another important consideration is that there is an existing payroll system which must interface with the financial management system.

An example of a reimbursable division is Instrument Fabrication Division, IFD, whose income from services to other government agencies represents 8% of the agency's budget. IFD relies on other divisions within the agency for functions such as procurement and accounting. IFD finances all management and support services by applying a fixed-rate surcharge to the labor base in some of its own units.

The following examples are intended to show some of the types of documentation which are gathered or produced in a logical database design.

These examples have been simplified so that the amount of detail does not obscure the intent of the example. However, in some instances enough detail is left in so that the reader may appreciate the sheer volume of the items of information to be gathered, analyzed and organized in logical database design. The result is, unfortunately, an uneven level of detail.

Even the sample system chosen, "Agency Financial Management System," is limited in scope, showing some aspects of normal in-house financial management for a service-oriented agency. Other federal agencies, whose mission is to administer or disburse government funds, would consider this example system a minor subsystem. In general, logical database design for financial management should consider the unique mission of the agency and the extent to which financial data can be used to support that mission.

INSTRUMENT FABRICATION DIVISION
Organizational Chart

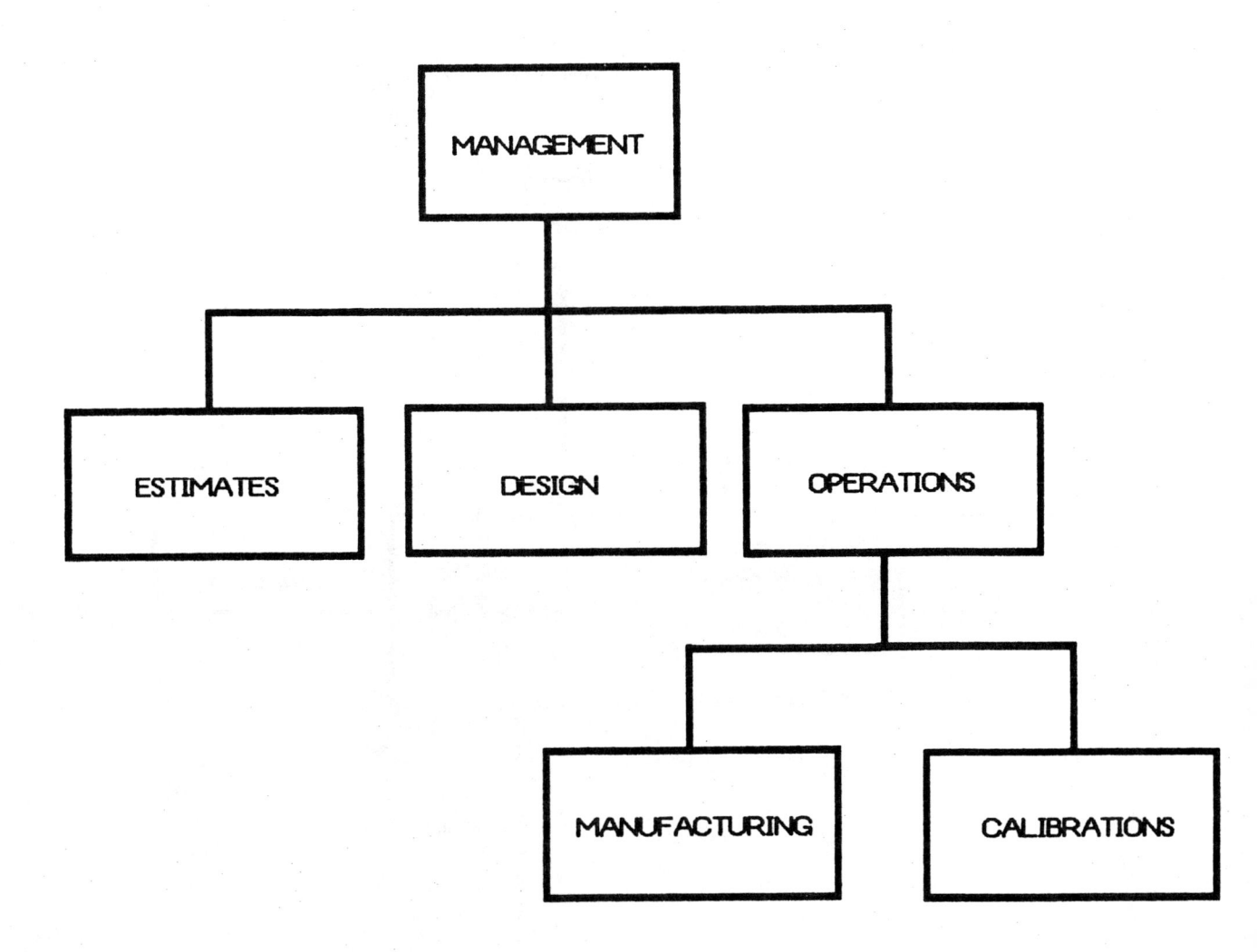

```
                    ┌──────────────┐
                    │  MANAGEMENT  │
                    └──────┬───────┘
           ┌───────────────┼───────────────┐
      ┌────┴─────┐   ┌─────┴────┐   ┌──────┴─────┐
      │ ESTIMATES│   │  DESIGN  │   │ OPERATIONS │
      └──────────┘   └──────────┘   └──────┬─────┘
                                  ┌────────┴────────┐
                           ┌──────┴──────┐   ┌──────┴──────┐
                           │MANUFACTURING│   │ CALIBRATIONS│
                           └─────────────┘   └─────────────┘
```

MISSION

The mission of Instrument Fabrication Division is to design and manufacture high-precision, one-of-a kind instruments in support of the agency's scientific research divisions. This service is available to other government agencies as well as the public. All instruments are manufactured on a reimbursable basis.

INSTRUMENT FABRICATION DIVISION
High Level Local Information-flow Model

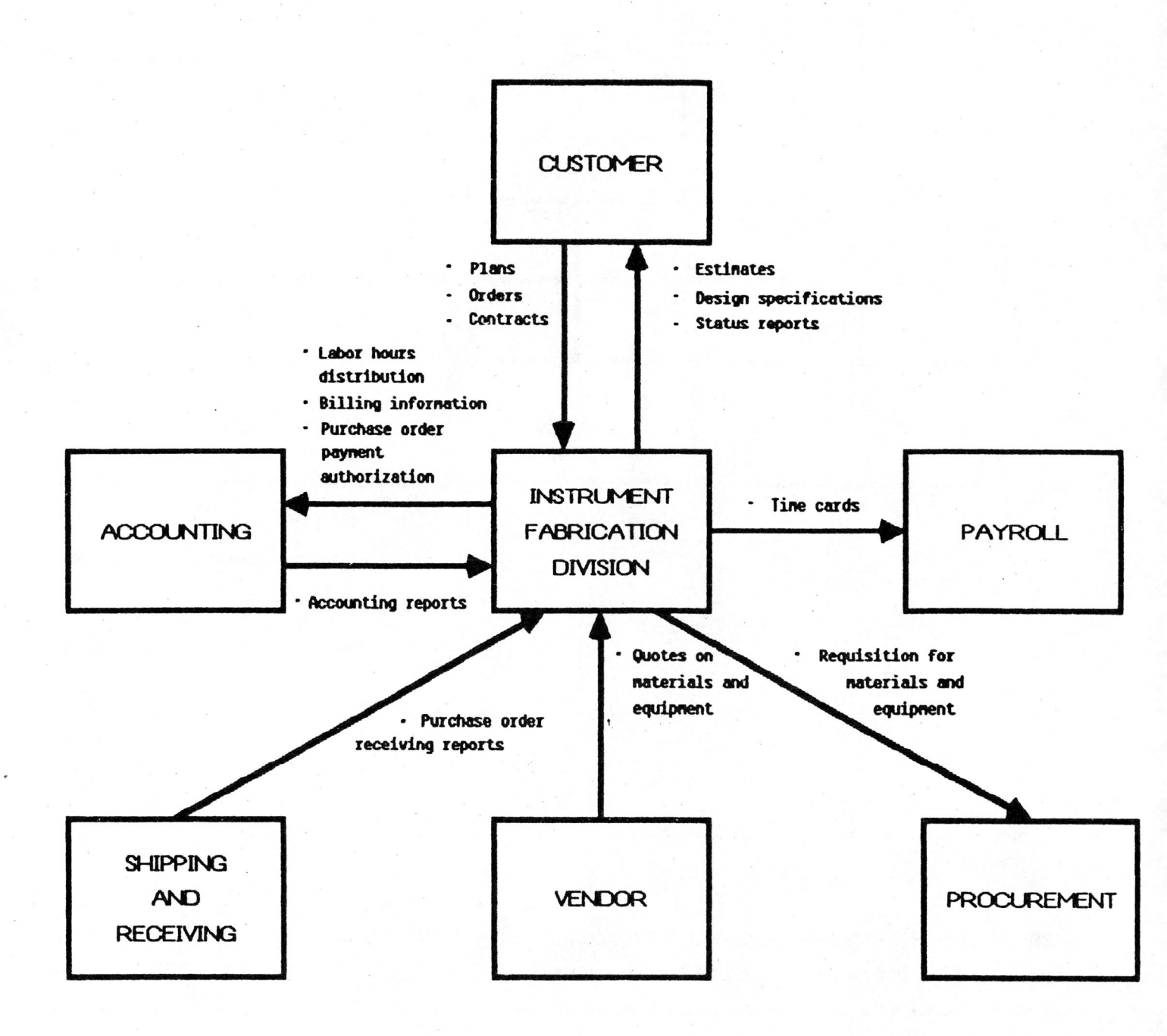

```
                          ┌──────────────┐
                          │   CUSTOMER   │
                          └──────────────┘
                    · Plans         · Estimates
                    · Orders        · Design specifications
                    · Contracts     · Status reports

           · Labor hours
             distribution
           · Billing information
           · Purchase order
             payment
             authorization
┌────────────┐                    ┌──────────────┐                    ┌──────────┐
│ ACCOUNTING │ ◄─────────────────│  INSTRUMENT  │── Time cards ─────►│  PAYROLL │
│            │ ─────────────────►│  FABRICATION │                    │          │
└────────────┘  · Accounting      │   DIVISION   │                    └──────────┘
                  reports         └──────────────┘
                                    ▲       ▲
                                    │       │     · Quotes on         · Requisition for
                                    │       │       materials and       materials and
                                    │       │       equipment           equipment
                          · Purchase order
                            receiving reports
┌────────────┐                    ┌──────────────┐                    ┌──────────────┐
│  SHIPPING  │                    │              │                    │              │
│    AND     │                    │    VENDOR    │                    │  PROCUREMENT │
│ RECEIVING  │                    │              │                    │              │
└────────────┘                    └──────────────┘                    └──────────────┘
```

-A.4-

INSTRUMENT FABRICATION DIVISION
Local Information-flow Model
ESTIMATES Unit

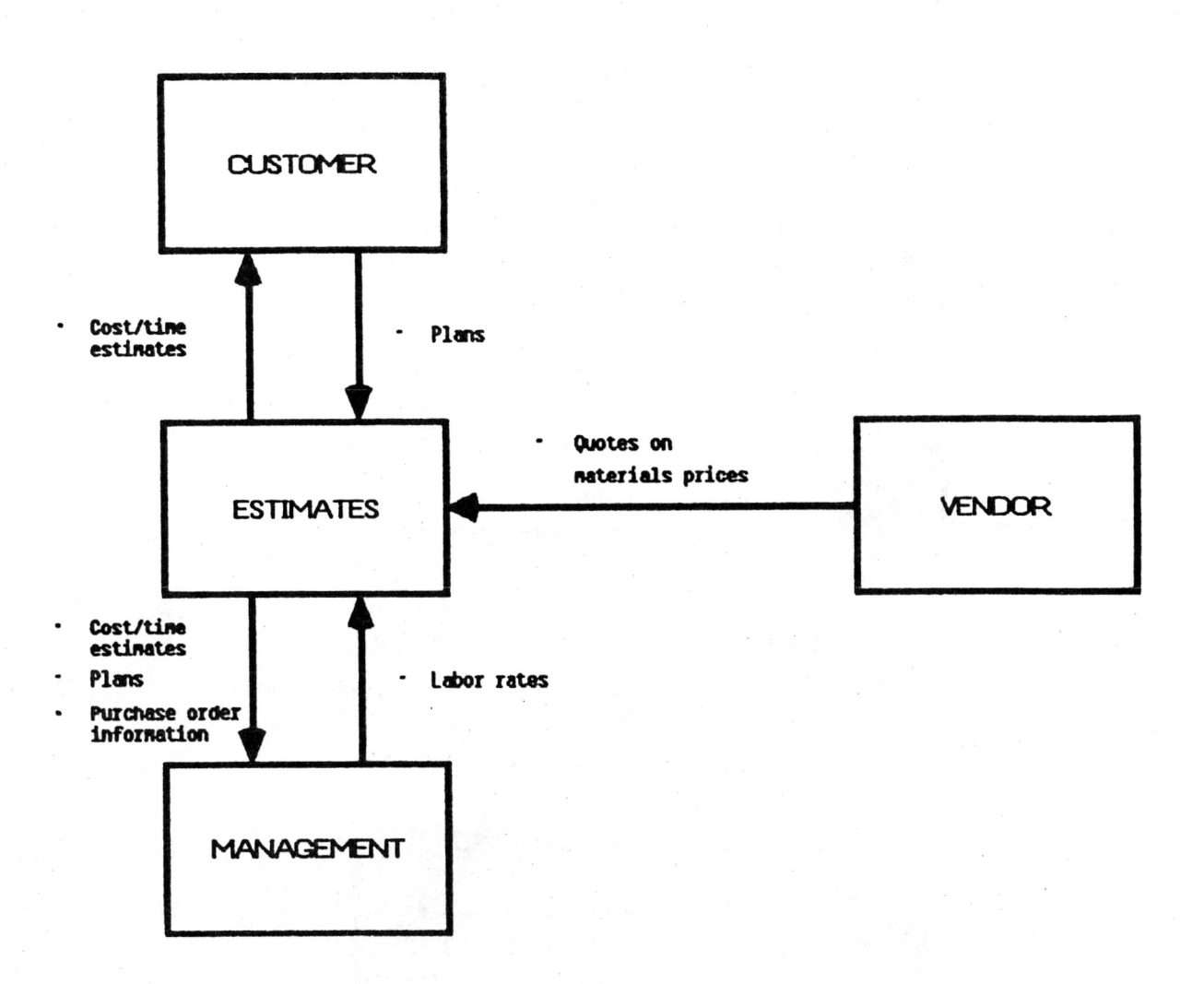

```
                    ┌──────────────┐
                    │   CUSTOMER   │
                    └──────────────┘
                      ▲          │
                      │          ▼
          · Cost/time      · Plans
            estimates
                    ┌──────────────┐         · Quotes on        ┌──────────┐
                    │　ESTIMATES　 │◄──────────materials prices──│  VENDOR  │
                    └──────────────┘                            └──────────┘
                      │          ▲
                      ▼          │
          · Cost/time      · Labor rates
            estimates
          · Plans
          · Purchase order
            information
                    ┌──────────────┐
                    │  MANAGEMENT  │
                    └──────────────┘
```

NOTES

Estimates are free to customers. The ESTIMATES unit is not reimbursed directly for services.

INSTRUMENT FABRICATION DIVISION

Local Information-flow Model
OPERATIONS Unit

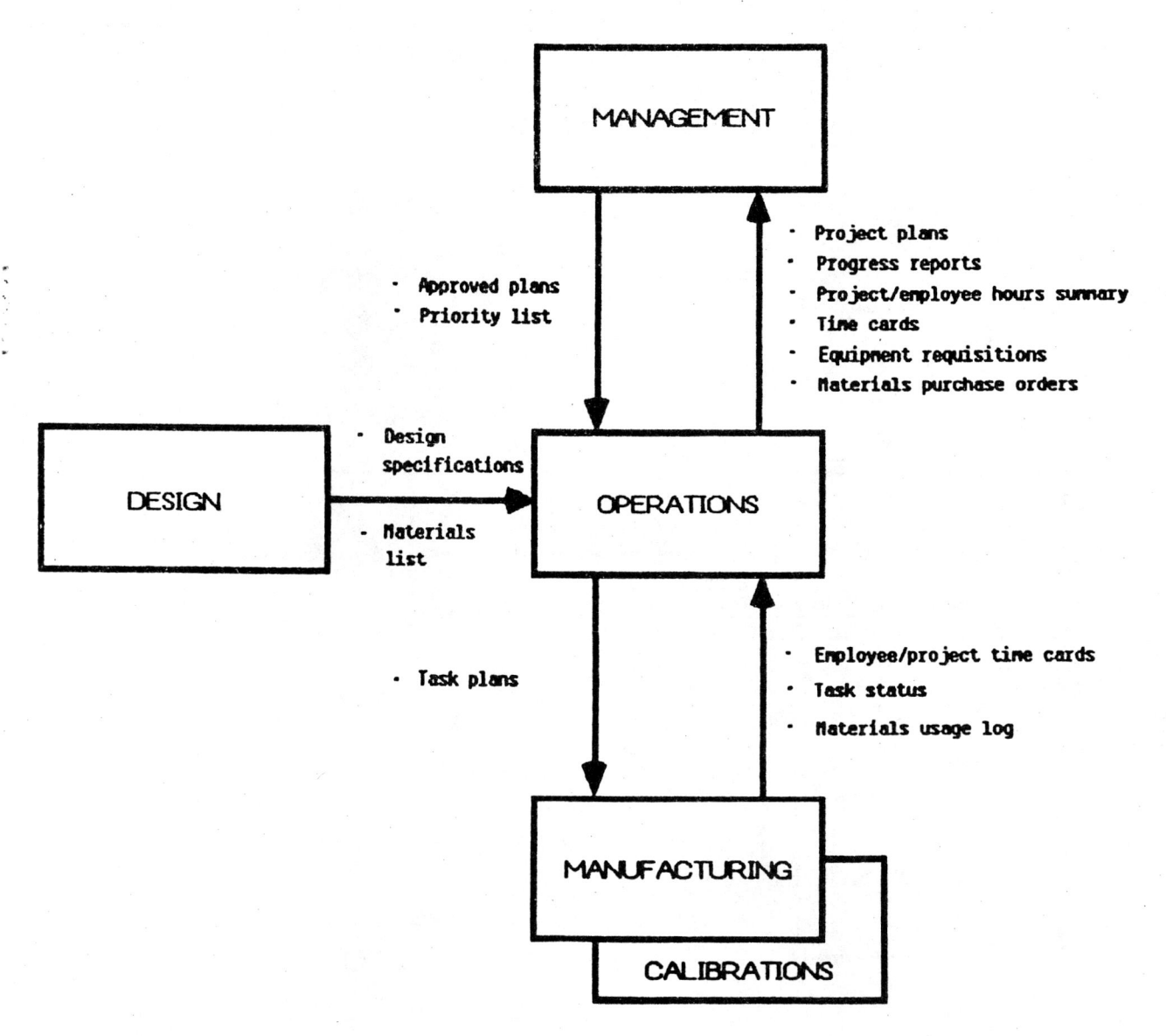

```
                    ┌──────────────┐
                    │  MANAGEMENT  │
                    └──────┬───────┘
                           │ ↕
              Approved plans    · Project plans
              Priority list     · Progress reports
                                · Project/employee hours summary
                                · Time cards
                                · Equipment requisitions
                                · Materials purchase orders

  ┌────────┐   · Design            ┌──────────────┐
  │ DESIGN │────specifications────▶│  OPERATIONS  │
  └────────┘   · Materials         └──────┬───────┘
               list                       │ ↑
                                          │
                          · Task plans    │   · Employee/project time cards
                                          │   · Task status
                                          ▼   · Materials usage log
                                   ┌──────────────┐
                                   │ MANUFACTURING│
                                   └──────┬───────┘
                                      ┌───┴────────┐
                                      │CALIBRATIONS│
                                      └────────────┘
```

NOTES

OPERATIONS is responsible for coordinating the efforts of MANUFACTURING and CALIBRATIONS, scheduling tasks, ordering materials and equipment, reporting material and labor spent on each project.

INSTRUMENT FABRICATION DIVISION
Local Information-flow Model

Function : Close Out Work Order

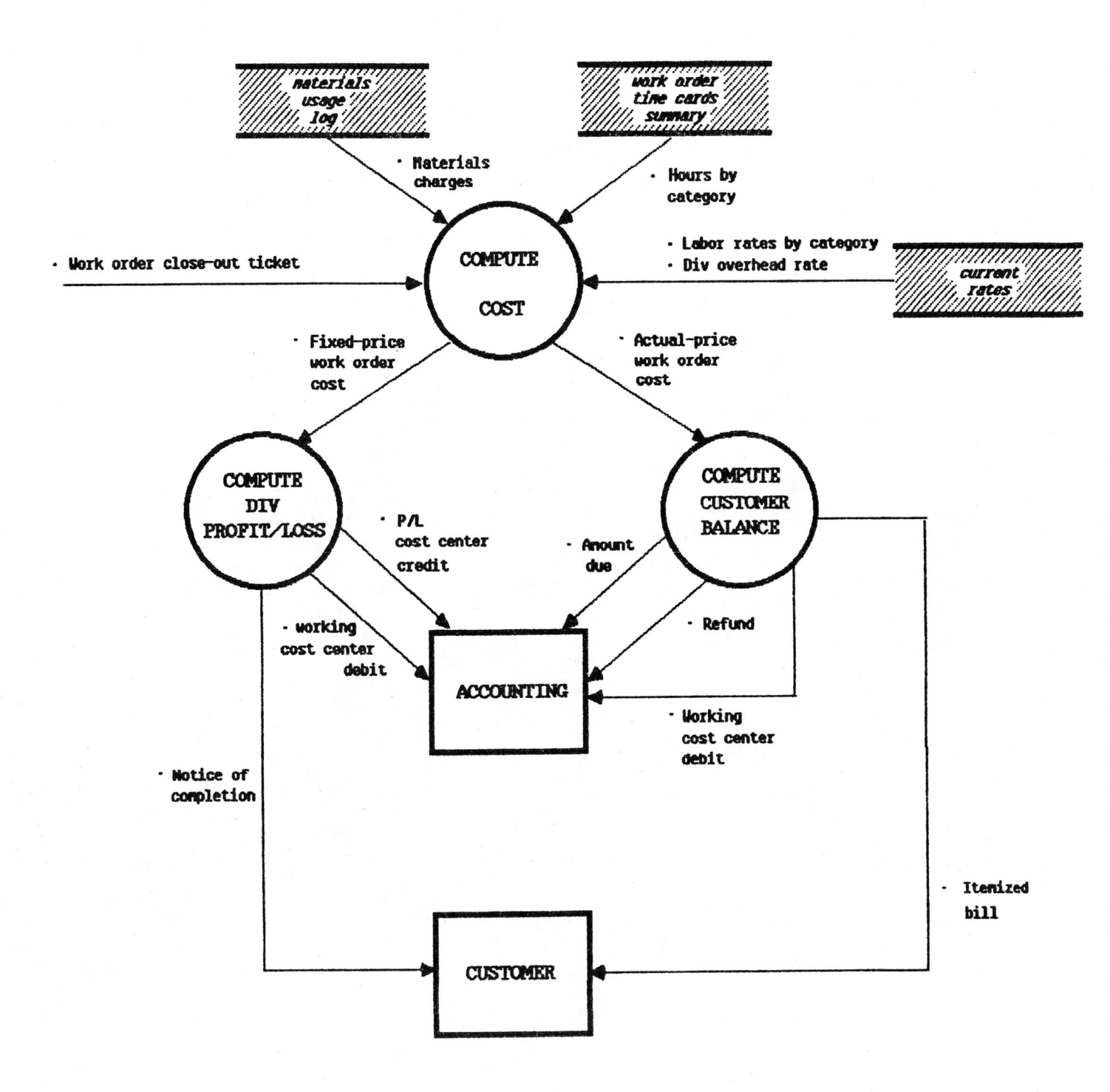

Data stores:
- materials usage log
- work order time cards summary
- current rates

Processes:
- COMPUTE COST
- COMPUTE DIV PROFIT/LOSS
- COMPUTE CUSTOMER BALANCE

External entities:
- ACCOUNTING
- CUSTOMER

Flows into COMPUTE COST:
- Materials charges (from materials usage log)
- Hours by category (from work order time cards summary)
- Labor rates by category (from current rates)
- Div overhead rate (from current rates)
- Work order close-out ticket

Flows out of COMPUTE COST:
- Fixed-price work order cost → COMPUTE DIV PROFIT/LOSS
- Actual-price work order cost → COMPUTE CUSTOMER BALANCE

Flows from COMPUTE DIV PROFIT/LOSS:
- P/L cost center credit → ACCOUNTING
- working cost center debit → ACCOUNTING
- Notice of completion → CUSTOMER

Flows from COMPUTE CUSTOMER BALANCE:
- Amount due → ACCOUNTING
- Refund → ACCOUNTING
- Working cost center debit → ACCOUNTING
- Itemized bill → CUSTOMER

-A.7-

AGENCY FINANCIAL MANAGEMENT SYSTEM

Global Information-flow Model

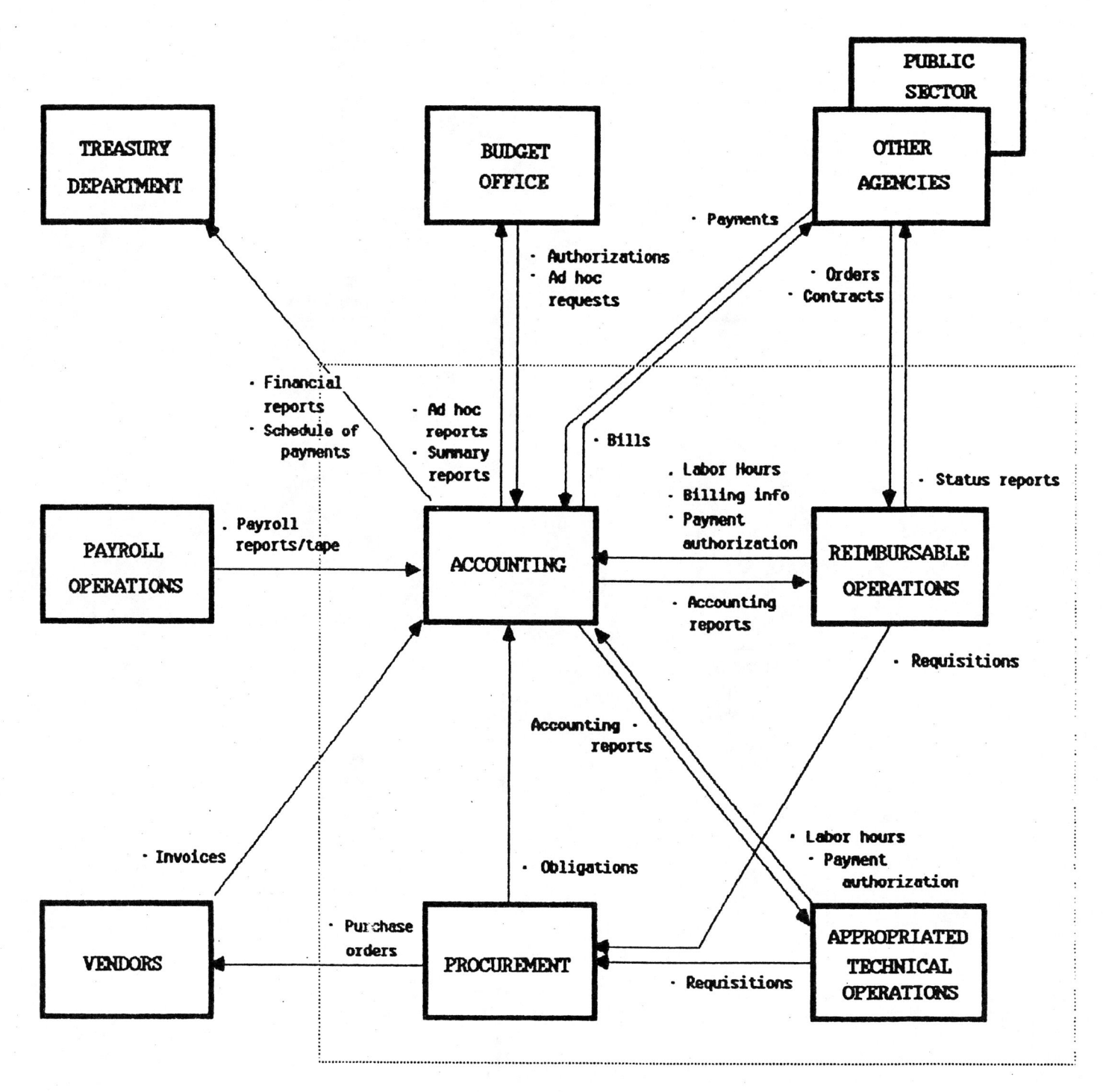

```
                                                              PUBLIC
                                                              SECTOR
  TREASURY              BUDGET                                OTHER
  DEPARTMENT            OFFICE                               AGENCIES
                                          · Payments
                        · Authorizations
                        · Ad hoc              · Orders
                          requests            · Contracts

   · Financial
     reports      · Ad hoc
   · Schedule of    reports      · Bills
     payments     · Summary
                    reports      · Labor Hours
                                 · Billing info       · Status reports
                                 · Payment
  PAYROLL       · Payroll          authorization    REIMBURSABLE
  OPERATIONS      reports/tape  ACCOUNTING          OPERATIONS
                                 · Accounting
                                   reports
                                                    · Requisitions

                               Accounting ·
                                 reports
                                                    · Labor hours
                                                    · Payment
                     · Invoices     · Obligations     authorization

                                                    APPROPRIATED
  VENDORS    · Purchase                              TECHNICAL
              orders    PROCUREMENT  · Requisitions  OPERATIONS
```

Boundary of Automation

-A.8-

AGENCY FINANCIAL MANAGEMENT SYSTEM
ENTITY-RELATIONSHIP DIAGRAM
OF CONCEPTUAL SCHEMA

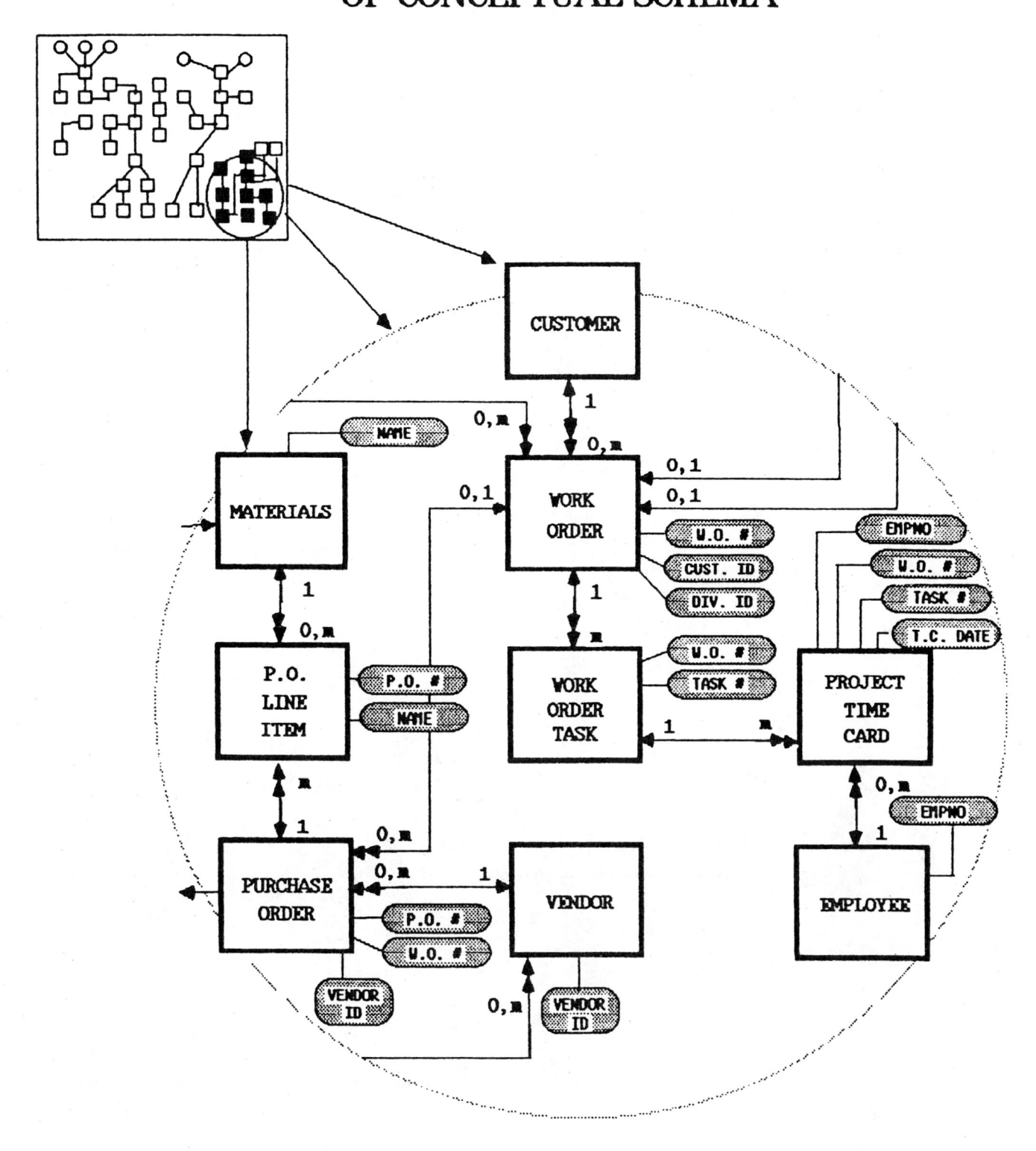

NOTES: Non-key attributes are not shown.
Data dictionary reports list all attributes.

-A.9-

Data Dictionary Display

Relationship : Time Charged To Task

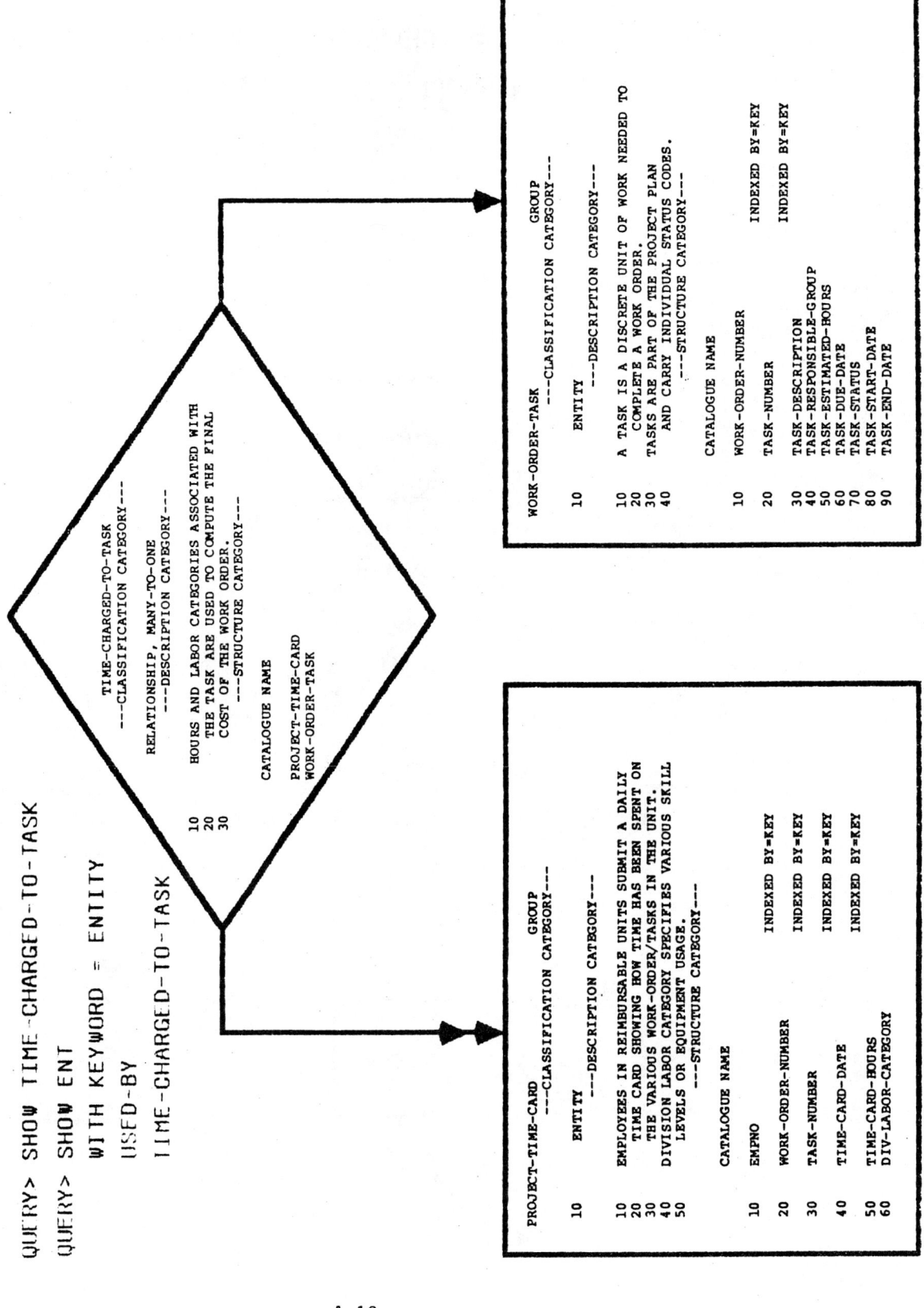

```
QUERY> SHOW TIME-CHARGED-TO-TASK
QUERY> SHOW ENT
       WITH KEYWORD = ENTITY
       USED-BY
       TIME-CHARGED-TO-TASK
```

```
                TIME-CHARGED-TO-TASK
                ---CLASSIFICATION CATEGORY---

                RELATIONSHIP, MANY-TO-ONE
                ---DESCRIPTION CATEGORY---

         10     HOURS AND LABOR CATEGORIES ASSOCIATED WITH
         20     THE TASK ARE USED TO COMPUTE THE FINAL
         30     COST OF THE WORK ORDER.
                ---STRUCTURE CATEGORY---

                CATALOGUE NAME

                PROJECT-TIME-CARD
                WORK-ORDER-TASK
```

```
WORK-ORDER-TASK          GROUP
                ---CLASSIFICATION CATEGORY---

   10    ENTITY
                ---DESCRIPTION CATEGORY---

   10    A TASK IS A DISCRETE UNIT OF WORK NEEDED TO
   20    COMPLETE A WORK ORDER.
   30    TASKS ARE PART OF THE PROJECT PLAN
   40    AND CARRY INDIVIDUAL STATUS CODES.
                ---STRUCTURE CATEGORY---

         CATALOGUE NAME

   10    WORK-ORDER-NUMBER           INDEXED BY=KEY

   20    TASK-NUMBER                 INDEXED BY=KEY

   30    TASK-DESCRIPTION
   40    TASK-RESPONSIBLE-GROUP
   50    TASK-ESTIMATED-HOURS
   60    TASK-DUE-DATE
   70    TASK-STATUS
   80    TASK-START-DATE
   90    TASK-END-DATE
```

```
PROJECT-TIME-CARD          GROUP
                ---CLASSIFICATION CATEGORY---

   10    ENTITY
                ---DESCRIPTION CATEGORY---

   10    EMPLOYEES IN REIMBURSABLE UNITS SUBMIT A DAILY
   20    TIME CARD SHOWING HOW TIME HAS BEEN SPENT ON
   30    THE VARIOUS WORK-ORDER/TASKS IN THE UNIT.
   40    DIVISION LABOR CATEGORY SPECIFIES VARIOUS SKILL
   50    LEVELS OR EQUIPMENT USAGE.
                ---STRUCTURE CATEGORY---

         CATALOGUE NAME

   10    EMPNO                      INDEXED BY=KEY

   20    WORK-ORDER-NUMBER          INDEXED BY=KEY

   30    TASK-NUMBER                INDEXED BY=KEY

   40    TIME-CARD-DATE             INDEXED BY=KEY

   50    TIME-CARD-HOURS
   60    DIV-LABOR-CATEGORY
```

AGENCY FINANCIAL MANAGEMENT SYSTEM
EXTERNAL SCHEMA

Function : Close Out Work Order

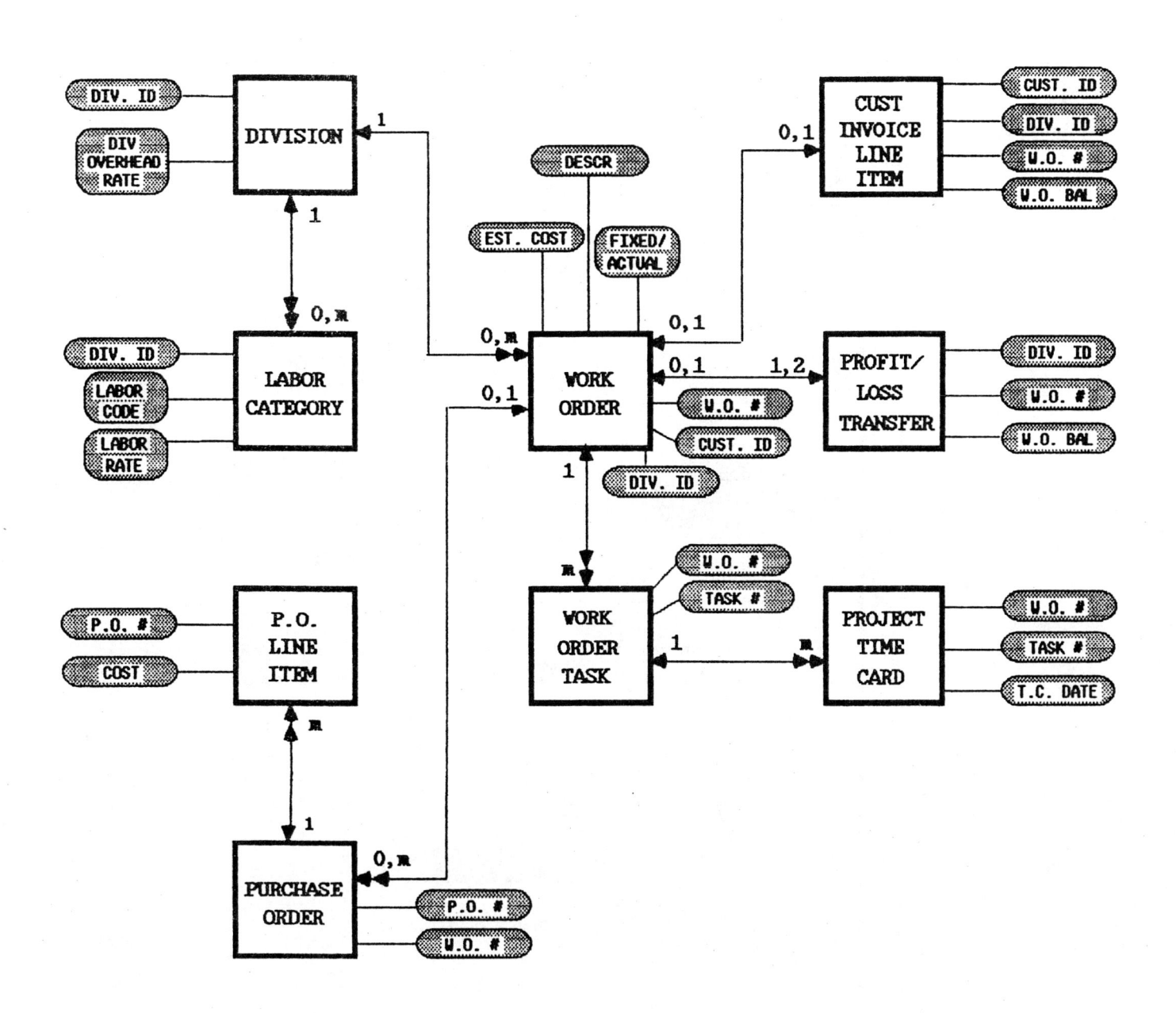

NOTE : Entities, relationships and attributes not used by this function are not shown. Complete details are available from the data dictionary.

-A.11-

EXTERNAL SCHEMA "OVERLAY" WORKLOAD FOR FUNCTION

"Close Out Work Order"
Biweekly Statistics for All Reimbursable Divisions

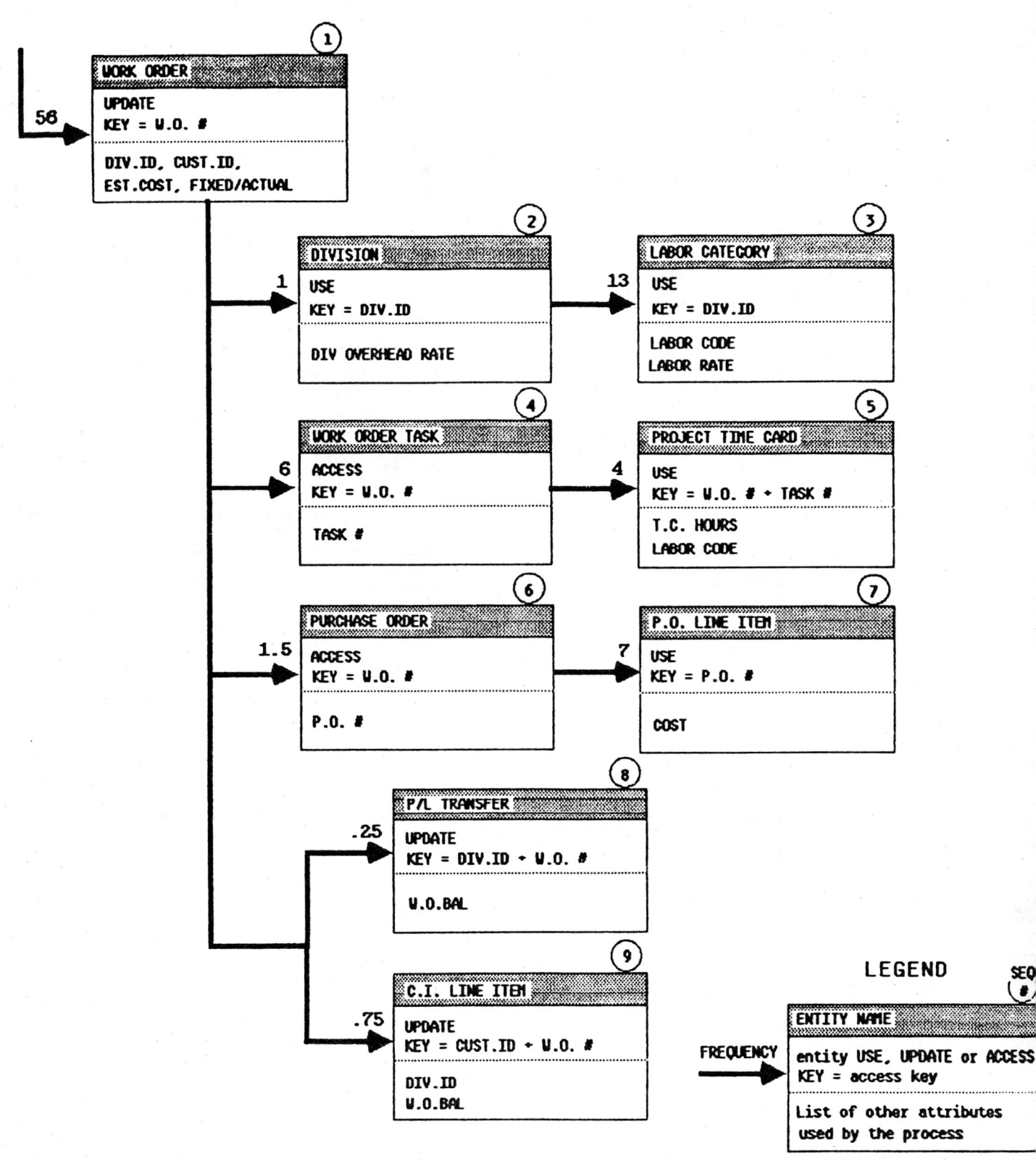

(1) WORK ORDER
56 →
UPDATE
KEY = W.O. #

DIV.ID, CUST.ID,
EST.COST, FIXED/ACTUAL

(2) DIVISION
1 →
USE
KEY = DIV.ID

DIV OVERHEAD RATE

(3) LABOR CATEGORY
13 →
USE
KEY = DIV.ID

LABOR CODE
LABOR RATE

(4) WORK ORDER TASK
6 →
ACCESS
KEY = W.O. #

TASK #

(5) PROJECT TIME CARD
4 →
USE
KEY = W.O. # + TASK #

T.C. HOURS
LABOR CODE

(6) PURCHASE ORDER
1.5 →
ACCESS
KEY = W.O. #

P.O. #

(7) P.O. LINE ITEM
7 →
USE
KEY = P.O. #

COST

(8) P/L TRANSFER
.25 →
UPDATE
KEY = DIV.ID + W.O. #

W.O.BAL

(9) C.I. LINE ITEM
.75 →
UPDATE
KEY = CUST.ID + W.O. #

DIV.ID
W.O.BAL

LEGEND

ENTITY NAME (SEQ #)
FREQUENCY →
entity USE, UPDATE or ACCESS
KEY = access key

List of other attributes
used by the process

-A.12-

DATA DICTIONARY DISPLAY

WORKLOAD FOR FUNCTION

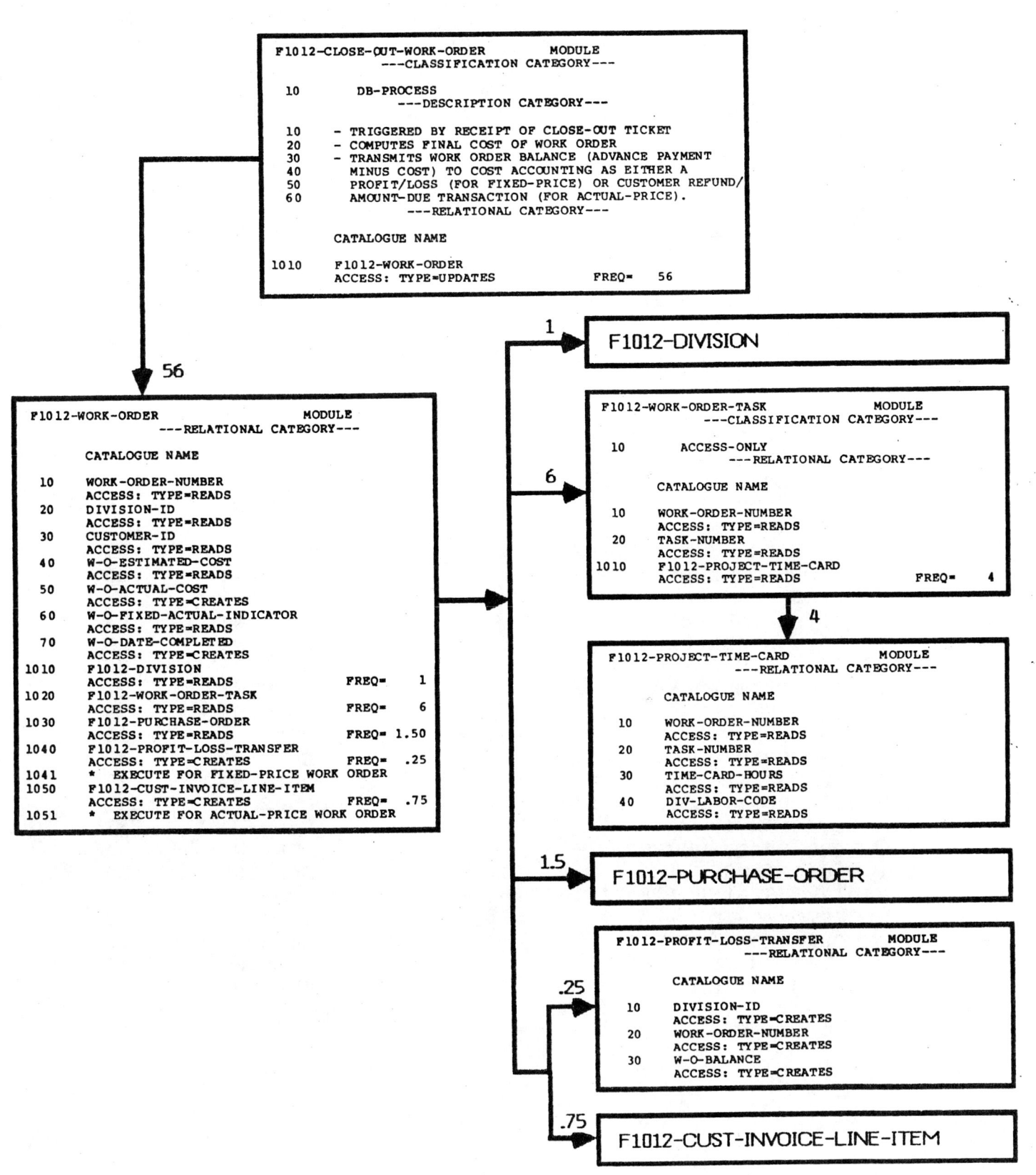

```
F1012-CLOSE-OUT-WORK-ORDER         MODULE
        ---CLASSIFICATION CATEGORY---

   10      DB-PROCESS
              ---DESCRIPTION CATEGORY---

   10    - TRIGGERED BY RECEIPT OF CLOSE-OUT TICKET
   20    - COMPUTES FINAL COST OF WORK ORDER
   30    - TRANSMITS WORK ORDER BALANCE (ADVANCE PAYMENT
   40      MINUS COST) TO COST ACCOUNTING AS EITHER A
   50      PROFIT/LOSS (FOR FIXED-PRICE) OR CUSTOMER REFUND/
   60      AMOUNT-DUE TRANSACTION (FOR ACTUAL-PRICE).
              ---RELATIONAL CATEGORY---

         CATALOGUE NAME

 1010    F1012-WORK-ORDER
         ACCESS: TYPE=UPDATES           FREQ=    56
```

── 56 ──▶

```
F1012-WORK-ORDER                    MODULE
        ---RELATIONAL CATEGORY---

         CATALOGUE NAME

   10    WORK-ORDER-NUMBER
         ACCESS: TYPE=READS
   20    DIVISION-ID
         ACCESS: TYPE=READS
   30    CUSTOMER-ID
         ACCESS: TYPE=READS
   40    W-O-ESTIMATED-COST
         ACCESS: TYPE=READS
   50    W-O-ACTUAL-COST
         ACCESS: TYPE=CREATES
   60    W-O-FIXED-ACTUAL-INDICATOR
         ACCESS: TYPE=READS
   70    W-O-DATE-COMPLETED
         ACCESS: TYPE=CREATES
 1010    F1012-DIVISION
         ACCESS: TYPE=READS             FREQ=     1
 1020    F1012-WORK-ORDER-TASK
         ACCESS: TYPE=READS             FREQ=     6
 1030    F1012-PURCHASE-ORDER
         ACCESS: TYPE=READS             FREQ=  1.50
 1040    F1012-PROFIT-LOSS-TRANSFER
         ACCESS: TYPE=CREATES           FREQ=   .25
 1041    *   EXECUTE FOR FIXED-PRICE WORK ORDER
 1050    F1012-CUST-INVOICE-LINE-ITEM
         ACCESS: TYPE=CREATES           FREQ=   .75
 1051    *   EXECUTE FOR ACTUAL-PRICE WORK ORDER
```

── 1 ──▶ **F1012-DIVISION**

── 6 ──▶
```
F1012-WORK-ORDER-TASK               MODULE
        ---CLASSIFICATION CATEGORY---

   10      ACCESS-ONLY
              ---RELATIONAL CATEGORY---

         CATALOGUE NAME

   10    WORK-ORDER-NUMBER
         ACCESS: TYPE=READS
   20    TASK-NUMBER
         ACCESS: TYPE=READS
 1010    F1012-PROJECT-TIME-CARD
         ACCESS: TYPE=READS             FREQ=     4
```

── 4 ──▶
```
F1012-PROJECT-TIME-CARD             MODULE
        ---RELATIONAL CATEGORY---

         CATALOGUE NAME

   10    WORK-ORDER-NUMBER
         ACCESS: TYPE=READS
   20    TASK-NUMBER
         ACCESS: TYPE=READS
   30    TIME-CARD-HOURS
         ACCESS: TYPE=READS
   40    DIV-LABOR-CODE
         ACCESS: TYPE=READS
```

── 1.5 ──▶ **F1012-PURCHASE-ORDER**

── .25 ──▶
```
F1012-PROFIT-LOSS-TRANSFER          MODULE
        ---RELATIONAL CATEGORY---

         CATALOGUE NAME

   10    DIVISION-ID
         ACCESS: TYPE=CREATES
   20    WORK-ORDER-NUMBER
         ACCESS: TYPE=CREATES
   30    W-O-BALANCE
         ACCESS: TYPE=CREATES
```

── .75 ──▶ **F1012-CUST-INVOICE-LINE-ITEM**

```
                    I N D E N T E D   I N D E X
        E X T E R N A L   S C H E M A   F O R   F U N C T I O N
                     F1012-CLOSE-OUT-WORK-ORDER

    RELATIVE LEVEL/DATA CATALOGUE NAME         ENTRY TYPE      PAGE


    . F1012-CLOSE-OUT-WORK-ORDER               MODULE            2
    . . F1012-WORK-ORDER                       MODULE            3
    . . . WORK-ORDER-NUMBER                    ELEMENT           4
    . . . DIVISION-ID                          ELEMENT           5
    . . . CUSTOMER-ID                          ELEMENT           6
    . . . W-O-ESTIMATED-COST                   ELEMENT           7
    . . . W-O-ACTUAL-COST                      ELEMENT           8
    . . . W-O-FIXED-ACTUAL-INDICATOR           ELEMENT           9
    . . . W-O-DATE-COMPLETED                   ELEMENT          10
    . . . F1012-DIVISION                       MODULE           11
    . . . . DIVISION-ID                        ELEMENT          12
    . . . . DIV-OVERHEAD-RATE                  ELEMENT          13
    . . . . F1012-DIV-LABOR-CATEGORY           MODULE           14
    . . . . . DIVISION-ID                      ELEMENT          15
    . . . . . DIV-LABOR-CODE                   ELEMENT          16
    . . . . . DIV-LABOR-RATE                   ELEMENT          17
    . . . F1012-WORK-ORDER-TASK                MODULE           18
    . . . . WORK-ORDER-NUMBER                  ELEMENT          19
    . . . . TASK-NUMBER                        ELEMENT          20
    . . . . F1012-PROJECT-TIME-CARD            MODULE           21
    . . . . . WORK-ORDER-NUMBER                ELEMENT          22
    . . . . . TASK-NUMBER                      ELEMENT          23
    . . . . . TIME-CARD-HOURS                  ELEMENT          24
    . . . . . DIV-LABOR-CODE                   ELEMENT          25
    . . . F1012-PURCHASE-ORDER                 MODULE           26
    . . . . WORK-ORDER-NUMBER                  ELEMENT          27
    . . . . PURCHASE-ORDER-NUMBER              ELEMENT          28
    . . . . F1012-PURCHASE-ORDER-LINE-ITEM     MODULE           29
    . . . . . PURCHASE-ORDER-NUMBER            ELEMENT          30
    . . . . . P-O-LINE-ITEM-COST               ELEMENT          31
    . . . F1012-PROFIT-LOSS-TRANSFER           MODULE           32
    . . . . DIVISION-ID                        ELEMENT          33
    . . . . WORK-ORDER-NUMBER                  ELEMENT          34
    . . . . W-O-BALANCE                        ELEMENT          35
    . . . F1012-CUST-INVOICE-LINE-ITEM         MODULE           36
    . . . . CUSTOMER-ID                        ELEMENT          37
    . . . . WORK-ORDER-NUMBER                  ELEMENT          38
    . . . . DIVISION-ID                        ELEMENT          39
    . . . . W-O-BALANCE                        ELEMENT          40

        * * *   E N D   O F   I N D E X   * * *
```

GLOSSARY OF DIGITAL LOGIC

CONTENTS

	Page
Absorption, Law of ...... Binary Digit	1
Binary Notation ...... Digitize	2
Distributive Law ...... Indempotent Law	3
Inhibit ...... Number System	4
Octal (Numbering System) ...... Vinculum	5

GLOSSARY OF DIGITAL LOGIC

ABSORPTION, LAW OF: In Boolean algebra, the law which states that the odd term will be absorbed when a term is combined by logical multiplication with the logical sum of the term and another term, or when a term is combined by logical addition with the logical product of the term and another term.

ACCURACY: The quality of freedom from mistake or error; that is, the degree of conformity to truth or to a rule.

ADDEND: The quantity that is added to another quantity (called the augend) to produce a sum.

ANALYSIS: The methodical investigation of a problem, and the separation of the problem into smaller related units for further detailed study.

AND: A logic operator having the property that if P is a statement, Q is a statement, R is a statement ... then the AND of P, Q, R ..., is true if ALL statements are true, false if ANY statement is false.

AND GATE: An electronic gate whose output is active only when every input is in its active state. An AND gate performs the function of the logical "AND." Also called AND-circuit.

ANODE: The positive electrode of an electrochemical device, such as a primary or secondary cell, toward which negative ions are drawn.

ARITHMETIC UNIT: The unit of a computing system that contains the circuits that perform arithmetic operations.

AUGEND: In arithmetic addition, a number that increases when another number (called the addend) is added to it.

AXIOM: A statement regarded as a self-evident truth.

BASE: (1) A reference value. (2) A number that is multiplied by itself as many times as indicated by an exponent. (3) Same as radix.

BASE NUMBER: The radix of a number system (10 is the radix, or base number, for the decimal system; 8 is the base number for the octal system).

BIAS: (1) An electrical force applied to a relay, vacuum tube, or semiconductor to establish an electrical reference level for the operation of the device. (2) The d.c. potential applied between elements of a transistor to make the device perform in the desired manner.

BIAS CURRENT: Current which flows through the base-emitter junction of a transistor. It can be adjusted to set the operating point of the transistor.

BINARY: (1) Pertaining to a characteristic or property involving a selection, choice, or condition in which there are at most two possibilities; (2) Pertaining to the number representation system with a radix of two.

BINARY CODE: A code that makes use of exactly two distinct characters, usually 0 and 1.

BINARY DIGIT: In binary notation, either of the characters 0 or 1.

GLOSSARY

BINARY NOTATION: Fixed radix notation where the radix is two.

BIT: A binary digit; for example, zero or one. It may be equivalent to an "on" or "off" condition.

BOOLEAN ALGEBRA: Mathematical logic that deals with classes, off-on circuit elements, and propositions. Uses logic gates such as AND, OR, NOT, etc. Introduced in 1847 by English mathematician George Boole.

CARRY: One or more digits, produced in connection with an arithmetic operation on one digit place of two or more numerals in positional notation, that are forwarded to another digit place for processing there.

CHARACTER: A letter, digit, or other symbol that is used as part of the organization, control, or representation of data.

CHECK: A process for determining accuracy.

COLLECTOR: (1) In a transistor, primary current flows through this electrode. (2) The external terminal of a transistor that is connected to this region.

COMPLEMENT: A number that can be derived from a specified number by subtracting it from a second specified number. For example, in radix notation, the second specified number may be a given power of the radix or one less than a given power of the radix. The negative of a number is often represented by its complement.

COMPLEMENTARY LAW: In Boolean algebra, this law states that the logical addition of a quantity and its complement will result in 1, and the logical multiplication of a quantity and its complement will result in a product of 0.

COMPUTER: A data processor that can perform substantial computation, including numerous arithmetic or logic operations, without intervention by a human operator during the run.

COMMUTATIVE LAW: In Boolean algebra this law states that changing the order of the terms in an equation will not affect the value of the equation.

Example: $A + B = B + A$; $A \cdot B = B \cdot A$

CUTOFF: The condition of a transistor when zero or a reverse bias is applied to the emitter-base junction and collector current ceases to flow.

DECIMAL: Pertaining to the number representation system with a radix of ten.

DECIMAL DIGIT: In the decimal number system, one of the characters 0 through 9.

DECIMAL NOTATION: A fixed radix notation where the radix is ten.

DECIMAL NUMERAL: A decimal representation of a number.

DECIMAL POINT: The radix point in decimal representation.

DEMORGAN'S THEOREM: A theorem which states that the negation or inversion of an expression that is ANDed is equal to the same expression of inverted OR implications, or the negation or inversion of an expression that is ORed is equal to the same expression of inverted AND implications. In symbols,

$$\overline{XYZ} = \overline{X} + \overline{Y} + \overline{Z} \text{ or } \overline{X+Y+Z} = \overline{X} \cdot \overline{Y} \cdot \overline{Z}$$

DIGIT: A symbol that represents one of the positive integers smaller than the radix.

DIGITAL: Pertaining to data in the form of digits.

DIGITAL COMPUTER: (1) A computer in which discrete representation of data is mainly used. (2) A computer that operates on discrete data by performing arithmetic and logic processes on these data.

DIGITIZE: To use numeric characters to express or represent data.

DISTRIBUTIVE LAW: In Boolean algebra, the law which states that if a group of terms connected by like operators contains the same variable, the variable may be removed from the terms and associated with them by the appropriate sign of operation.

DIVIDEND: The number that is divided by another number.

DIVISOR: The number by which the dividend is divided.

DOUBLE NEGATION, LAW OF: In Boolean algebra, the law which states that the complement of the complement of a term is the equivalent of the term.

DUALIZATION, LAW OF: See DEMORGAN'S THEOREM.

DUODECIMAL: The number system with a radix of twelve.

EMITTER: (1) An element in a transistor that sends current carriers into the base of the transistor. (2) In a vacuum tube, the cathode.

EXCLUSIVE OR: A logical operator which has the property that if A and B are two logic statements, then the statement $A \oplus B$, where the $\oplus$ is the Exclusive OR operator, is true if either A or B, but not both are true, and false if A and B are both false or both true. The boolean expression for the Exclusive OR operation is $f = A\overline{B} + \overline{A}B$.

EXCLUSIVE-OR CIRCUIT: A circuit that produces an active output signal when any one, but not more than one, input is in its active state.

EXPONENT: In a floating point representation, the numeral written in superscript (10^2), representing a number that indicates the power to which the base is to be raised.

EXPRESSION: A series of variables that are connected by operating symbols to describe a desired computation.

FACTOR: Any of the numbers, quantities, or symbols which, when multiplied together, form a product.

FLIP-FLOP: A device having two stable states and two inputs (or types of input signals), each of which corresponds with one of the two states. The circuit remains in either state until caused to change to the other state by application of a pulse.

FORWARD BIAS: A bias voltage applied to a semiconductor junction with polarity such that the junction is activated.

GATE: As applied to logic circuitry, one of several different types of electronics devices that will provide a particular output when specified input conditions are satisfied. (AND, OR, Inverter)

GATING: The application of a particular waveform used to perform electronic switching.

GROUND: The point in a circuit used as a common reference point for measuring purposes.

HARVARD CHART: In terms of logic expression simplification, lists all the possible variable combinations under consideration and the complements of these variable combinations.

HEXADECIMAL: A number system with a base of sixteen.

HEXADECIMAL SYSTEM: Pertaining to the number system with a radix of sixteen. (It uses the ten digits of the decimal system and the first six letters of the alphabet.)

IDENTITY, LAW OF: In Boolean algebra, the law which states that, when combining three or more terms, in either logical addition or logical multiplication, the order in which the terms are combined will not affect the result.

IDEMPOTENT LAW: In Boolean algebra, combining a quantity with itself either by logical addition or logical multiplication will result in a logical sum or product that is the equivalent of the quantity. Example: $A + A = A$; $A \cdot A = A$

GLOSSARY

INHIBIT: To prevent the occurrence of an event.

INPUT: The current, voltage, power, or activating force applied to a circuit or device.

INPUT/OUTPUT: (I/O) Pertaining to either input or output or both.

INSTRUCTION: A statement that specifies an operation and the values or locations of its operands.

INVERTER CIRCUIT: A circuit which performs the NOT operation. With an input of A the output is $\overline{A}$, and with an input of $\overline{A}$ the output is A.

LOGIC: The basic principles and applications of truth tables, interconnections of off-on circuit elements, and other factors involved in mathematical computation in automatic data processing systems and other devices.

LOGIC CIRCUIT: The primary units in a digital equipment, made up of electronic gates.

LOGIC DIAGRAM: In computers and data processing equipment, a diagram representing the logical elements and their interconnections.

LOGIC ELEMENT: A device that performs the logic function. The smallest building blocks which can be represented by operators in an appropriate system.

LOGIC INSTRUCTION: Any instruction that executes an operation that is defined in symbolic logic, such as AND, OR, NOR.

LOGIC OPERATION: A non-arithmetical operation in a computer, where logical YES or NO quantities are involved.

LOGIC SWITCH: A diode matrix or other switching arrangement that is capable of directing an input signal to one of several outputs.

LOGIC SYMBOL: A symbol used to represent a logic element graphically. Also a symbol used to represent a logic operator.

MATRIX: In computers, a logic network in the form of an array of input leads and output leads with logic elements connected at some of their intersections.

MINUEND: The number from which another number is to be subtracted.

MISTAKE: A human action that produces an unintended result.

MODULUS: The total number of different numbers or stable conditions that a counting device can indicate.

MULTIPLICAND: The number that is to be multiplied by another number (called the multiplier).

MULTIPLIER: The number by which another number is multiplied.

NAND GATE: Basically, the circuit operates by ANDing a number of logic signals together; it then uses its output signals as the input to Inverter circuit which complements or negates the results.

NEGATION: The process of inverting or complementing the value of a function or variable.

NEGATIVE LOGIC: When the signal that activates the circuit (a 1, high, or true) has an electrical level that is _relatively_ more NEGATIVE than the other logic state, the logic polarity is considered to be NEGATIVE.

NOR GATE: The NOR gate combines the functions of an OR gate and the Inverter circuit. It produces a circuit in which the output is a logic 1 only if ALL inputs are a logic 0.

NOT: A logic function having the property that it inverts its input to provide the opposite output.

NUMBER: A symbol (called a numeral), or group of symbols, representing a sum of units.

NUMBER SYSTEM: Any set of symbols or characters used for the purpose of counting objects and performing arithmetic operations.

OCTAL (NUMBERING SYSTEM): A numbering system with a radix of 8.

PARTIAL PRODUCT: In mathematics, the intermediate sum obtained when the multiplicand is multiplied by each digit in a multiplier having more than one digit.

POLYNOMIAL EXPANSION: Method which uses the positional notation process to derive the equivalent new number. It includes changing the individual digits of the number being converted to digits acceptable in the new system and changing the old base to the new base equivalent.

POSITIONAL NOTATION: See POSITIONAL VALUE.

POSITIONAL VALUE: The principle of positional value consists of assigning a digit a value which depends on two factors: (1) the digit's basic value, that is, the number of units it represents by itself; and (2) a weighting value, which is determined by the digit's position within a given number.

POSITIONAL WEIGHTING: The value given a digit based on the digit's position within a given number.

POSITIVE LOGIC: When the signal that activates the circuit (a 1, high, or true) has an electrical level that is relatively more POSITIVE than the other logic state, the logic polarity is considered to be POSITIVE.

POSTULATES: In mathematics or logic, an axiom or hypothesis.

PRODUCT: The number resulting from the multiplication of two or more numbers.

QUANTITY: In mathematics it designates a positive or negative number.

QUOTIENT: The number which results when one number is divided by another.

RADIX (OR BASE): The number of symbols a number system uses including zero. The value of the radix is always one unit greater than the largest basic character being used.

REGISTER: A number of flip-flops arranged in a chain.

REMAINDER: In division, the number left after the quotient has been found which cannot be divided by the divisor without resulting in a fraction.

REVERSE BIAS: An external voltage applied to a diode or semiconductor junction to reduce the flow of current across the junction. (Also called back bias.)

SUBTRAHEND: The number which is subtracted from the minuend.

SUM: The results of an addition.

THEOREM: A formula or statement in mathematics or logic which is based on or deduced from other formulas or statements.

TRUTH TABLE: A table that describes a logic function by listing all possible combinations of input values and indicating, for each combination, the true output values.

UNIT: A single object or thing.

V_{CC}: Collector supply voltage.

VARIABLE: A representative symbol that can assume any of a given set of values.

VEITCH DIAGRAM: A diagram used to find the simplest logic equation needed to express a given function.

VINCULUM: A straight horizontal line placed over terms of an expression; it serves the same grouping purpose as parenthesis and brackets and indicates negation.

ANSWER SHEET

TEST NO. ______________ PART ________ TITLE OF POSITION ______________________________
(AS GIVEN IN EXAMINATION ANNOUNCEMENT - INCLUDE OPTION, IF ANY)

PLACE OF EXAMINATION ______________________ (CITY OR TOWN) ______________________ (STATE) DATE ______________

RATING

USE THE SPECIAL PENCIL. MAKE GLOSSY BLACK MARKS.

1	A B C D E	26	A B C D E	51	A B C D E	76	A B C D E	101	A B C D E
2	A B C D E	27	A B C D E	52	A B C D E	77	A B C D E	102	A B C D E
3	A B C D E	28	A B C D E	53	A B C D E	78	A B C D E	103	A B C D E
4	A B C D E	29	A B C D E	54	A B C D E	79	A B C D E	104	A B C D E
5	A B C D E	30	A B C D E	55	A B C D E	80	A B C D E	105	A B C D E
6	A B C D E	31	A B C D E	56	A B C D E	81	A B C D E	106	A B C D E
7	A B C D E	32	A B C D E	57	A B C D E	82	A B C D E	107	A B C D E
8	A B C D E	33	A B C D E	58	A B C D E	83	A B C D E	108	A B C D E
9	A B C D E	34	A B C D E	59	A B C D E	84	A B C D E	109	A B C D E
10	A B C D E	35	A B C D E	60	A B C D E	85	A B C D E	110	A B C D E

Make only ONE mark for each answer. Additional and stray marks may be counted as mistakes. In making corrections, erase errors COMPLETELY.

11	A B C D E	36	A B C D E	61	A B C D E	86	A B C D E	111	A B C D E
12	A B C D E	37	A B C D E	62	A B C D E	87	A B C D E	112	A B C D E
13	A B C D E	38	A B C D E	63	A B C D E	88	A B C D E	113	A B C D E
14	A B C D E	39	A B C D E	64	A B C D E	89	A B C D E	114	A B C D E
15	A B C D E	40	A B C D E	65	A B C D E	90	A B C D E	115	A B C D E
16	A B C D E	41	A B C D E	66	A B C D E	91	A B C D E	116	A B C D E
17	A B C D E	42	A B C D E	67	A B C D E	92	A B C D E	117	A B C D E
18	A B C D E	43	A B C D E	68	A B C D E	93	A B C D E	118	A B C D E
19	A B C D E	44	A B C D E	69	A B C D E	94	A B C D E	119	A B C D E
20	A B C D E	45	A B C D E	70	A B C D E	95	A B C D E	120	A B C D E
21	A B C D E	46	A B C D E	71	A B C D E	96	A B C D E	121	A B C D E
22	A B C D E	47	A B C D E	72	A B C D E	97	A B C D E	122	A B C D E
23	A B C D E	48	A B C D E	73	A B C D E	98	A B C D E	123	A B C D E
24	A B C D E	49	A B C D E	74	A B C D E	99	A B C D E	124	A B C D E
25	A B C D E	50	A B C D E	75	A B C D E	100	A B C D E	125	A B C D E

ANSWER SHEET

NOV - - 2016

TEST NO. _____ PART _____ TITLE OF POSITION _____
(AS GIVEN IN EXAMINATION ANNOUNCEMENT - INCLUDE OPTION, IF ANY)

PLACE OF EXAMINATION _____ DATE _____
(CITY OR TOWN)   (STATE)

RATING

USE THE SPECIAL PENCIL. MAKE GLOSSY BLACK MARKS.

Make only ONE mark for each answer. Additional and stray marks may be counted as mistakes. In making corrections, erase errors COMPLETELY.